Appreciation for

THE BOOK OF JOB
TRANSLATED WITH COMMENTARY BY ROBERT D. SACKS

Sacks's prose is eminently approachable and has the effect of bringing the reader into intimate contact with the characters in the book. Sacks introduces us to Job and each of Job's friends as individuals. We get to know what each holds to be important and what are the motivations that underlie their questions and arguments. The complicated interplay of interlocutors becomes sensible and lucid in Sacks's capable hands. Sacks's knowledge of the Hebrew language and tradition further brings the book to life and adds depth to the reader's understanding.

Susan Paalman, St. John's College, Annapolis

Reading Robert Sacks's translation and commentary on The Book of Job is a wonderful experience, both for its delicate and penetrating exploration of the book's language and for its powerful illumination of the book's meaning. In coming to see the world as a cosmos beyond the reach of human justice, Sacks argues, Job learns to recognize natural right, and in particular the equality of men and women.

Abraham Anderson, Sarah Lawrence College

Robert Sacks's translation and commentary combines a lucid translation that respects the strangeness of the original with a compelling philosophical reading of The Book of Job. At the heart of his extensive commentary is an account of the discovery of nature—of "a world beyond man." Scholars and students alike will benefit from this remarkable book.

Frank Hunt, St. John's College, Santa Fe

Those of us whose understanding of the Bible has been immensely enriched by Robert D. Sacks's *The Lion and the Ass* and *Beginning Hebrew: Intentionality and Grammar* are now able to learn from his translation and discussion of The Book of Job. Sacks's insights into this extraordinary biblical book, especially his astute critical judgment that Job is the book of the Hebrew Bible that most puts us in contact with the question of the relation between Greek philosophy and the Hebrew Bible, makes his book an enduring source of wisdom pertaining to the time-honored inquiries of our civilization.

Terence J. Kleven, Central College, Pella, Iowa

The Book of Job

The Book of Job

A New Translation
with In-Depth Running Discussion

by

Robert D. Sacks

Kafir Yaroq Books
an imprint of Green Lion Press
Santa Fe, New Mexico

www.kafiryaroq.com

Set in 11-point Minion Pro

Book design and production by Howard J. Fisher. Managing
editor, Dana Densmore. Cover design executed by William H.
Donahue; photograph courtesy of NASA. Author photo courtesy
of Berel Levertov.

Printed and bound by Sheridan Books, Inc.,
Chelsea, Michigan

Cataloging-In-Publication data:
Sacks, Robert D.

The Book of Job: A New Translation with In-Depth Running
Discussion / by Robert D. Sacks
Includes index, bibliography, biographical note.

ISBN-13: 978-1-888009-50-7 (sewn softcover binding)

1. Bible 2. Wisdom literature 3. Bible commentary
Sacks, Robert D. (1931–). II. Title

Library of Congress Control Number: 2016935167

Ainsi il n'y a rien d'inculte, de stérile, de mort dans l'univers, point de chaos, point de confusion qu'en apparence....

Thus there is nothing fallow, nothing sterile, nothing dead in the universe, no chaos, no confusion save in appearance....

Leibniz, *La Monadologie*, 69

Contents

Translator's Introduction

We of the Western tradition have the blessing and the curse of finding ourselves heirs to two quite different ways of thought and hence to two quite different ways of life. Though they sit uneasily together, the struggle between them has formed much of the life behind the growth of both our daily language and our highest contemplations. They are, then, the foundation of both our deepest insights and our deepest prejudices. As such, they have given rise to that particular horizon within which we live, and beyond which we constantly strive to peer. The circumstance to which I refer is often spoken of as the problem of Science versus Religion, or of Reason versus Faith. More fundamentally, and perhaps less prejudicially, we may call it the question of Athens and Jerusalem, or of Greek philosophy and the Hebrew Bible.

Any attempt to understand the relation between these two roots of our civilization as they were before they met is all the more difficult, since rarely can they be caught addressing the same question in ways that can be compared with true clarity of thought. This consideration, among others, eventually led me to the Book of Job since, of all the books of the Bible, it seemed to me to be most in contact with those problems which gave rise to Greek philosophy.

The language of Job is strange and difficult, and translators often disagree. In my notes and discussions, I have most frequently acknowledged the renditions of Robert Alter, Robert Gordis, and Moshe Greenberg;[1] and wherever I have felt it necessary to differ greatly from my predecessors

---

[1] Alter, Robert, *The Wisdom Books: Job, Proverbs, and Ecclesiastes: A Translation with Commentary* (W. W. Norton and Co., 2010). Greenberg, Moshe, tr., *The Book of Job* (Jewish Publication Society of America, 1980). Gordis, Robert, *The Book of Job: Commentary, New Translation, and Special Study* (Jewish Theological Seminary of America, 1978).

I have tried to give the arguments in favor of each translation—insofar as I am able to reconstruct them—in order
that readers might have some basis for forming their own
conclusions. At times I have made reference to certain other
translations in order to bring out points of interest; chief
among these are the King James Version (KJV), the Revised
Standard Version (RSV), and that of the Jewish Publication
Society, 1985 (JPS). I have also tried to make my remarks
intelligible even to those readers who cannot follow the
Hebrew they contain.

I wish to thank both Mr. Hilail Fradkin of the Bradley
Foundation and Mr. Antony Sullivan of the Earhart
Foundation for having supplied my table while I was prepar-
ing material for this volume in the late 1970's. Thanks as well
to Eve Adler and those others in Vermont who were so help-
ful during that time.

The present 2016 edition (the second) was prepared at
the suggestion of Dana Densmore, for which I thank her
heartily. Many thanks as well to my editor Howard Fisher for
his ever-friendly advice, his close and tireless reading, and
for all those prodding emails that began, "You promised to..."
My grateful thanks go also to Frank Hunt for his generous
attention to the text of this edition and for numerous know-
ledgeable suggestions and corrections.

As readers of the first edition will notice, I have omitted
a lengthy interlude of commentary on the word אָוֶן (perversion), which I hope will one day appear as an article on
its own. Although I still believe in its importance, I am no
longer convinced that it is relevant to the Book of Job.

Robert D. Sacks
Santa Fe, New Mexico

Translator's Notes

On the Names of Man

In Hebrew there are four words each of which might justifiably be translated *man*, but I thought it best to preserve the difference wherever I could. The first two are איש (ish) and אנוש (anosh). Ultimately they both come from the same root which means *weak* or *mortal*, as in the expression *a mortal wound*. איש no longer retains any sense of the meaning of its root, and I have translated it as *man* in the generic sense, not specifically male. The second, אנוש, is more poetical, and perhaps retains a hint of the root. I have used *mortal*. They share a common plural, so that *men* and *mortals* translate the same Hebrew word.

For the word אדם (adam) I have used *human* except where that seemed inappropriate; such instances are acknowledged in footnotes.

The fourth word, גבר (gever), is from a root meaning *strong*. Generally the word means *man*, specifically male. A more forceful form of the word means *hero*, but that word does not appear in the Book of Job. Nevertheless, in most cases, though not all, *hero* seems to catch the poet's intent. Except where otherwise noted, therefore, I have used *hero* consistently for גבר so that each reader can judge.

On the Names of God

The following chart lists the Hebrew names of God, along with the corresponding translations I have adopted:

יהוה	YHWH	the Lord	1:6–2:7, 38:1–42:11
אלהים	*elohim*	God	1:6–2:10, 5:8, 28:23, 34:9, 38:7
אל	*el*	God	3:3–40:1
שדי	*shaddai*	the Almighty	5:17–40:2
אדני	*adonai*	the Lord	28:28
קדוש	*qadosh*	the Holy One	6:10

The name יהוה generally appears on occasions of meeting
with God, as in 1:6, 2:1, 2:7; or when referring to God speaking or being directly spoken to: 1:7, 1:8, 1:9, 1:12, 2:2, 2:3, 2:4,
2:6. There is, however one important exception to this rule in
the passage:

> The LORD (יהוה) *gives, and the* LORD *takes; blessed be the
> name of the* LORD. [1:22]

The name אלהים, GOD, on the other hand, except insofar
as it is used in the expression "The Sons of GOD," consistently
refers to man's awareness of God, as in the following passages:

> *He was a simple and straightforward man, a* GOD-*fearing
> man who turned away from evil.* [1:1]

> *Then the* LORD *said to the Satan: "Did you happen to notice
> my man Job? There is no one like him on Earth. He is a
> simple and straightforward man, a* GOD-*fearing man and
> one who turns away from evil."* [2:3]

> *He himself would get up early in the morning to make a
> burnt offering for each of his children; "For perhaps," Job
> said, "my children have sinned, and cursed* GOD *in their
> hearts."* [1:5]

> *One day the Sons of* GOD *came to present themselves before
> the* LORD, *and the Satan came along with them.* [1:6, 2:1]

> *Then the Satan answered the* LORD *and said: "What, do
> you think that Job fears* GOD *for nothing?"* [1:9]

> *But throughout all that Job never sinned or even charged*
> GOD *with folly.* [1:22]

> *Curse* GOD *and die!* [2:9]

> *If we accept the good from* GOD, *must we not also accept
> the evil?* [2:10]

Pronouns referring to God are not capitalized in this translation.

Fear and Awe

Two Hebrew words, פחד (pachad) and ירא (yira), often become confused in English translation. פחד generally means

fear; ירא denotes *awe,* but it has more of a moral sense than the English word conveys. I will almost always translate פחד as "fear," and ירא as "awe and trepidation" (or, as a verb, "being in awe and trepidation of"). I will, however, retain the time-honored phrase "GOD-fearing," even when ירא is employed. Any other departures from this practice will be noted.

Translation

Chapter One

¹*A* MAN THERE WAS from the land of Uz, and his name was Job. He was a simple and straightforward man, a GOD-fearing man who turned away from evil. ²He had seven sons and three daughters. ³He owned seven thousand sheep, three thousand camels, ten thousand head of cattle, five hundred she-asses and was the head of a very large estate. He was the richest man in the East. ⁴His sons used to make feasts in the home of each man on his day, and send word to their three sisters to come and eat and drink with them. ⁵Now when the days of feasting had gone full circle, Job sent word to them to sanctify themselves. He himself would get up early in the morning to make burnt offerings for each of his children; "For perhaps," Job said, "my children have sinned, and cursed GOD in their hearts." Thus did Job all of his days.

///

1 *man*. See the translator's note on the names of man, page xiii above

GOD. See the translator's note on the names of God, page xiii above.

simple. םָּת (tam). Like its English equivalent, םָּת has a range of meanings, from *whole* to *guileless* or even *foolish*; and even these examples do not adequately suggest the breadth of its usage. The word will importantly reappear in 31:40 and will be treated more fully in the discussion of that verse beginning on page 215 below.

⁶One day the Sons of GOD came to present themselves before the LORD, and the Satan—that is, the Adversary—came along with them.

⁷"Well," said the LORD to the Satan, "where have you been?" "Oh," said the Satan to the LORD, "wandering around Earth. I just went down there to go for a stroll." ⁸Then the LORD said to the Satan, "Did you happen to notice my man Job? There is no one like him on Earth. He is a simple and quite a straightforward man, a GOD-fearing man and one who turns away from evil."

⁹Then the Satan answered the LORD and said: "What, do you think that Job fears GOD for nothing? ¹⁰Haven't you been protecting him and his house, and everything that he has? You have blessed all of his labors, and everything he owns is spreading out all over the land. ¹¹But just reach out your hand to take it away and he will curse you to your face for sure."

¹²"Well, all right," said the LORD, "all that he has is in your hands now; just don't harm him." Then the Satan went out from the presence of the LORD.

¹³One day, when his sons and his daughters were eating and drinking wine in the house of their oldest brother, ¹⁴a messenger came to Job and said, "The oxen

―――――――――――――――――――――――――――――――

⁶ *the Satan.* שׂטן is a root bearing various meanings, including *to oppose* and *to accuse.* As noted in the discussion of Chapter 1, page 99 below, it does not necessarily function here as a proper name.

⁹ *fears.* The Hebrew root is ירא, which would normally be rendered *awe,* as I explained in the Translator's Notes. But "awe" seems too noble a word to appear in the banter which is here taking place between Satan and God.

were plowing and the asses were grazing alongside them, ¹⁵when the Sabeans attacked, taking them all and putting the boys to the sword; and I alone have escaped to tell thee." ¹⁶While he was still talking, another one came in and said, "The fire of GOD fell from heaven. It burnt the sheep and shepherds and devoured them; and I alone have escaped to tell thee." ¹⁷While he was still talking, yet another one came in and said, "The Chaldean sent out three companies, poured down on the camels, carried them off and put the boys to the sword; and I alone have escaped to tell thee." ¹⁸While he was yet talking, another one came in and said, "Your sons and your daughters were eating and drinking wine in the house of their oldest brother, ¹⁹when a mighty wind came in from the wilderness and struck the four corners of the house. It fell down on the young people. They are dead, and I alone have escaped to tell thee."

²⁰Then Job rose up and tore his cloak, shaved his head, and fell to the ground and worshiped. ²¹He said, "Naked I came out of my mother's belly and naked I shall return there. The LORD gives, and the LORD takes; blessed be the name of the LORD." ²²But throughout all that Job never sinned or even charged GOD with folly.

Chapter Two

¹ ONE DAY the Sons of GOD came to present themselves before the LORD, and the Satan came along with
them.

² "Well," said the LORD to the Satan, "where have you
been?"

"Oh," said the Satan to the LORD, "wandering around
Earth; I just went down there to go for a stroll."

³ Then the LORD said to the Satan: "Did you happen to
notice my man Job? There is no one like him on Earth.
He is a simple and quite a straightforward man, a GOD-
fearing man and one who turns away from evil. He is still
holding tight to his simplicity, and you have beguiled me
into destroying him for nothing."

⁴ Then the Satan answered the LORD and said: "Well,
skin beneath skin! Everything a man has he will give for
his life. ⁵ Just reach out your hand and get to his bones
and his flesh, and he will curse you to your face for sure."

⁶ "Well, all right," said the LORD, "he is in your hands
now; just don't kill him."

⁷ Then the Satan went out from the presence of the
LORD and struck Job with boils from the sole of his foot

---

³ *beguiled.* The word תַּסִיתֵנִי (tasiteni), *you beguiled me*, suggests but
does not derive from the root שׂטן (satan)—although they may ultimately
be connected etymologically.

to the crown of his head, *8*and he took a potsherd and scratched himself as he sat in the ashes. *9*His wife then said to him, "You are still holding tight to your simplicity. Curse GOD and die!"

*10*But he said to her: "You talk like a worthless woman. If we accept the good from GOD, must we not also accept the evil?" And throughout all that Job never sinned in speech.

*11*Now when Job's three friends heard about all the evils that had come upon him, they came each man from his own place—Eliphaz the Temanite, Bildad the Shuhite, and Zophar the Na'amathite. They conferred with one another and planned to come together to console him and to show him compassion. *12*But when they raised their eyes even from far off they could hardly recognize him. They lifted up their voices and cried. Then each man tore his robe and threw dust over his head heavenward. *13*Seven days and seven nights they sat with him on the ground and no one spoke a word because they saw how very great his suffering was.

Chapter Three

¹ ℭHEN JOB OPENED his mouth and spurned his day.

²Job answered and said:

³May the day of my birth be lost in oblivion and with it that night in which it was said: "A hero has been conceived." ⁴May that day be a day of darkness. May God from on high not seek it out nor any brightness radiate upon it; ⁵but let darkness and the Shadow of Death redeem it, and may a cloud dwell above it. May that which warms the day terrify it. ⁶Let murk consume that night that it not be counted among the days of the year or enter into the number of its months.

⁷Thus shall that night become hard and sterile with no sound of joy in it. ⁸Those who despise the sea and those who are determined to lay Leviathan open will curse it. ⁹Let its morning stars darken. Let it hope for the light,

///

³ *hero.* I discussed my choice of *hero* as a translation for the Hebrew word גֶּבֶר (gever) in the note on the Names of Man, page xiii above. See also the Discussion of Chapter 3, page 106.

⁵ *Shadow of Death.* צַלְמָוֶת (tzalmavet). Here and elsewhere, I capitalize this phrase to indicate that it translates what I regard as a proper noun. In Hebrew, compound words, of which צַלְמָוֶת is an example, are often proper nouns; improper nouns, on the other hand, are *never* compounds. For more on this word, see the Discussion of Chapter 3, pages 107–108.

⁸ *sea.* Traditionally the word is יוֹם, which certainly means *day*; but the text is doubtful, and some editors have suggested an emendation to יָם, *sea*, because of its association with Leviathan.

but let there be none. May it not see the eyelid of dawn open, *10* for it closed not the doors of my mother's belly but hid my eyes from toil.

11 Why did I not come out of the womb and die, exit the belly and perish? *12* Why were there knees to receive me, and what were those breasts to me that I should have sucked? *13* Else would I have been at ease and had my quiet. *14* I could have slept and had my rest with kings and counselors of the earth, who rebuild ruins for themselves, *15* or with princes who had silver and yet filled their houses with gold.

16 Why was I not like a stillborn hidden away or as a scion that never came into the light? *17* There the guilty cast off their rage and there rest those whose power is spent. *18* There prisoners are wholly at ease, for they do not even hear the driver's voice. *19* Small and great, all are there, and the slave is free of his lord.

20 Why does he give light to those whom toil has consumed, or life to the bitter of soul? *21* Or to those who wait for death when there is none? Or who dig for it even more than for subterranean treasure? *22* Whose delight reaches exaltation, and who rejoice because they have found the grave? *23* Or to a hero whose way has been lost and whom God has hedged about? *24* Sighs do as my

―――――――――――――――――――――――――――――

19 *all*. In general the reader should be aware of the use of the word *all* in this translation. Hebrew is more likely to use *Men are X* where English would use *All men are X*. In these cases we have often decided to follow normal English usage.

bread and my roaring pours out as water. [25] I feared a fear and it came to pass, and what I dreaded has come upon me. [26] I was not at ease, I was not quiet, I had no rest, but rage came.

Chapter Four

1 THEN ELIPHAZ THE TEMANITE answered and said:

2 How can one speak without being more than wearisome? But who can refrain from words? *3* It was you who always [taught] restraint and strengthened so many frail hands, *4* you who had the words to pick up those that were stumbling and bolster the knees that were about to bend. *5* But now it has come upon you, and it is indeed wearisome. It has found you out and you are stunned. *6* But may not that dread itself be your surety and your hope, the simplicity of your ways? *7* Think back now, who being innocent was ever lost? Where have the upright been annihilated? *8* So far as I can see, those who plow evil and sow tribulation reap them. *9* One breath from God, and they are lost, a puff of his nostrils and they are finished. *10* An old lion may roar and the savage lion give voice, but the teeth of that spirited lion will be broken. *11* The lioness is lost for lack of prey, and the young ones will be scattered.

12 A word stole upon me but my ear caught only a trace, *13* as when one gropes in a night vision when deep

―――――――――――――――――――――――――――――――――

3 *[taught].* Words in square brackets [ ] do not appear in the Hebrew text; I have supplied them where necessary for a complete English sentence.

9 *nostrils.* Literally, *nose.* Usually used to signify *anger,* and often translated as such.

sleep falls upon mortals. *14* Fear came upon me and a trembling, making all my bones to quake. *15* A wisp of a breath fluttered over me fixing each hair upon my flesh. *16* It halted. I could not recognize its form, just a shape there before my eyes, and then there was silence. Then I heard a voice saying: *17* "Shall a mortal be more just than his God? or a hero more pure than his maker?"

18 If he puts no trust in his servants and even to his angels lays charge of folly, *19* what of those who dwell in a house of clay, whose foundation is but dust? He will crush them like a moth. *20* They are beaten from morning till evening. Forever they are lost and no note is taken. *21* Their tent rope is pulled out from under them and they die without reason.

Chapter Five

1 CRY OUT! Is there anyone to answer you? To which of the holy ones will you turn now? *2*For indignation can kill a fool and jealousy murder a dunce. *3*I have seen the fool take root and I suddenly broke into his hut. *4*His sons shrank back from help. They were beaten at the gate; and to save them there was none. *5*All that he has harvested the hungry shall devour, even taking out from under the thorns; and the thirsty shall go panting after their wealth. *6*Evil does not come out of the dust nor does tribulation sprout from the ground: *7*but a human is born to tribulation sure as sparks fly upwards.

*8*None the less I would make my appeal to God and put my matter before that GOD *9*who accomplishes deeds great beyond inquiry, marvels which have no number. *10*He who gives out rain over the face of the earth and sends water into the fields, *11*he can raise the despondent on high, giving sanctuary to the mournful. *12*He has shattered the devices of the crafty and their own hands cannot save them. *13*He traps the wise in their own craftiness as the advice of those contorted ones dashes headlong. *14*They encounter darkness by day and grope in the noonday sun as if it were night. *15*But the needy he

---

3 broke into. Literally, *pierced.*

5 The meaning of this verse is exceptionally obscure.

saves from the cutting edge of the sword, and the poor from the hands of the mighty. ¹⁶ The downtrodden will have hope, and the mouth of injustice will be stopped.

¹⁷ Indeed, happy is the mortal whom God restrains, who has no contempt for the bonds of the Almighty. ¹⁸ For he causes pain, but he binds up; he wounds, but his hands heal. ¹⁹ From six troubles he will deliver you, even in seven no evil will touch you. ²⁰ In famine he will redeem you from death, and in war even from the power of the sword. ²¹ When tongues scourge, you will be secure and shall have no dread of violence when it comes; ²² but at violence and starvation you will laugh. Have no dread of the beasts of the earth, ²³ for you have a covenant with the rocks in the field, and the beasts of the fields will bring you peace. ²⁴ You will be certain of harmony in your tent. You shall tend to your flock. and nothing will go amiss. ²⁵ You shall know that your seed will be great and your offspring will be as the grass of the earth. ²⁶ You shall come to your grave in full vigor like a whole shock of wheat standing tall in the time of its harvest. ²⁷ We have searched it out, and thus it is. Listen and you shall know for yourself.

//

²¹⁻²² *dread.* The Hebrew root ירא would ordinarily convey more of awe than of dread. But it seems clear that Eliphaz actually has fear and dread in mind in this speech. To render it as "awe" would imply that Eliphaz regards *being in awe of nature* as the danger he wishes Job to avoid; but such a conception is probably beyond Eliphaz's imaginative power.

Chapter Six

¹ THEN JOB ANSWERED and said:

² Oh, would that my indignation could truly be weighed, my calamities all laid out together on the pan of a scale! ³ Then would it raise up even the sands of the seas. And thus I speak without care, ⁴ for the arrows of the Almighty are upon me, and my spirit drinks in their venom. The terrors of God are arrayed against me. ⁵ Will the wild ass bray when there is grass? Does the ox bellow at his fodder? ⁶ Can what is tasteless be eaten without salt, or does the slime of an egg white have any taste? ⁷ My soul refuses to touch them. They are like a contagion in my daily bread.

⁸ Who will see to it that my request comes to light, that God grant my hopes? ⁹ Would that God were pleased to crush me, loose his hand and cut me off! ¹⁰ That would come to me as compassion. Let me spring up in my writhing though he spare me not; for never have I disavowed the words of the Holy One. ¹¹ What strength have I, that I should wait in expectations? What is my end that I should prolong my life? ¹² Is my strength the strength of a rock? Do I have flesh of bronze? ¹³ No, I have no support within me and all resourcefulness has been driven out.

¹⁴ To those in despair the kindness of friends is due, but trepidation and awe of the Almighty has forsaken them all. ¹⁵ My brothers have betrayed me like a wadi,

a running brook that has gone dry. *¹⁶*They crystal over with ice and invert to black. They hide themselves in snow. *¹⁷*They thaw and disappear. In the heat they vanish from their place.*¹⁸*Their beds twist and turn. They flow out into the vastness and are lost. *¹⁹*The caravans of Tema look to them; the band from Sheba hopes for them *²⁰*but find themselves lost because they trusted. They arrived and were confounded.

*²¹*So now you are as nothing, and at sight of terror you have taken fright. *²²*But did I ever say to you, "Give me"? "Offer the bribe for me out of your wealth"? *²³*"Deliver me from the hand of the foe"? or "Redeem me from the hands of the Most Terrifying"?

*²⁴*Teach me and I will hold my peace. Only show me where I have erred. *²⁵*How forceful honest words are, but what proofs are they that come from you! *²⁶*Are you busy devising a proof in words while taking the testimony of a despairing man to be no more than the wind? *²⁷*Would you cast down an orphan, out a friend? *²⁸*Come, face me; I'll not lie to you. *²⁹*Stop, I beg you! Let there be no injustice. Give in! For yet my stand smacks of what is right. *³⁰*There is no injustice on my tongue, and yet does not my palate know the taste of ruination?

///

²¹ at sight of terror you have taken fright. תְּרְאוּ חֲתַת וַתִּירָאוּ. With "sight" and "fright" I am attempting to capture the musicality underlying Job's play on the words תִּרְאוּ (tir'u, *you see*), and תִּירָאוּ (tir'a'u, *you fear*). Remember that Job is answering Eliphaz, whose concern is fear and not awe; recall my remark on 5:22.

Chapter Seven

¹ *D*OES NOT A MORTAL have a term of duty to serve here on earth, and are not his days like the days of a hired servant? ² Like a slave he yearns for the shadows, like a hireling he hopes for his wages. ³ So have I been allotted months of emptiness. Nights of toil have they apportioned me. ⁴ I lie down and say, "When shall I arise?" and night drags on and I am sated with tossing till morning twilight.

⁵ My flesh is clothed in maggots and clumps of earth. My skin has become hard and begins to ooze. ⁶ The days fly by me swifter than the weaver's shuttle, and reach their culmination in bare empty hope.

⁷ Remember that life is but a wind and that never will the sight of happiness return to my eyes. ⁸ The eye that sees me takes no note of me; your eye is upon me, and I am not. ⁹ As a cloud that reaches to its fullness and is gone, so he who descends into the Pit arises no more. ¹⁰ He will not return home again, and no one there would recognize him any longer.

¹¹ No, I cannot restrain speech, but will speak out of the narrowness constricting my spirit. I will complain in the bitterness of my soul. ¹² Am I the sea or some

---

⁹ the Pit. שְׁאוֹל (sheol).

monster that you set watch over me? *13* When I said that my bed will show me compassion and my couch bear my complaint, *14* you frightened me with dreams and terrified me with visions; *15* and I preferred strangulation and death to my own substance. *16* I have contempt; I will not live forever. Then just let me be, for my days are but the mist of a breath.

17 What is a mortal that thou shouldst magnify him? And that thou shouldst set thine heart upon him? *18* Yes, and inspect him every morning and test him every minute. *19* When will you let me be? You'll not even let me alone to swallow my own spit. *20* Supposing I have sinned, what have I done to you, O thou Great Watcher of Man? Why have you set me on course against you so that I have become a burden even unto myself? *21* Why can you not pardon my transgressions or bear my perversions? For now I shall lie down in the dust. You will seek for me, but I am not.

///

13 *bear*. Hebrew נשׂא. I translate this verb as *bear* except as otherwise noted.

20 *Man*. Here translating אדם (adam).

Chapter Eight

1 THEN BILDAD THE SHUHITE answered and said:

2 How long will you continue to recite these things with words of such mighty wind? *3* Will God pervert judgment? Will the Almighty pervert right? *4* If your sons have sinned against him will he not drive them into the hands of their transgression? *5* But if you seek God out and implore the Almighty, *6* and if you are pure and upright, surely then he will rouse himself up for you. He will make your righteous hut to flourish. *7* And though your beginnings be small, your legacy will grow great indeed.

8 Only ask of the first generations. Seat yourself firmly upon what their fathers had searched out; *9* for we are only of a yesterday and know nothing, our days are but a shadow passing over the land. *10* Will they not teach you and speak to you as the words come tumbling out of their heart?

11 Can papyrus flourish where there is no marsh? Or can reed flourish without water? *12* While yet in their tender days, they wither before any grass, still unpicked. *13* Such is the course for all those who forget God. For him all hope will vanish. The profane man is lost, *14* for he who feels a loathing for his own sense of trust will come to rely upon a spider web.

15 He will lean upon his house but it will not hold; he will hold fast to it but it will not stand. *16* It may sit fresh under the sun and shoots may spring up in his garden, *17* with roots twining round a knoll and clinging to the house of stone. *18* Yet his own habitat will devour him and deny him, saying, "I have never seen you!" *19* Such are the delights of his ways, and out of the dust another will spring. *20* But surely God will neither have contempt for a simple man nor strengthen the hand of the evil-doer. *21* He will fill your mouth with laughter, and your lips with shouts of joy. *22* Those who hate you will be clothed in shame, and the tent of the guilty will vanish.

//

14 feels a loathing. The English Standard Version translates: "His confidence is severed, and his trust is a spider's web"; most translators have some variant of this understanding. But Young's Literal Translation renders: "Whose confidence is loathsome, and the house of a spider his trust." The heart of the problem is the word יָקוֹט (yaqut), from the root קוֹט. The difficulty is that there are two such roots. The first is an assumed variant form of קטט, to *break* or *snap*. Although קטט appears nowhere else in the Bible, its cognate can be found in Arabic. The second root קוֹט is a rather common variant form of קוץ, to *feel a loathing*. This form can be found in Job 10:1, as well as three times in the Book of Psalms, and four times in Ezra; and such is the rendering I have adopted in this verse.

Chapter Nine

¹ THEN JOB ANSWERED and said:

² Yes, all that I know; but then what can make a mortal's justice apparent to God? ³ Even if one wanted to go to trial with him, he would not answer, no, not one in a thousand. ⁴ Wise of heart—mighty in power, who can stand fast against him and remain unbroken? ⁵ He who can transport the mountains and they feel it not; or overturn them in his anger, ⁶ who can cause the earth to reel from its place till its pillars rage! ⁷ He who says a word to the sun, and it does not rise; who seals up the stars, ⁸ and who by himself spreads out the heavens and tramples on the tier of the sea; ⁹ who made Arcturus and Orion, the Pleiades, and the Chambers of the South; ¹⁰ who accomplishes great things, there is no finding them out—wonders without number.

¹¹ He passes by me, but I cannot see him. He moves on, but I do not comprehend him. ¹² He snatches up, and who can stop him? Who can say to him, "What is it you are about to do?" ¹³ But God will not turn back his anger. Under his rule even the ministers of Rahab bend low.

///

⁵ *anger.* For the sake of consistency I have held to the following conventions, even though they seem somewhat arbitrary at times:

אף (af)	כעס (ka'as)	חמה (chamah)	גור (gur)	חת (chat)
anger	indignation	fury	terror	dread

¹⁴I would now answer him, choosing my words against him with care, ¹⁵but even though I am in the right, still I cannot do it. Yet I must plead for what seems to me just.

¹⁶Even if I were to summon him and he were to answer me, even then I do not believe that he would pay me any mind, ¹⁷for he is the one that can crush me for a hair or multiply my wounds, gratis. ¹⁸He will not even let me catch my breath, but sates me with bitterness. ¹⁹If trial be by strength, he is the mighty one; and if by court of law, who will plead my case? ²⁰Though I am just, my own mouth would condemn me. I am simple but he will show me twisted. ²¹I am simple but I no longer care and have only contempt for my life.

²²It's all one. Therefore I say that, simple or guilty, he destroys all. ²³When the whip suddenly brings death, he mocks as the innocent despair. ²⁴The earth has been placed into the hands of the guilty. He has covered the eyes of its judges. If it be not he, then where is that one?

²⁵My days are swifter than the post. They take flight for they have seen no good. ²⁶They pass through with the reed boats; they swoop down like an eagle upon its prey. ²⁷Even if I should say, "Let me forget my complaint, abandon my long visage and put on a cheerful look," ²⁸even then would I yet feel the dread of all my grief, since I know that you will never find me pure. ²⁹I will still be found guilty. Why then toil for an airy nothing? ³⁰If I were to wash in snowy waters and cleanse my hands with lye, ³¹you would dip me in the muck till even my clothes would hold me in abomination.

³²He is not a man as I am, that I can answer him, that we can come together under judgment. ³³There is no

arbitrator between us who can lay his hand on us both!
[34] But let him turn his rod away from me and not frighten me with his terror; [35] then I could speak without trepidation and awe of him, for in myself I am none of these things.

Chapter Ten

*¹M*Y SPIRITS feel a loathing towards life. I will unleash my complaint and speak in the bitterness of my soul. *²*To God I say: Do not condemn me, but let me know the cause of this struggle against me. *³*Does it seem good to you that you oppress, that you have contempt for the toil of your own hand, but radiate upon the counsel of the guilty? *⁴*Do you have eyes of flesh? Can you see as mortals see? *⁵*Can time mean to you what it means to a mortal? Do your years pass by as the years of a human, *⁶*that you probe back into my perversions and track down my every sin? *⁷*Somewhere in your mind I am not guilty, and yet there is none to save me from your hand.

*⁸*Your hands toiled over me and made me and yet from all about they devour me. *⁹*Remember that you made me as clay and that you will return me to dust. *¹⁰*You poured me out like milk and thickened me like cheese. *¹¹*With skin and flesh you clothed me, and knit me all together with bones and sinews. *¹²*Your dealings with me were full of life and full of loving care. Your guardianship watched

//

⁵ *mortal.* אנוש (anosh). See the translator's note on the Names of Man, page xiii above.

   human. גבר (gever). As I explained in the translator's note on the Names of Man, גבר generally has the force of "hero" in the Book of Job. In this instance, however, Job means to contrast what is mortal with what is immortal , and therefore I have rendered the word as *human*.

over my spirit, *13*and you treasured all these things up in your heart. But I know what you have in mind; *14*if I sin you will be watching and you will not clear me from my perversion. *15*Well, if I have been guilty, the grief is mine; but even when I am innocent I have been so sated with reproach that no feeling of honor is left in me and I see only my own feebleness. *16*You must feel the majestic pride of a lion in hunting me. Must you always use me to manifest your wonders? *17*Continually you bring new witnesses against me, feeding your indignation against me. Army after army is upon me.

*18*Why did you bring me out of the womb? Had I only perished without ever an eye to see me, *19*I would be as though I had not been, as though I had been led from the belly to the grave. *20*So little time remains. Forbear! Leave me a bit that I may be cheerful. *21*Well, I will be going soon, going to a land of darkness and the Shadow of Death, and I will not return; *22*to a land, a darkness of murk, the Shadow of Death and without order—a land whose light is murk.

Chapter Eleven

1 THEN ZOPHAR THE NA'AMATHITE answered and said:

2 Will this multitude of words never be answered? Must the man with the quick lip always be in the right? *3* Do you think that this claptrap of yours should bring all men to silence? Do you really believe you can mock without being rebuked? *4* You say, "My tenets are spotless. I am pure in Thy sight." *5* Oh, if only God himself would open his lips and speak to you, *6* tell you the secrets of wisdom; for discernment is many-sided, and you must know that God will bear some of your perversions for you.

7 The deepest things of God, can you find them out? Would you discover the utmost things of the Almighty? *8* It is higher than heaven—what can you do? Deeper than the Pit—what can you know? *9* Longer than the earth is its measure and broader than the sea. *10* If he should pass by and separate or close up, who can turn him back? *11* He knows the worthless man. Can he see wickedness and not ponder it? *12* Hollow man will become thoughtful when the wild ass gives birth to a human.

13 But if you direct your heart firmly and spread out your hands to him *14* and if, when there is wickedness in your hand, you remove it, and let no injustice dwell in your tent, *15* then shall you bear your countenance high above all blemish. You will be firm and have no trepidation. ¹⁶ You will forget all toil and think of it only as water that has flowed by. ¹⁷ Life will arise out of the noonday sun and soar as the morning. ¹⁸ You will be secure because there will be hope. You will burrow in and lie at ease. ¹⁹ You will be in repose and none shall make you afraid. Many will seek your favor. ²⁰ But the eyes of the guilty will fail. For them, all escape is lost, and their one hope is to exhale the spirit.

Chapter Twelve

¹ THEN JOB ANSWERED and said:

² You are indeed of the people, and with you learning will die; ³ but like you, I too have some understanding which does not fall short of yours. Who is not capable of such things? ⁴ But now I have become a joke to my friends, one who would "call on God and have him answer"; simple and just, yet still a joke! ⁵ For those who can think at their ease there is always scorn for calamity. But it's out there waiting for anyone whose foot should happen to slip. ⁶ Oh, there is peace enough in the tents of robbers and security for those who enrage God, which God himself has placed in their hand.

⁷ Just ask the beasts and they will show you; or the birds in the sky, they can tell you, ⁸ or have a chat with the earth and it will teach you. Even the fish in the sea can relate the tale for you. ⁹ Who among all these does not know that it was the hand of the LORD that has done all this?

¹⁰ In his hand is the soul of every living thing and the breath of each bodily man. ¹¹ Does not the ear try words as the palate tastes food? ¹² Is wisdom with the old, or does length of days make for understanding?

---

⁶ The meaning of this verse is obscure.

13 With him are wisdom and valor. His are counsel and understanding, *14* and what he tears down can never be rebuilt. He closes in on a man and nothing is ever reopened. *15* He restrains the waters and all is parched. He sends them out again and the land is overturned. *16* With him are strength and soundness. Both the one who errs and the one who causes the error are his. *17* He makes counselors to go about ravaged, and even the judges he drives into madness. *18* He undoes the restraint of kings and restrains by a strip about their loins. *19* He makes priests to go about ravaged, and subverts the mighty. *20* He obliterates the speech of the trustworthy and takes taste from the elders. *21* He pours out disgrace upon noble men and closes the girdle of the well armed. *22* He unveils deep things from out of the darkness; he leads the Shadow of Death out into the light. *23* He makes nations great, and then he destroys them. He expands nations, and there he leaves them. *24* He obliterates the heart from the heads of the peoples of the earth. He makes them to wander through chaos with no path. *25* They grope in the darkness without a light. He makes them wander like a drunken man.

Chapter Thirteen

1 ALL THIS MY EYE HAS SEEN; my ear has heard all and understood. *2* Whatever you know, I know, nor do I fall short of you. *3* I would speak with the Almighty! I wish to argue with God. *4* But you are a bunch of worthless doctors who plaster over with lies. *5* Who can move you to silence? It would be wisdom on your part. *6* Hear my argument; listen to my quarrel.

7 Would you speak unjustly for God's sake? For his sake would you speak words of treachery? *8* Would you show him favor, or even argue his case for him? *9* Will it turn out to be good when he comes to examine you? Do you think you can deceive him as you can deceive a mortal? *10* Certainly he himself would argue against you. If you were to show him even hidden favor, *11* would his preference not be to terrify and let his fear fall upon you? *12* Your aphorisms are proverbs of ash, your bulwarks, bulwarks of clay.

13 Be silent now for my sake, and I will speak, let come upon me what may. *14* For what reason do I take my flesh between my teeth and my life in my hands? *15* It may be that he will slay me. I have no higher expectations.

―――――――――――――――――――――――――――――

15 It may be … no higher expectations. This is the כתיב (*ketiv*—what is actually written). The קרי (*keri*—how tradition says it is actually to be read) gives: "Though he slay me, yet will I trust in him."

Nonetheless I will defend my ways before him. [16] That too has become for me salvation, for the impious do not approach him.

[17] Listen, listen to my words. With your ears attend to my declaration. [18] I have laid out my case and I know I shall be vindicated. [19] Who is he that would contend with me? Now, as things are, I can only remain silent and perish. [20] Do but two things for me and I shall no longer be hid from your face. [21] Remove your hand from me, and let not your terror frighten me. [22] Then summon me up and I will reply, or let me speak and you shall give answer.

[23] How many are my perversions and my sins? Let me know my transgression and my vices. [24] Why do you hide your face from me and think of me as your enemy? [25] Would you terrorize me like a driven leaf? Or put me to flight like a piece of dry straw, [26] that you write bitter things against me and bring up the perversions of my youth? [27] You put my feet in the stocks. You scrutinize my every wandering. You circumscribe the foundation under my feet, [28] and it all becomes worn out like a rotten thing—like a piece of cloth that the moths have eaten.

Chapter Fourteen

¹A HUMAN IS BORN OF WOMAN, short-lived and full of rage. ²He sprouts up as a fresh bud and withers. He flits by as a shadow and cannot endure. ³Can you open your eyes even to one such as that, and yet come along with him to proceedings raised against you? ⁴Who can bring a clean thing out of an unclean thing? Not one! ⁵His time is fixed. You keep the number of his months. You have set him a limit which he cannot overstep. ⁶Then turn your gaze from him and let him be, so long as his days as a hireling are acceptable.

⁷For a tree there is hope. If it is cut down, it renews itself and its sprouting never wanes. ⁸When its roots become old in the land and its stump is left in the dust to die, ⁹then even at the mere scent of water it bursts into bloom and sends out branches like a young sapling. ¹⁰But when a hero dies, he perishes and is no more. A human expires, and where is he? ¹¹The waters are gone from the sea. The river becomes a wasteland and is dried up. ¹²A man lies down and rises not. Till the heavens are no more they shall not wake nor be roused from their slumber.

¹³Who can move you to hide me in the Pit and conceal me till your anger passes? Set me a fixed limit and remember me. ¹⁴If a hero dies, will he come back to life again?

All the days of my service I have waited in expectation for my release to come. ¹⁵You would call, I would answer, and you would have love for the work of your hands. ¹⁶ Then no longer would you keep track of my every step and scrutinize my sin. ¹⁷ My transgression would be sealed up in a pouch and you would plaster over my perversions.

¹⁸ A mountain has fallen and crumbled away, a rock dislodged from its place. ¹⁹ The waters have worn the stones away and its torrents have washed away the dust of the land. So you have trashed all mortal hope. ²⁰ You have overpowered man, and he has resigned. You have mangled his face and sent him off. ²¹ His sons were honored but he never knew of it. They were in disgrace, but he was unaware. ²² His body surrounds him with pain, and his spirit is eaten away.

Chapter Fifteen

¹*Then* Eliphaz the Temanite answered and said:

²Should a wise man even answer such blustery thoughts and fill his own belly with the east wind? ³Should he argue with such barren words and idle talk that goes nowhere? ⁴You have abandoned awe and deserted the grounds of all discourse with God. ⁵Your perversion has taught your mouth and you have chosen a crafty tongue. ⁶Your own mouth condemns you, not I, and your own lips have testified against you.

⁷Were you the first human to be born? Did you come writhing into being before the hills? ⁸Have you been listening in on God's secret council? Why, you have set all wisdom aside for yourself. ⁹What do you know that we do not know or understand that we are not able to? ¹⁰Both the hoary-headed and the aged are among us, more resplendent in days than your father. ¹¹Are the compassion of God and his gentle words too meager for you? ¹²What has taken hold of your heart and so dazzled your eyes ¹³that you have turned your spirit on God and dredged

///

¹² *What has so dazzled your eyes...?* וּמַה־יִּרְזְמוּן עֵינֶיךָ. The root רזם, here rendered as *dazzle*, is unknown outside of this verse but is assumed to have some connection with light. RSV construes "your eyes" (עֵינֶיךָ) as the subject, rendering: "Why do your eyes flash?" But while the Hebrew word מַה can mean *why*, its primary meaning is *what*. Thus I take "your eyes" as the object, yielding the present rendition.

up such words out of your mouth? *14* What is a mortal that he should be clean, or one born of woman that he should consider himself just?

15 If he puts no trust in his holy ones and even the heavens are not clean in his sight, *16* what of man—that abhorred and corrupted one—who drinks up injustice like water!

17 I will show you. Listen to me! This thing have I surely seen and will relate, *18* a thing which the wise have reported from their fathers and have not withheld. *19* To them alone has the land been given, and no stranger has gone among them.

20 The guilty one writhes in pain all his days and the number of his years lies hidden from those who can terrorize. *21* Sounds of fear are always in his ear. When he is at ease, a robber will fall upon him. *22* He can have no trust that he will return from the darkness, and he is ever on guard against a sword. *23* He wanders for bread, not knowing where. He knows only that the day of darkness is ready at hand.

24 Narrowness and anguish oppress him. They overwhelm him like a king set for battle, *25* for he has stretched out his hand against God and played the hero against the Almighty. *26* Neck down, he charges against him with his thickly-bossed shield, *27* his face covered with fat and his haunches bloated.

28 He dwells in cities of desolation, in houses not fit to be lived in and bound for the trash heap. *29* He will not become rich. What wealth he has will not last, nor will his possessions spread themselves over the earth. *30* He will not be turned from the darkness, but a flame turned aside by the breath of his own mouth will dry up his young saplings. *31* Let him not trust in a deceitful nothing, for his compensation will be nothing.

32 He will be finished before his time. His fronds will never turn to moisty green, *33* but like a vine he will cruelly cast off his unripe grapes and reject his own blossoms like the olive—*34* for the congregation of the polluted is a barren place, and the tents of bribery are a consuming fire. *35* They conceive toil and give birth to wickedness. Their belly brews deceit.

Chapter Sixteen

1 ⸆HEN JOB ANSWERED and said:

2 I have heard too much of this rot. Bringers of a toilsome compassion, the whole lot of you! *3* Is there no end to such blustery talk? What ails you that you answer me so? *4* I too could speak as you do if it were you instead of me! I could heap words upon you and shake my head; *5* strengthen you with my words or hold you in check by the motion of my lips. *6* But when I speak, my own pain is not held in check, nor does it subside when I am quiet.

7 Oh, how he has worn me out! You have wiped out my whole community. *8* You have shriveled me up as a witness, and this distortion has risen up to testify against me. *9* His malevolent anger tears at me. He gnashes his teeth. My foe hones his eyes against me. *10* They gape at me with their mouths. They strike my cheeks to taunt me. They gather en masse against me. *11* God sets the wicked to close in on me and casts me into the hands of guilty men. *12* I was at ease and he shattered me. He grabbed me by the neck and shattered me. He set me out as a target.

13 His bowmen surrounded me. He cleaved open my kidneys without mercy and spilled my bile out on the ground. *14* He broke me breach after breach. He rushed at me as a conqueror. *15* I have sewed sackcloth over my skin. I have driven my horns into the dust. *16* My face is red with weeping and my eyes are covered over with shadowy death, *17* though I have no injustice on my hands and my prayer is pure. *18* Let not the earth cover over my blood or find a place for my outcry. *19* For now my witness must be in heaven. The one who can testify for me must be on high. *20* Oh, my advocates, my friends, my eyes weep before God. *21* Will no one argue for a hero before God as a human should do for a friend? *22* For but a few years will pass by, and then I shall go the way that I shall not return.

Chapter Seventeen

¹MY SPIRIT HAS BEEN DESTROYED and my days snuffed out. The grave is ready for me now. ²Mocking men are always about me and my eye lives under their discontent. ³Put up now, go my surety. Who will be the one to take my hand on it? ⁴So you have protected their hearts from insight, and that is why even you no longer have any respect for them ⁵Why, he would even turn in a friend to get his own cut, but the eyes of his children will comprehend.

⁶Now he has made a folk adage of me, and I've become as Tophet of old. ⁷My eyes are blind from indignation

///

⁵ *comprehend.* תִּכְלֶנָה (tikhlenah). RSV renders: "The eyes of his children will fail." Greenberg translates: "The eyes of his children will pine away." Alter: "and his sons' eyes waste away." The root כלה has as its foundation the notion of *all,* or *a whole.* As a verb it can mean either *to be complete* or *to be all* as in the Pennsylvania Dutch expression "Papa is all," that is, "Papa is dead." I have taken it in the former sense, RSV and Greenberg in the latter.

⁶ *Tophet.* The text is quite unclear at this point, but if the translation is correct, the reference is to one of the valleys below the walls of Jerusalem.

> *And they have built the high place of Tophet, which is in the valley of the son of Hinnom, to burn their sons and their daughters in the fire; which I did not command, now did it come into my mind. Therefore, behold, the days are coming, says the Lord, when it will no more be called Tophet, or the valley of the son of Hinnom, but the valley of Slaughter: for they will bury in Tophet, because there is no room elsewhere. (Jer. 7:31–32)*

(continued overleaf)

and all form appears to me but as shadows. *8* The upright are appalled by that. The pure raise up against such impiety. *9* The righteous hold tight to their ways. The man of clean hands adds to his strength. *10* Then let them all pass by in review. No, I find no wise man among you.

11 My days have passed by. My ambitions have been snapped, all that my heart possesses. *12* They claim it is day when it is night, and in the face of darkness they say that light is near. *13* If then I must take the Pit to be my home and spread out my couch in darkness, *14* call out to the muck, "Thou art my Father," and call out "Mother" and "Sister" to the maggots, *15* where then is my hope? O my hopes, who will ever take note of them? *16* They have all sunk down into the Pit and together they lie in the dust.

And he defiled Tophet, which is in the valley of the sons of Hinnom, that no one might burn his son or his daughter as an offering to Molech. (II Kings 23:10)

Tophet did, indeed, become a kind of byword:

Thus will I do to this place, says the Lord, and to its inhabitants, making this city like Tophet. The houses of Jerusalem and the houses of the kings of Judah—all the houses upon whose roofs incense has been burned to all the host of heaven and drink offerings have been poured out to other gods shall be defiled like the place of Tophet. (Isa. 19:12–13)

Chapter Eighteen

¹ THEN BILDAD ANSWERED and said:

² How long will you continue to set these traps in speech? Try to understand and then we will speak. ³ Why are we considered beasts and made unclean in your eyes? ⁴ You, you who tear yourself apart in anger, is the earth to be abandoned for your sake? Or the rock dislodged from its place?

⁵ The light of the wicked will be smothered and there will be no glow around his fire. ⁶ Light will turn dark in his tent. His candle will fail him. ⁷ The stride of his perversion will be hobbled. His plans will trip him up, ⁸ for his own feet will lead him into a net, and he will stroll himself right into the trap. ⁹ A snare will grab him by the heel, a web tighten about him. ¹⁰ His appointed rope lies hidden in the ground, a snare on his path. ¹¹ Terror falls upon him from everywhere sending his feet at odds. ¹² His vigor will know starvation: disaster is headed straight for his ribs. ¹³ His skin will be eaten away; death's firstborn will consume his members. ¹⁴ He will be torn from his tent of safety and marched off to the King of Terror. ¹⁵ It takes up lodging in his tent uninvited, brimstone scattered over his hut.

¹⁶ His roots will be dried up from beneath, and his branches parched from above. ¹⁷ All recollection of him will be lost from the land and he will have no name

abroad. ¹⁸He will be thrust from light into darkness and driven from this fruitful ground. ¹⁹For him there will be no heir or scion, not a shred left in all his haunts. ²⁰They of the west are horrified by his days, and they of the east are seized by confusion. ²¹These are indeed the dwellings of the unjust, for this is the place that knew not God.

///

¹⁸ *fruitful ground.* תֵבֵל (tayvayl). This word is often translated *face of the earth*. The initial ת, along with the vocalic pattern, would suggest that it is a noun derived from יבל, *produce* (of land).

Chapter Nineteen

¹ THEN JOB ANSWERED and said:

²How long will you torment my spirit and crush me with words? ³These ten times you have humiliated me! Do you feel no shame to be so harsh towards me? ⁴Even if I have erred, that error must lodge within me; ⁵but if you must place yourselves above me to prove my disgrace, ⁶know that it is God himself who has perverted me.

⁷He has encircled me with his net. I scream, "Violence!" but I get no answer. I cry out, but there is no place of judgment. ⁸He has barred the road and I cannot pass through. He has covered my path with darkness, ⁹stripped all glory from me, and removed the crown from my head.

¹⁰He tears at me from all sides round and so I retreat. He uproots my hopes like a tree. ¹¹His anger burns against me, and he accounts me as one of his foes. ¹²Together, his troops advance. They erect a highway toward me and encamp round about my tent.

¹³He made my brothers withdraw from me, and of my friends he has made strangers. ¹⁴Those who were close to me have left; and those who knew me have

---

⁴ *erred.* שָׁגִיתִי. The word implies a wrong done inadvertently.

all forgotten. ¹⁵ Those who lived in my house and the women who served me account me an alien and to them I have become no more than a stranger. ¹⁶ I called to my servant, but he gave no answer, and now must I curry to him for favor. ¹⁷ My breath is repulsive to my wife, and to the sons of my own belly I am loathsome. ¹⁸ Even children have contempt for me. When I rise, they speak against me. ¹⁹ All those who were closest to me abhor me and those I loved have turned against me. ²⁰ My bones stick to my skin and to my flesh. Only the skin of my teeth ceases to hold.

²¹ Be gentle with me, you, my friends, be gentle, for the hand of God has struck me. ²² Why do you pursue me like God, taking satisfaction out of my flesh?

²³ Who will find a place that my words may be written down? Who will see to it that they are inscribed in the Book: ²⁴ with stylus of iron and with lead incised in rock forever? ²⁵ Yet I know that my vindicator lives and that one day he will stand up upon the dust.

²⁶ Even after my skin has been stripped away, yet from out of my raw flesh shall I behold God. ²⁷ It is I myself who shall see. My own eyes must behold, and not those of a stranger, although the vitals within my bosom are finished. ²⁸ You have said: "How are we persecuting him?" The root of the matter, they say, lies within me.

---

²⁰ *skin of my teeth*. I take this phrase to refer to Job's gums.

[29] But stand in terror of the sword, for fury is a perversion meet for the sword, that you may know that there is judgment.

//

[29] *But stand in terror of the sword...* It seems quite impossible to say what this verse could mean, coming from the mouth of Job at this time. Many people think that it has either been transposed from somewhere else in the poem or that the text has been terribly garbled. All this and more is possible; I thought it best to follow the received text as assiduously as I could, in hopes of traveling at least approximately in the direction intended by the poet.

Chapter Twenty

1 THEN ZOPHAR THE NA'AMATHITE answered and said:

2 It is my disquietude that would have me answer; all for a feeling that lies within me, *3* for I seem to hear the admonition of my own shame; a spirit out of my own understanding would have me reply.

4 Do you know this, that from timeless time, since humankind was set upon the earth, *5* the joy of the guilty has been quick, and the delight of the defiled but of a moment. *6* Though his loftiness rise to the heavens, his head reaching to the clouds, *7* like his own dung he will be lost in eternity. Even those who see him will ask, "Where is he?" *8* He flies off as a dream and no one can find him. He recedes like a vision of the night. *9* The eyes that observed him have given o'er; they no longer even take note of him in his place.

10 His sons find favor with the poor; their hands return his wealth. *11* His bones are full of vigor, yet they lie with him in the dust. *12* Though evil bring sweetness to his lips and he hide it under his tongue, *13* cherish it, never to abandon it, but retain it on his palate, *14* the bread in his bowels will become the gall of an asp within him. *15* He devours wealth only to vomit it back, for God has seized it from out of his belly. *16* He will suck the poison of asps and the tongue of a viper will slay him.

17 He shall not see the streams, the rivers, or brooks of honey and butter. *18* The fruit of his labors he shall return and never consume. Oh, he will receive the full compensation of his labors but it will bring no joy. ¹⁹He may steal a house, but he cannot cause it to flourish; for he has crushed and abandoned the poor. ²⁰Since he knew no peace from his belly he cannot escape through his pleasure.

²¹There will be no survivor to enjoy it and thus nothing of his good shall endure. ²²Though all his needs are fulfilled, he will feel hard pressed. The hand of toil will be upon him. ²³As he is about to fill his belly, he will send out his burning anger upon him and rain it down upon him into his bread. ²⁴He will flee a weapon of iron only to be overturned by a bow made of brass. ²⁵Drawn, and through his body it goes, lightning swift into the gall, and terror strikes at him.

²⁶The whole of darkness has been stored up to be his treasure. He will be consumed by an unblown fire and all shall go ill with the remnant left in his tent. ²⁷The heavens will expose his perversion, and the earth shall rise up against him. ²⁸The harvest of his land will be exposed, trickled away on the day of his wrath. ²⁹Such is the portion of the wicked human; an inheritance left him by the word of God.

---

²³ *As he is about to fill his belly, he will send out his burning anger.* The first "he" refers to man, specifically to the guilty man of verse 5; the second "he" refers to God. The Hebrew pronoun easily switches its subject, even in the course of a single sentence. We find another such example in 21:19 below.

Chapter Twenty-One

¹ *T*HEN JOB ANSWERED and said:

²Listen well to my words; let that be your compassion. ³Bear with me while I speak, and after I have spoken, then you may mock. ⁴Is my complaint against humankind? If it were, why has my spirit not worn itself out? ⁵Turn to me and be appalled. Clap your hand to your mouth. ⁶When I remember, I am filled with terror and a palsy grips my flesh.

⁷Why do the wicked live on, ancient, yet heroic in power, their seed firmly established by their side, ⁸their progeny spread out before their eyes? ⁹Their homes are at peace, without fear, for the stave of God is not upon them. ¹⁰Their bull breeds and is not rejected. His cow drops her calf with never a miscarry. ¹¹They set their babes free as sheep; their children dance. ¹²They strike up with timbrel and with lute and rejoice to the strains of a pipe. ¹³They spend their days in good cheer and in peace they descend into the Pit. ¹⁴They say unto God: "Turn yourself away from us. We have no desire to know your ways. ¹⁵What is this Almighty that we should serve him? How shall we profit if we do come to terms with him?" ¹⁶Is not good fortune in their hand? Though such counsel of the wicked

///

¹⁶ *Is not good fortune in their hand?* הֵן לֹא בְיָדָם טוּבָם. Greenberg translates: "Their happiness is not their own doing." In the Book of Job it is often difficult to distinguish a negative statement from a negatively worded rhetorical question, which, as in English, implies a strongly

is beyond me, [17]how often is it that the lamp of wicked is put out, or that calamities come upon them; or how often does he allot them pain in his anger? [18]Are they as straw before the wind, or as chaff that the storm has made off with?

[19]God, you say, will treasure up all his wickedness to lay upon his sons. Why then, let him complete the bargain now and then shall he learn. [20]Let his eyes see his own ruin and let him drink of the Almighty's cruet of fury: [21]for what does he care for his house after he has gone, and the number of his months has been cut off?

[22]Would he teach understanding even to that God who can judge those who are on high? [23]One dies in his simplicity, wholly at ease and secure. [24]His skin is sleek; the marrow of his bones still moist. [25]Another dies in the bitterness of his soul, never having eaten of goodness, [26]yet together they lie in the dust, and the worms cover them over.

[27]Oh, I know what you are thinking, the machination you have devised against me. [28]For you say, "Where is

---

worded positive answer. For example: "Is that not so?" strongly implies that it *is* so. But the author of Job often leaves it up to the reader to distinguish between "Is that not so?" and "That is not so!" It is a very common problem throughout the whole of the book, and each translator must deal with it as best he can. RSV and KJV translate about the same as I do.

[18] *made off with.* What was said in the note to verse 16 applies equally to verses 17–19, and translations differ greatly.

[20] *drink of the Almighty's cruet of fury.* וּמֵחֲמַת שַׁדַּי יִשְׁתֶּה. I have taken מֵחֲמַת (mechamat) as a kind of play on words. It could mean *from anger*, from the root חמס, meaning *hot*; but together with the word יִשְׁתֶּה, *drink*, as here, one cannot help also hearing its homonym, from the otherwise unknown root חמת; that word denotes some kind of drinking vessel, perhaps a wineskin.

the house of this prince? Where is this tent, this dwelling place of the evil ones?" ²⁹ Have you not inquired of every passer by, and did you not recognize his sign ³⁰ that the wicked man is spared on the day of calamity, rescued from the frenzy? ³¹ And who can make him face his ways? Well, his deeds are done now, and who will repay him? ³² When he is brought to the grave, they will set a vigil over his tomb. ³³ The clods of the wadi will fall sweetly upon him. Every human will march along after him, and those who precede him will be without number.

³⁴ How, then, can you offer me such empty compassion when your answers remain full of treachery?

Chapter Twenty-Two

¹ T HEN ELIPHAZ THE TEMANITE answered and said:

²Can a hero be of use to his God as a prudent man can be of use to a friend? ³When you act justly, does it give the Almighty any kind of pleasure? Does he profit when your ways become simple? ⁴Do you really think that it is because of your awe and trepidation that he has rebuked you and hauled you up for judgment? ⁵Oh, you are evil. Are there no bounds to your perversions? ⁶You have impounded your brothers on a whim, and whatever clothed the naked you have stripped away. ⁷You have given no water for the weary to drink, and bread you have withheld from the hungry. ⁸And so the land goes to the man of arms. The favored occupy it; ⁹but the widow you have sent away empty-handed, and the arms of the fatherless have been crushed. ¹⁰And for that you have been surrounded by snares, fear strikes you of a sudden, ¹¹or darkness so that you cannot see, and a flood of waters has covered you over.

¹²Is not God high in the heavens? Only look to the utmost star. See how far off it is. ¹³And so you say: "How much can God know? Can he judge from behind that thick mist? ¹⁴Clouds have obscured him and he can see nothing as he strolls round the circuit of heaven."

---

⁸ *favored.* נְשׂוּא פָנִים. Literally, "of raised countenance."

15 Have you kept to that primordial path which the men of wickedness have trod, *16* men who were snatched up before their time? Their foundation flows off in a stream. *17* Those who say to God, "Leave us be!"—how can the Almighty do anything about that, *18* when it was he who filled their houses with all kinds of good? Though the counsel of the guilty is beyond me, *19* the righteous see it and rejoice; even the innocent show derision, *20* saying, "Has not our enemy been destroyed, their remains consumed by fire?"

21 Please, come close to him and be at peace. All good things will come your way. *22* Receive guidance from his mouth and keep his saying in your heart. *23* If you will return to the Almighty and be rebuilt, if you keep injustice far from your tent, *24* take gold dust for sand and nuggets as mere rocks in a stream, *25* the Almighty will be your gold and most precious silver; *26* for then you shall have taken delight in the Almighty and raised your countenance up unto God. *27* If you supplicate to him, he will hear you, and you will have fulfilled your vows. *28* Proclaim your words and thus it shall be. A light will shine upon your path. *29* When men have sunk low you will say, "Audacity!" But he will save the humbled. *30* Even the guilty he will deliver; they will be delivered through the purity of your hands.

///

21 come close to. הַסְכֶּן. This is a play on words. It is the same word that was translated *be of use to* in verse 2. Although, as that verse implies, a man cannot "be of use to" God, he can nonetheless "come close to" God.

Chapter Twenty-Three

¹ THEN JOB ANSWERED and said:

²My musings are bitter again today. My hand is heavy from all my groaning. ³Who can tell me how to find him! How I might come to his appointed place! ⁴I would lay out my case before him, and fill my mouth with arguments. ⁵I would know with what words he would answer me! I want to understand what he would have to say to me. ⁶Would he strive against me with his great power? No, surely he would place his confidence in me. ⁷There an upright man can reason with him, and there would I be released from my judge forever.

⁸So, onward I went, but he was naught; to the rear, but I discerned him not.

⁹To the left among his works I could not grasp hold. He enveloped the right, but I saw not. ¹⁰But he knows the way I have taken. He has tried me and I have come through as gold. ¹¹My foot held tight to his track; I kept to his ways and did not swerve. ¹²Nor have I departed from the commandments of his lips. From within my breast I have treasured up the words of his mouth. ¹³But he is of but one purpose, and who can dissuade him? His soul need only desire, and it is done. ¹⁴He will fulfil what has been prescribed for me, and he has many such things about him. ¹⁵It is because of all this that his presence leads me into confusion. When I reflect, I fear him. ¹⁶God has softened my heart, the Almighty

has led me into confusion. [17]I was not destroyed by the darkness only because he had concealed its thick murk from me.

Chapter Twenty-Four

¹ WHY HAS NOT THE ALMIGHTY set aside specific times for judgment? Now, even those who know him cannot recognize his timing.

² Boundary-stones are carried off, flocks seized and peacefully sent to pasture. ³ Men lead away the donkeys of the fatherless. They have impounded the widow's ox. ⁴ᵃ The destitute they turned from the roads. ⁹ They pluck the fatherless from the breast and take a pledge of the poor. ⁴ᵇ The poor of the land hide themselves together.

⁵ They are wild asses in the desert, going off about their labors of snatching up at dawn. They have only the wasteland to provide food for their young. ⁶ They harvest in the fields and glean the vineyards of the guilty.

⁷ Naked, they pass the night without clothing; and shelter from the cold there is none. ⁸ Drenched by torrents in the hills, they cling to a rock for want of shelter. ¹⁰ Without clothing, they go about naked. Hungry, they bear the sheaves; ¹¹ confined within walls, they labor at the olive press; trampling down in the wine-vats, they thirst. ¹² From out of the city the dead groan, wounded souls cry out; yet in all that God sees nothing unsavory.

¹³ They were rebels against the light who could neither recognize its path nor remain within its course. ¹⁴ In the

---

⁹ This verse is in fact 24:9. I, like others, place it after 24:4a.

light a murderer arises, killing the poor and the needy; and at night he turns thief. *¹⁵* An adulterous eye watches at twilight, saying, "No eye will take note of me," and he conceals his face. *¹⁶* In the dark he tunnels his way into houses which are sealed up tight against him by day, since he does not know the light. *¹⁷* For him morning and the Shadow of Death are all the same, for he recognizes nothing but the terrors of the Shadow of Death.

¹⁸ Let him be held in disrepute over the entire face of the waters and his lot be accursed upon the land. He cannot turn down the path to the vineyards. *¹⁹* As drought and heat steal away snowy waters, so does the Pit those who sin. *²⁰* The womb will forget him and the worms will find him sweet. Let him no longer be remembered, that injustice may be broken as a tree. *²¹* He is mated to a barren woman who cannot give birth, and life shall not go well for his widow.

²² By his might, he can make the valiant bend, and though he may stand tall for a time he has no steadfast

///

¹⁶ *he.* The Hebrew text switches to the plural for the rest of the passage.

²² וּמָשַׁךְ אַבִּירִים בְּכֹחוֹ יָקוּם וְלֹא־יַאֲמִין בַּחַיִּין: יִתֶּן־לוֹ לָבֶטַח וְיִשָּׁעֵן וְעֵינֵיהוּ עַל־דַּרְכֵיהֶם. Greenberg translates: "Though he have the strength to seize bulls, May he live with no assurance of survival. Yet [God] gives him the security on which he relies, and keeps watch over his affairs."

Alter: "He who hauled bulls with his strength will stand up and not trust in his life, Though God grant him safety on which he relies."

RSV translates: "Yet [God] prolongs (pulls/bends) [the life of] the mighty by his power; they rise up when they despair of life. [He] gives them security, and they are supported: and his eyes are upon their ways."

I render: "By his might, he can make the valiant bend, and though he may stand tall [for a time] he has no steadfast belief in life. His world may seem secure, and he may [come to] rely upon it, but his eyes are upon its ways." I have put brackets around words that do not actually appear in the Hebrew text to facilitate comparison.

belief in life. ²³ His world may seem secure, and he may come to rely upon it, but his eyes are upon his ways. ²⁴ He may be exalted for a while; but then he is gone, brought low, and shriveled up like a mallow, withered away like heads of grain. ²⁵ If it be not so, then prove me a liar and make my words worth nothing.

Chapter Twenty-Five

1 THEN BILDAD THE SHUHITE answered and said:

2 Dominion and fear are his. He makes peace in his high place. *3* Is there any number to his troops? Upon whom does his light not fall? *4* Can a mortal think himself just before God? Or what can cleanse anyone born of woman?

5 Look high as the moon, nothing shines. Even the stars are not pure in his sight. *6* And now, what of these mortals, the maggots; or the son of mortal man, the worm?

Chapter Twenty-Six

¹ THEN JOB ANSWERED and said:

²Oh, why must you try to help when you are so power-less? You would save me with a mighty arm, but you have not the strength! ³What kind of advice is it that you give without wisdom, providing guidance to every passer by? ⁴To whom have you uttered all these words? Whose spirit is it that has been coming out of you?

⁵Ancient specters writhe beneath the waters and those who dwell in them. ⁶The Pit stands naked before him and there is no cover for Abaddon. ⁷He stretches the northern lands out over the chaos and suspends the earth above the nothingness. ⁸He binds up the waters in thickened murk, and yet the cloud is not burst by them. ⁹He covers over the face of his throne, shrouding it in his clouds. ¹⁰He cuts a boundary round the face of the waters, reaching out to where the light finds its end in darkness. ¹¹The pillars of heaven tremble, astounded by his rebuke. ¹²By his power the sea comes to rest. By his skill he struck down Rahaba. ¹³By his breath the heavens turn fair. His hands have made the fleeing serpent writhe. ¹⁴Yet these are but a touch of his way, only a whisper of what can be heard in him. Oh the thunder of his mighty deeds, who can reflect upon it!

///

⁶ *Abaddon* (אֲבַדּוֹן), from a root meaning *to perish* or *to destroy*, appears in Job, Proverbs, and Psalms in reference to the dwelling place of the dead, more often named שְׁאוֹל (sheol).

Chapter Twenty-Seven

¹And again Job took up his proverb and said:

²By the life of that God who has merely thrown aside the whole of my case, the Almighty has embittered my soul!

³Yet so long as there is breath within me, or the spirit of God in my nostrils, ⁴never will my lips speak any injustice, or my tongue utter deceit. ⁵No, I'll not pretend that you have been just. Even till I perish, I shall not turn my simplicity from me. ⁶I shall not disavow my integrity, but cling tight to my righteousness and not let go; for my heart has never felt pangs of reproach.

⁷My enemies are as the wicked, and he that rises up against me as the unjust; ⁸for what hope does the impious man have when he is cut off, when God will have drained his soul away? ⁹Will God hear his cries when trouble comes his way? ¹⁰Will he rejoice in the Almighty, even if he should call upon God at all times? ¹¹But I will teach you what is in the hands of God; and what belongs to the Almighty I shall not conceal. ¹²Well, you have all seen what has happened. Oh, why are you so utterly useless?

///

² *my case.* מִשְׁפָּטִי. As noted in the discussion of Chapter 8 below, there are occasions on which one might be tempted to translate this word as *my right* rather than *my case.* The present verse is not such an instance.

¹³ Such is the lot of the guilty human from God, a heritage from the Almighty set aside for those who can terrorize. ¹⁴ If his sons become great, the sword will be out for them, for his offspring will never be satisfied with bread. ¹⁵ When death buries those that remain, even their widows shall not weep for them. ¹⁶ If he should pile up silver like dust and lay out his clothing as if it were clay, ¹⁷ then once he has laid it out the righteous shall wear it, and the innocent will share the silver.

¹⁸ He built his house like a moth. It is like a shack that some night watchman might make. ¹⁹ He lies down a rich man; but nothing more will be gathered, for when his eyes are opened all will be gone. ²⁰ Terrors will overtake him like a flood of waters, and by night a sea-storm will make off with him. ²¹ The east wind will hoist him up and be on its way. It will sweep him from his place, ²² turn and hurl itself at him without mercy. With the whole of his spirit he flees from its hand, ²³ but it claps down its palm upon him and whistles him off from his place.

Chapter Twenty-Eight

1 THERE IS A MINE FOR SILVER and a place where gold is made pure. *2* Iron is taken from the earth, and the rock is made to flow with copper. *3* Man brings an end to the darkness. He explores everything to its limit, even to this rock of murk and the Shadow of Death. *4* Far from any habitation, he blasts out channels. Abandoned by every passer by, destitute of all humanity, they wander.

5 There is a land which gives us our daily bread, but underneath it churns like fire. *6* Its stones are the home of sapphires, and its dust is of gold. *7* No bird of prey knows the trails. The eye of the falcon has never caught sight of it, *8* nor have the sons of pride ever trampled it over. The lion can bear it no witness, *9* but man has put his hand to the flint and overturned mountains by the root. *10* He rips open channels through the rocks. His eye sees every precious thing. *11* He binds up the flowing rivers and the hidden things come to light.

12 Yet wisdom, where can she be found? Which is the place of understanding? *13* No mortal knows its value, nor can it be found in the land of the living. *14* The Deep says, "It is not within me"; and the Sea says, "I have it not." *15* It cannot be gotten for gold, nor silver be weighed out as its price. *16* It cannot be measured by the gold of Ophir, or by the precious onyx, or by sapphire. *17* Nor gold nor glass can match its value, nor vessels of fine gold be its wage. *18* Neither crystal nor coral can call it to mind, for gathering wisdom is more precious than pearls. ¹⁹The topaz of Nubia cannot express its value, nor can its weight be taken in pure gold.

²⁰Wisdom, where does she come from? Which is the place of understanding? ²¹She is hidden from the eye of every living thing. She is concealed even from the birds of heaven. ²²Abaddon and Death have said: "Now we have heard only rumors of it with our ears." ²³But GOD understands the way to it; he knows the place, ²⁴for he can look to the ends of the earth and see all things that are under the sky. ²⁵When he established the weight of the wind, and set out the waters according to its measure, ²⁶when he gave a law for the rain and a passageway for the voice of the thunderbolt, ²⁷then it was that he saw it, counted it, measured it, and delved into it. ²⁸And then he said unto humankind, "Behold, awe of the Lord, that is Wisdom, and to turn away from evil is understanding."

///

²³ GOD. אֱלֹהִים. This is the first time we have met the name אֱלֹהִים (elohim) since Chapter 2. Morphologically it is a plural and is commonly used outside the Book of Job to refer to the one God of Israel. The name אֵל, *God*, is in the singular and can have a more generic meaning.

²⁸ *Lord.* אֲדֹנָי. This is the only time in the text that the name אֲדֹנָי (adonai) appears. In contrast, the word *YHWH*, the LORD, which we frequently saw in Chapters 1 and 2, and which will begin to re-emerge in Chapter 38, is more like a personal name for the God of Israel. Its root seems to be a word meaning *to be* or *to become*. The distinction between *being* and *becoming* can be made in Hebrew, but not with the clarity that one has in either Greek or English.

Outside the Book of Job, אֲדֹנָי is a very common name for the God of Israel, especially in the Book of Psalms. Its literal meaning is *my lords*. In the singular it is often applied to a human being; and in such cases its meaning lies somewhere between the two English words *mister* and *master*.

Chapter Twenty-Nine

*¹*And again Job took up his proverb and said:

²Who can return to the months gone by, to the days when God watched over me, ³when his lamp shone over my head and I walked in the darkness by his light; ⁴back to my autumnal days when God was at home inside my tent, ⁵when the Almighty was yet with me, and I with my lads all about me; ⁶when my feet were bathed in cream, and the rock poured out its streams of oil for me?

⁷When I went to the city gates and was about to take my seat on the square, ⁸the young men would see me and retire, elders would rise and stand. ⁹Princes refrained from words and put their hands over their mouths. ¹⁰The voice of the nobles was hushed, and their tongue stuck to their palate, ¹¹for an ear had heard and it blessed me; an eye had seen and it approved, ¹²because I had saved a poor man when he cried out, and an orphan when there was no one else to help him.

¹³The blessings of those who had been lost came to me, and I made the widow's heart sing. ¹⁴I put on judgment, and it covered me. A just cause fit like a coat or a hat. ¹⁵I became eyes to the blind, and feet to the lame. ¹⁶I was a father to the needy, and often I would search out a case for a man whom I did not know. ¹⁷I would break the jaw of the unjust and wrest the prey from his teeth.

¹⁸I thought to myself: "I shall perish in my own little nest, my days having multiplied as sand, ¹⁹my roots opening me up to the waters, and the dew resting upon

my branches." ²⁰ My dignity was ever fresh, my bow would renew itself in my hand. ²¹ Men would hear me and wait in expectation, falling silent to hear my counsel. ²² After I spoke they had no changes. My words fell gently upon them. ²³ They waited for me in expectation as for the rain; their mouths opened wide as if to catch the spring rain. ²⁴ I joked with them a bit, so that my kindness would not overwhelm them since they had no self-confidence. ²⁵ I chose their way, and sat as chief. I dwelt as a king among his troops or as one who has compassion for mourners.

///

²⁴ *I joked with them ... they had no self confidence.* אֶשְׂחַק אֲלֵהֶם לֹא יַאֲמִינוּ וְאוֹר פָּנַי לֹא יַפִּילוּן. Greenberg translates: "When I smiled at them, they would not believe it; they never expected a sign of my favor." Alter has: "I laughed to them—they scarcely trusted—but my face's light they did not dim." RSV renders: "I smiled on them when they had no confidence and the light of my countenance they did not cast down."

The first problem is that יַפִּילוּן (yappilun) may come from פלל, which normally means to pray or to intervene; but compare Gen. 48:11—"I never expected to see your face"—that is how Greenberg takes it. However, it could as well come from נפל, to fall, and in the causative form could mean either *to cast down* or *to overthrow* or *disarm*.

A further problem is whether וּן is an objective or a subjective ending. I take it as objective; RSV as subjective.

Chapter Thirty

1 **B**UT NOW THEY HAVE TURNED ME into the joke, those younger than I, whose fathers I would have felt contempt to put with my sheep dogs. *2* What is the strength of their hands to me, those men from whom all vigor has been lost, a wasteland in want and starvation? *3* They gnaw at a parched land and destroy as they are destroyed.

4 They gather mallow and leaves from the bushes. Broom root has become their food. *5* Driven from the heart of things, they are cried upon like thieves. *6* They find their quarter in river beds, in holes in the dust and the rock. *7* Braying in the bushes, they huddle together under a weed. *8* Sons of Fools and Sons of Nobodies! They have been whipped from the land.

9 And now they have made a ditty of me and I have become a byword to them. *10* Oh, how they abhor me and keep their distance; they do not even refrain from spitting in my face. *11* They unfasten my tent-rope and down they have brought me. They have thrown off all restraint. *12* On my right, flowering youths rise up and put me to flight. They pave roads of destruction against me. *13* They tear up my path and foster my demise, but it does them no good. *14* They come in a great burst, wave after wave of destruction. *15* Terror turns upon me; it pursues my gentility like the wind, and my salvation passes me by like a cloud. *16* Now, my soul has poured itself out, and days of misery have taken hold of me. *17* By night my

bones are whittled away, and the gnawing never ceases.
¹⁸ My clothing envelops me in great constraint and the collar of my tunic chokes at me. ¹⁹ It throws me into the mire and I become as dust and ashes.

²⁰ I cry out to you, but you give no answer. I stand there, but you only stare at me. ²¹ You have turned brutal, and with the might of your hand you persecute me. ²² You hoist me up onto the wind and set me astride to be tossed about in the wreckage. ²³ I know that you will deliver me to death, the house prepared for all that lives; ²⁴ yet will not those in turmoil reach out their hand and cry out in their calamity?

²⁵ Did I not weep for those who had seen hard times? My soul grieved for the poor. ²⁶ I had hoped for the good, but there came only evil; I waited in expectation for the light, but there came only a murk. ²⁷ My bowels churned, never at rest. Days of poverty were ever before me.

//

¹⁸ בְּרָב־כֹּחַ יִתְחַפֵּשׂ לְבוּשִׁי כְּפִי כֻתָּנְתִּי יַאַזְרֵנִי. Greenberg translates: "With great effort I change my clothing; the neck of my tunic fits my waist." Alter reads: "With great power He seizes my garment, He grabs hold of me at the collar." RSV translates: "With violence it seizes my garment; it binds me about like the collar of my tunic," but gives, as an alternative translation: "My garment is disfigured."

Here the first problem is the meaning of the word יִתְחַפֵּשׂ. Its root, חפשׂ, means *to search*. In the reflexive, it means *to distort* or *to disguise* oneself by a change of clothing; compare I Sam. 28:8, I Kings 20:38, 22:30. That would account for Greenberg's translation. However, in each of these cases the emphasis is on the act of disguising, not on the change of clothing. It must also be pointed out that the verb is in the third, not the first person. On the other hand, while אזר does mean *to gird*, the emphasis seems to be on the strength rather than on the waist. I, then, take Job to be saying that he feels his clothing pulling at him and distorting him. This means taking לְבוּשִׁי as the subject rather than the object of the verb.

28 I walked in gloom with no sun above. I stood up in the assembly and cried out; 29 and thus I became a brother to the Jackal and friend to the Ostrich. 30 My skin turned black and is now peeling off; my bones are scorched by the heat. 31 My lyre has turned to mourning and my flute to the voice of tears.

Chapter Thirty-One

¹ *I* HAVE MADE A COVENANT with my eyes, for how could I gaze upon a maiden? ² What part have I in God above, or heritage from the Almighty on high? ³ Is not calamity for the unjust, and disaster only for those who work wickedness? ⁴ Does he not see my ways or take count of my every step?

⁵ Have I walked along in falsehood, or has my foot hurried to deceit? ⁶ Let him weigh me on the scales of justice, and then God will know of my simplicity. ⁷ If my step has wandered from the way, my heart gone after my eyes, or a taint stuck to my hand, ⁸ then let me sow but another eat, or let my crop be uprooted.

⁹ If my heart was seduced by a woman and I set ambush at my neighbor's entrance way, ¹⁰ may my wife grind with another, and let others bow down over her, ¹¹ because that would have been licentiousness and a juristic perversion. ¹² It would be a fire consuming down to Abaddon, uprooting all that I have ever accomplished.

¹³ If ever I felt contempt for the cause of one of my servants, man or maid, when they brought case against me— ¹⁴ what would I do when God rose up? How would

---

¹¹ *juristic perversion.* עָוֹן פְּלִילִים. The phrase is as oxymoronic in Hebrew as it is in English. It hovers between the legal and the pre-legal.

I answer him if he should ever call me to account? ¹⁵Did not he who made me in my mother's belly make him as well? Did he not form us in the same womb?

¹⁶How could I withhold pleasures from the poor or drain a widow's eye, ¹⁷or even eat a crust of bread alone, not sharing it with the fatherless, when they had grown up with me for a father? ¹⁸From my mother's belly I was their mother's guide. ¹⁹Whenever I saw a man who was lost, without clothing, nothing to cover his pitiful state— ²⁰didn't his loins bless me because he [knew that he could always] warm himself with the shearing of my sheep!

²¹If ever I brandished a hand against the fatherless because I saw help standing at the gate, ²²let my shoulder fall from its socket or my arm break at the joint, ²³because divine torment would fill me with fear and I could not bear its weight.

²⁴If ever I placed my confidence in gold, or called fine gold my security, ²⁵or rejoiced in the greatness of my wealth or in the bounty found in my hand; ²⁶if ever I have seen the radiance of the light or the moon walking in splendor, ²⁷and with my heart secretly attracted, placed my fingers to my lips to kiss them, ²⁸even that

///

¹⁵ *womb.* This translation requires reading בְּרֶחֶם for בָּרֶחֶם; see Robert Gordis, *The Book of Job* (Jewish Theological Seminary of America, 1978), p. 348.

¹⁸ *mother's.* Literally, *her.*

would have been a juristic perversion, for I would have forsaken God the most high. ²⁹ Could I have rejoiced when hardship struck at those that hate me or come to life because evil had found them, ³⁰ without giving my palate over to sin by asking for his life with a curse? ³¹ Even the men of my own tent would have said, "Who will let us at his flesh? We will not be satisfied."

³² I left no stranger sleeping out-of-doors but opened my doors to the traveler. ³³ Would I have covered over my transgressions like [some] human or concealed perversion in my bosom ³⁴ through terror of the great multitude? Or was I so shattered by family disgrace that I would stand petrified, not daring to go out the opening way?

³⁵ Who will find someone to listen? Well, here is my writ: Let the Almighty answer, or let the man who has a quarrel against me write it down in a book. ³⁶ I'll hoist it up on my shoulders, or wear it round me like a crown. ³⁷ But I will also give him an account of my every step and I will present it to him as a prince.

³⁸ But if my own land cries out against me, its furrows weeping together, and ³⁹ claims that I have eaten its produce without payment and snuffed out the life of its

///

²⁹ *Could I.* Greenberg begins this sentence with "Did I"; RSV and Alter translate the phrase as an "if" clause; but neither one works as well in light of the verse as a whole.

³⁶ *hoist.* alternatively, *raise.*

owners, [40]then may thorns grow in that place for wheat, and foul weeds for barley.

The words of Job are *tam*.

///

[40] *tam*. This is the same Hebrew word תָּם that was used to characterize Job as "simple" in 1:1. I leave it untranslated here in an attempt to preserve its wide range of meanings; these are extensively reviewed in the discussion of 31:40, which begins on page 215 below.

Chapter Thirty-Two

¹ Now the three men ceased to reply to Job because he was right in his own eyes. ² But Elihu the son of Barachel the Buzite, of the House of Ram was angry at Job, fuming because he considered himself more just than God. ³ And his anger burned against his three friends because they could find no answer but merely condemned Job. ⁴ Now Elihu held back his words and waited for Job, because they were all older. ⁵ But when Elihu saw that no answer came from the mouths of these three men, anger burned within him.

⁶ Then Elihu son of Barachel the Buzite answered and said:

I am but young in years, and you are most venerable; so I shrank back and was in awe to declare my thoughts in front of you. ⁷ I said to myself, "Let the generations speak, and the fullness of years proclaim wisdom." ⁸ But surely there is a spirit in mortals, a breath of the Almighty that gives him understanding. ⁹ It is not the great who are wise, nor is it the elders who understand judgment.

¹⁰ So I say unto you, "Hear me; I myself shall declare my thoughts." ¹¹ I have waited in expectation for your words and listened for your understanding, while you searched for something to say. ¹² I observed you carefully, and there was none to confute Job, nor was there an answer to his assertions from any of you.

[13] Beware of saying we have found wisdom; God will defeat him, not man. [14] Now he has set out no words against me; and I shall not reply using your reasonings, [15] for they have been shattered and can no longer reply. All meaning has left them.

[16] I waited in expectation till they had finished speaking, till they stood and could no longer reply. [17] But now I shall give my side of the matter. I myself shall declare my thoughts. [18] I am full of words, and the wind in my belly presses upon me; [19] my belly is like wine that has no vent, like jugs of new wine ready to burst. [20] I shall speak, and it will expand me; I shall open my lips and reply. [21] I will show no favor nor flatter any man; for I know no flattery, [22] or may my maker soon carry me off.

Chapter Thirty-Three

¹ATTEND MY WORDS, JOB. Listen well to each utterance that I now make. ²Behold, I open my lips and the tongue in my palate begins to speak. ³My speech is an upright heart. The thoughts of my lips speak with clarity. ⁴The spirit of God has made me, and the breath of the Almighty gives me life.

⁵Answer me, if you can. Lay your case out before me and take your stand. ⁶Here I am, just as you wished, standing in for God; though I too was nipped from clay, ⁷so terror of me will not overwhelm you, nor will the pressure I put upon you weigh heavily.

⁸Oh, you have spoken it into my ear, and I still hear the sound of each word.

⁹"I am pure, free of transgression." "I am clean." "There is no perversion about me." ¹⁰"He finds ways to oppose me," and "He thinks of me as his enemy." ¹¹"He puts my feet in the stocks." "He scrutinizes my every wandering."

¹²But in this you have not acted justly. I will answer you, for God is greater than any mortal. ¹³Why do you

---

⁶ *standing in for God.* הֵן־אֲנִי כְפִיךָ לָאֵל (hen 'ani kephikha le'el). Translations of this verse differ widely. See in the Discussion of Chapter 33 below.

nipped. This is a good word which I confess to have "nipped" from Greenberg.

vie with him? He is not obliged to answer on every count. *14* Yet God speaks once, even twice, but none take note. *15* It may be in a dream, or in a vision of the night, when heavy sleep falls upon mortals as they slumber in their beds.

16 He unveils the ears of mortals and places his seal upon their conduct *17* to turn a human away from action and conceal pride from the hero. *18* He will bring his soul back from the Pit, and his life from perishing by the sword.

19 He is tried by pain in his bed, and his bones ceaselessly twist in strife. *20* His life renders his bread loathsome, and his soul takes no delight in fine food. *21* His flesh is devoured, no longer to be seen, and his bones are ground away and disappear. *22* His soul draws near to the muck and his life is [attracted] to [all that] brings death.

23 If there only were a messenger, an interpreter—one in a thousand, to tell a human what is right for him, *24* he would have mercy on him and say: "Redeem him from descending into the muck, for I have found his ransom." *25* Let his flesh become brighter than youth, and let him return to his springtime days.

26 Let him but supplicate unto God and he shall be accepted and see his face with shouts of joy, for he shall return to mortal man his sense of righteousness. *27* Let him only stand squarely in front of mortals and say I have sinned; I have dealt perversely with what was right, and my accounts have not been settled. *28* Thus he shall redeem his soul from passing into the muck; and his life shall see in the light.

²⁹ Yes, God will do all these things two or three times for a hero, ³⁰ to bring his soul back from the muck to be made bright by the light of life.

³¹ Pay heed, Job, and hear me; be silent now and I will speak. ³² If you have the words, respond to me. Well, speak! For I wish to justify you. ³³ But, if you have nothing, then listen to me. Be silent and I will teach you wisdom.

Chapter Thirty-Four

¹ THEN ELIHU ANSWERED and said:

²Hear my words, ye wise men; give ear to me, all you who know, ³for the ear tests words as the palate tastes food. ⁴Let us choose for ourselves what is lawful so that we may know among ourselves what is good. ⁵Now Job has said: "I am just" and "...that God who has thrown aside the whole of my case"; ⁶"I declare false the judgment made against me" and "The arrow was mortal, though I was without transgression."

⁷What hero is there like unto Job who drinks up mockery as if it were water, ⁸joins company with those who deal in wickedness, and walks with men of evil? ⁹For he has said: "It is of no use to a hero that he be in GOD's favor."

¹⁰And so, ye men of heart, hear me; far be God from injustice and the Almighty from evil. ¹¹As a human labors, so shall he be recompensed; and wherever a man wanders, that is where he will find himself. ¹²Now, surely, God does not cause wickedness; nor does the Almighty turn judgment aside.

¹³Who laid charge upon him to care for the earth? Or who placed upon him the whole of this fruitful ground? ¹⁴If he cared to, he could gather his spirit and his breath back into himself. ¹⁵Then all flesh would perish and mankind would return to dust.

¹⁶If there be such a thing as understanding, then listen to this. Attend to the sound of my words. ¹⁷Shall he

that hates judgment bind up? Would you condemn the Magnificent Just One, *18* he who can say to a king, "You are worthless," or to the nobles, "You are guilty men"? *19* Who shows no favor to any liege, or recognizes the prince above the pauper, since they are the works of his hand, every one?

20 They can die in a moment; the people tremble at midnight, and pass on. The mighty are turned aside, but by no [human] hand, *21* for his eyes are upon the ways of man, and he watches his every step. *22* There is no darkness and there is no Shadow of Death for the worker of wickedness to hide in, *23* nor has he ever yet accorded it to man that he go with God into judgment.

24 He shatters the magnificent, no knowing how many, and sets others up in their place. *25* Surely he can recognize their deeds. Everything turns to night, and they are crushed. *26* He slaps them down along with the guilty in full view of all *27* because they turned away from him and do not comprehend his *28* ways of bringing the cries of the poor unto himself; for he hears the cry of the needy.

29 But when he is silent, who can condemn? If he should hide his face, who can even take note of him, be it a nation or be it a single human? *30* Lest a polluted human reign; lest he ensnare the people. *31* For has he said unto God, "I will bear it all and offend no more." *32* What I have not seen, teach me. If I have done injustice, I shall persist in it no longer. *33* Should not payment for it be required of you because you had such contempt? It is you must answer, not I. Whatever you know, then, speak!

34 Men of heart will say to me, and a wise hero will listen to me, [saying,] *35* Job has spoken without knowledge, his words are lacking insight. ³⁶ May Job's trials know no limit, because his answers are no different from those of the men of wickedness. ³⁷ He adds sin upon transgression, slaps us in the face, and continually speaks against God.

Chapter Thirty-Five

¹ THEN ELIHU ANSWERED and said:

²Is that what you think to be judgment? To say, "My righteousness is greater than God's?" ³Or when you say, "How does all this benefit you? How am I better off than if I had sinned?" ⁴I will answer your words, and your friends along with you. ⁵Look up into the heavens and see. Only take note of the nebula, how high above you it is. ⁶If you have sinned, how could you perturb it; and even if you multiply your transgressions, how could you affect it? Or if you were righteous, what would you add to it? What could it gain from your hand? ⁸Your evils fall upon men like yourself, and your righteousness is for sons of man.

⁹Under great oppression they cry out; they scream to be saved from mighty arms; ¹⁰but none say, "Where is God my maker, the one who makes songs in the night; ¹¹who teaches us more than the beasts of the earth and makes us wiser than the birds of the sky?"

¹²There they cry out, but he gives no answer to the majestic pride of evil men. ¹³Oh, how pointless! God will not listen, nor will the Almighty take note. ¹⁴Particularly since you have said that you do not regard him, the case

///

⁸ *sons of man.* Another case where it seems better to render אָדָם as *man* rather than *human*.

is before him, and for him you must writhe [in uncertainty]. *15* But since for the present he does not exert his anger, he foolishly misunderstands. *16* And Job, futility pours from his mouth. He grows heavy with words but has no comprehension.

Chapter Thirty-Six

1 AND ELIHU CONTINUED to speak:

2 But wait a bit for me, and I will show you. There is still another word to be said for God. *3* I will fetch my knowledge from afar to show my maker righteous. *4* Indeed, my words are not false. One who has simple knowledge is among you.

5 God is mighty and shows no contempt—mighty in strength of heart. *6* He gives no life to the guilty, but grants judgment to the poor *7* and does not turn his eyes from the righteous. As for kings about to ascend the throne, he seats them forever and they are exalted.

8 But if they have been bound in fetters and trapped in cords of affliction, *9* he reminds them what they have done and that they can prevail over their transgressions. *10* He unveils their ears to admonition. *11* If they can hear and obey, they will complete their days in prosperity and their years in delight. *12* But if they cannot hear they will perish by the sword and pass on without ever knowing why.

13 The impious of heart put on anger and will not cry out for help when he afflicts them. *14* They died when their soul was yet young, for it lived among whores. *15* But the poor he tears from their poverty and unveils their ears by force, *16* and you he has lured away from the edge of narrowness into a broad place, free of stress, and your table is laden with sumptuous fare.

17 You are filled with the judgment of the guilty, and so judgment and justice have laid hold of you. *18* Beware lest fury turn you to derision, or a great ransom pull you aside. *19* Will your cries for help, though made with determination of strength, bring order to life in narrowness? *20* Do not pant by night, eager to raze people from their base.

21 Beware, do not turn to wickedness, for that is what you have chosen rather than poverty. *22* Behold, God is exalted in his power. Who can guide like him? *23* Who can oversee his ways? or say to him, "Thou hast done injustice"? *24* Remember then to exalt his works of which mortals sing. *25* All humans have beheld him. Mortals have looked upon him from afar.

26 Behold, God is exalted but we cannot know. The number of his years cannot be unearthed. *27* He draws up droplets of water, and the moisture refines itself into his mist *28* that flows together into the nebula and trickles back down upon humankind.

29 Who can comprehend the expanse of the clouds, the roarings under his canopy? *30* He spreads out his light over it, and covers over the roots of the sea; *31* for with them he pronounces judgment upon the nations and provides food in abundance. *32* He covers over the lightning in his hand and commands it to strike at its mark. *33* But the roarings tell of him, amassing anger against injustice.

Chapter Thirty-Seven

¹ AT THIS TOO, my heart trembles and leaps from its place. ² Listen, listen well to the rage in his voice and the groaning that comes up out of his mouth. ³ Straight down it comes, under the whole of heaven. His light goes out to the ends of the earth, ⁴ and then, a roaring voice. He thunders with the voice of his majestic pride, and when they are heard he does not hold them back. ⁵ God thunders marvels with his voice, working great things, though we can never know them. ⁶ For to the snow he says, "Fall to the ground," and to the rain, "Pour down"; and the rain is a downpour of his might.

⁷ He has sealed up the hand of every human so that each mortal of his making may know ⁸ that a beast goes in for shelter and settles down into its lair ⁹ when the tempest comes out of its chamber, cold from its scattering-place. ¹⁰ The breath of God turns all to ice, and the wide waters are cast like bronze. ¹¹ He weighs down the clouds with moisture, and the lightning-cloud spews out its bolt. ¹² On a topsy-turvy course he steers them to accomplish all that he has commanded them upon the face of this fruitful ground, ¹³ whether by lash or by love, so he founds it upon his land.

¹⁴ Hear this, Job. Stand at attention and contemplate the wonders of God. ¹⁵ Do you know how God lays

///

¹² *fruitful ground.* See the note on 18:18 above.

charge upon his cloud when the radiance appears? ¹⁶Do you know how the clouds are kept in balance, the wonders of simple knowledge? ¹⁷Or even how it is that your clothing keeps you warm when the land has respite from the southern wind?

¹⁸Can you beat the nebula into a great expanse, firm as a mirror cast like molten metal? ¹⁹Tell us, then: what shall we say to him? We cannot lay out our case because of the darkness. ²⁰Does anything get through to him when I speak? Can a man speak when he is about to be swallowed up?

²¹Now not a man sees the light, though it shine blinding bright in the nebula, not till a passing spirit shall make them pure. ²²Out of the north there comes a golden splendor. A frightful majesty rests upon God. ²³The Almighty—none will find him. He is ever multiplying in might and in right, abundant in judgment, giving neither wrack nor reason. ²⁴Thus mortals hold in awe the one whom even the wise of heart have never seen.

//

²³ *neither wrack nor reason.* For this phrase, see the Discussion of Chapter 37.

Chapter Thirty-Eight

*1*AND THE LORD ANSWERED JOB out of the tempest and said:

*2*Who now is this one that makes counsel dark by words without knowledge? *3*Come, gird up your loins like a hero. I will question you, and you must inform me.

*4*Where were you when I laid the foundations of the earth? Speak up, if you know! *5*Who fixed its measurements, if you have any understanding? Who stretched a measuring line round it, *6*and into what were its pylons fixed? Who set the cornerstone *7*as the morning stars sang together, and the sons of GOD all shouted for joy?

*8*Who closed up the sea behind the double door, when first it burst out of the womb *9*and I clothed it in a cloud and swaddled it in mist, *10*imposing my law upon it, and put up the bars and the double doors, *11*and said: "To this point you may come, but no farther. Here your majestically proud waves must come to rest."

*12*Have you yet commanded the morning, or taught the dawn to know its place, *13*to grab hold of the corners of the earth, and to winnow out the wicked? *14*It is as transformed as clay stamped by a seal, and fixed as dye in a garment. *15*The light is withheld from the wicked, and the uplifted arm is broken.

*16*Have you ever come upon the source of the seas, or gone for a stroll down by the cranny in the deep? *17*Have the gates of death unveiled themselves to you, or have you seen the gates of the Shadow of Death? *18*Have you pondered the expanse of the earth? If you know all these things, declare them!

*19*Which is the road to the dwelling of light? And which is the place of darkness, *20*that you may take it to its borders and know the way to its home? *21*You know, for even then you were born, and the number of your days is great!

*22*Have you come upon the storehouses of snow, or seen the vaults of hail *23*which I have laid aside for a time of narrowness and for the days of battle and of war?

*24*By what paths is light dispersed? How is the east wind cast about the earth? *25*Who cleaved canals for the flooding torrent and made a pathway for the voice of thunder, *26*that it might rain in no-man land, a wilderness with no human in it, *27*to make a surfeit of the devastation and the devastated, and make a budding field bloom?

*28*Does the rain have a father? And who begets the drops of dew? *29*From whose belly does ice emerge, and who gave birth to the frost of heaven? *30*Water draws itself up tight as stone, and the face of the deep clutches to itself.

*31*Did you bind the Pleiades together with a chain, or untie the reins of Orion? *32*Can you lead out the Mazzaroth in its time or guide the Bear with her

//

32 *Mazzaroth*. מַזָּרוֹת. The exact meaning of this word is not known. It would appear to be the name of one of the constellations; or it may simply mean *constellations*.

children? ³³ Do you know the laws of the heaven, and can you impose its authority on the earth?

³⁴Can you raise your voice to the clouds and be covered in a torrent of water? ³⁵ If you send out the lightnings, will they go? Will they say to you, "Here we are!"? ³⁶ Who placed wisdom in the secret core and gave intelligibility to the outward form? ³⁷ And who is wise enough to tell the tale of the nebula? Who can tip the bottles of the sky, ³⁸ to liquify the dust and cast it into congealed clods?

³⁹ Can you hunt up prey for the lioness, and bring to fulfillment the life in its cubs ⁴⁰ as they crouch in their dens or lie in ambush in their lairs? ⁴¹ Who prepares a catch for the raven when his young cry out to God for help, while he wanders about without food?

Chapter Thirty-Nine

¹Do you know when it is time for the mountain goat to drop? And have you watched the hind writhing in the dance of birth? ²Can you number the months they fulfill? And do you know the season for them to deliver, ³when they couch and split open to give birth to their young and thus come to the end of their travail? ⁴Their children thrive and flourish in the wild. They come out and return unto her no more.

⁵Who sent the wild ass off to be free? And who has untied the reins of the untamed jenny, ⁶whose home I have made the wilderness, and who dwells off in the salt lands? ⁷He laughs at the bustling of the city, and does not even hear the drivers shout, ⁸but roams the hills as his pasture, and every green thing is his to search out.

⁹Would the wild ox agree to serve you? Would he spend the night at your crib? ¹⁰Can you hitch him up with a rope and hold him to the furrow? Will he plow up the valleys behind you? ¹¹Would you rely upon him? Remember, his strength is great. Could you leave him your toils? ¹²Would you trust him to bring in the grain and gather it into the barn?

¹³The Ostrich whimsically flaps her wing as if she had the pinions and plumage of a stork, ¹⁴but leaves her eggs

---

¹³ *stork.* חֲסִידָה (chasidah). See an account of this bird, as well as the hawk (verse 26) and the eagle (verse 27) in the Discussion of Chapter 39.

on the ground for the dust to keep them warm. ¹⁵ She has forgotten that a foot can crush them, or that a wild beast might trample them down. ¹⁶ She treats her children roughly, as if they were not even hers. Her toils were all in vain. You see, she had no fear ¹⁷ because God had caused her to forget all wisdom, and she has no share in understanding. ¹⁸ She just flaps her wings as if on high, and laughs at a passing horse and its rider.

¹⁹ Did you give to the horse its strength, or clothe its neck with a mane? ²⁰ Can you make him leap like a locust when the glory of his snort breeds terror? ²¹ He digs up the valleys, and exults in his strength as he goes out to meet armed combat. ²² He laughs at fear and is not dismayed, nor is he turned back by the edge of the sword. ²³ A quiverful of arrows whizzes by—the flashing spear and the javelin. ²⁴ With clattering and rage, he gouges into the earth. He pays no homage to the trumpet's blast, ²⁵ but when the trumpet-call is replete he cries, "Huzzah!" He smells the battle from afar. Oh, the roars of the captains and the shoutings!

²⁶ Is it by your wisdom that the hawk soars and spreads its wing out to the south? ²⁷ Does the eagle mount at your command, building its nest on high? ²⁸ He dwells upon the rock. He takes up lodging on the highest pinnacle, making it his stronghold. ²⁹ From there he searches out his prey. His eye spots it from afar, ³⁰ and his fledglings swill down the blood. Whenever death defiles, he is there.

Chapter Forty

¹And the Lord answered Job and said:

²Should a man of restraint wrangle with the Almighty? One who would convict God must give answer.

³Then Job answered the Lord and said:

⁴I have become so weak. How can I answer you? I lay my hand upon my mouth. ⁵I have spoken once, but I have no answer; twice, but I cannot continue.

⁶And the Lord answered Job out of the tempest and said:

⁷Gird up your loins like a hero: I will question you, and you are to let me know. ⁸Would you shatter my judgment? Would you condemn me in order that you might be right? ⁹Have you an arm like God's, and can you thunder in a voice such as his?

¹⁰Go ahead, deck yourself out in majestic pride and dignity. Put on glory and splendor. ¹¹Let fly the outbursts of your anger. Look upon every man of majestic pride and abase him. ¹²Look upon everyone of majestic pride and bring him low and tread down the guilty. ¹³Bury them all in the dust. Bind their faces in obscurity. ¹⁴Then even I would praise you, for your own right hand would have saved you.

15 But look now, here is Behemoth whom I made along with you. He eats fodder just like the cattle, *16* but just look at the strength in his loins. His might is in the muscles of his belly. *17* He can stretch out his tail stiff as a cedar. The sinews of his thighs are all knit together. *18* His bones are ducts of brass, and his limbs are like rods of iron. *19* He is the first of God's ways. Only his maker can approach him with a sword.

20 The mountains yield him produce, and all the beasts of the field come there to play. *21* He lies down under the lotuses, hiding in the reeds and the fen. *22* The lotuses blanket him with their shade, and the willows of the brook surround him. *23* Though the river rage, he is unalarmed, confident that the Jordan will burst into his mouth. *24* Can he be taken by the eyes? Or pierced in the nose with a snare?

25 Can you haul Leviathan in with a fishhook? Can you press down his tongue with the line? *26* Can you put a ring through his nose, or pierce his jaw with a barb? *27* Would he make you many pleas, or speak to you

―――――――――――――――――――――――――――――――

15 *Behemoth.* The word בְּהֵמוֹת is the normal plural of the feminine noun בְּהֵמָה (behemah), which means any large domesticated animal like a cow or an ox. We have already seen it in the Book of Job:

Just ask the beasts (בְּהֵמוֹת) *and they will show you* [12:7]

In the present passage, however, the word is a masculine singular proper noun, as indicated by the masculine singular verb of the second verset: "He eats fodder."

softly? ²⁸ Will he make a covenant with you to be your eternal servant?

²⁹ Can you play with him like a bird or tie him on a string for your young ladies? ³⁰ Or can the dealers get hold of him and trade their shares in the market? ³¹ Can you fill his hide with harpoons, or his head with fishing spears? ³² Merely place your hand upon his head, and you will remember war no more.

Chapter Forty-One

¹ *T*HUS, [ALL] EXPECTATION is an illusion. Do men not reel at the sight of him? ²No one is so brutal as to rouse him up. Now, who is that one who would stand before me? ³Who confronts me and [demands that] I give exact restitution? Is not everything under the heavens mine?

⁴I will no longer be silent about him or his exploits, or the grace of his frame. ⁵Who can unveil his outer garment, or come before his double-folded jaw? ⁶Who

///

¹ *expectation.* The Hebrew root יחל has meanings that range from *hoping* to *waiting.* Here I render it *expectation*, as lying midway between those extremes. Other instances of this root in the Book of Job include:

> *What strength have I, that I should **wait in expectation**? What is my end that I should prolong my life?* [6:11]

> *It may be that He will slay me. I have no higher **expectations**. None the less I will defend my ways before him.* [13:15]

> *If a man dies, will he come back to life again? All the days of my service I have **waited in expectation** for my release to come.* [14:14]

> *Men would hear me and **wait in expectation**, falling silent to hear my counsel.* [29:21]

> *They **waited** for me **in expectation** as for the rain; their mouths opened wide as if to catch the spring rain.* [29:23]

> *I looked for the good but there came evil; I **waited in expectation** for the light, but there came only a murk.* [30:26]

> *I have **waited in expectation** for your words and listened for your understanding while you searched for something to say.* [32:11]

> *I **waited in expectation** till they had finished speaking, till they stood and could no longer reply.* [32:16]

can open the doors of his face—his teeth surrounded by terror! ⁷But his pride is the strength of his shields, narrowed up and closed by a seal, ⁸each touching the next, and not a breath between them. ⁹Each one clings to his brother. They clutch each other and cannot be parted.

¹⁰Lights flash at his sneeze. His eyes are like the cracking of dawn. ¹¹Out of his mouth comes a flaming torch, as sparks of fire escape. ¹²From his nostrils there comes smoke as from a stream or boiling cauldron. ¹³His breath ignites the coals, and flames come out of his mouth. ¹⁴His strength resides in his neck, and terror dances before him. ¹⁵Festoons of flesh, fused all together, lie on him cast as metal, and they do not quiver. ¹⁶His heart is cast hard as stone, cast as a nether millstone.

¹⁷When he rises up, the gods are afraid. They shatter and are in confusion. ¹⁸No sword that will reach him can stand, nor spear, nor javelin, nor lance. ¹⁹Iron he counts as straw, and bronze as rotten wood.²⁰No son of the bow can put him to flight. Slingstones turn to stubble ²¹and clubs are rated as straw. He laughs at the sound of the javelin.

²²His underparts are jagged shards. He sprawls himself out, implacable, on the mud ²³and makes the deep to seethe like a cauldron. He makes the sea his ointment-pot ²⁴and leaves a shining wake till the abyss seems all hoary-headed. ²⁵No one of the dust will have dominion over him, for he was made to be without fear. ²⁶He sees every towering thing. He is king over all the sons of pride.

Chapter Forty-Two

¹ THEN JOB ANSWERED THE LORD and said:

² I know that you can do all, and that no design can be withheld from you. ³ "Who is this one that conceals counsel without knowledge?" I have spoken though I had not understood. There is a world beyond me, a world full of wonders that I had never known. ⁴ "Now listen and I will speak; I shall question and you will inform me." ⁵ I had heard of you as ears can hear; but now my eyes have seen you. ⁶ Wherefore I have both contempt and compassion for dust and ashes.

⁷ And it was so, that after the LORD had spoken these words unto Job, the LORD said to Eliphaz the Temanite: "My anger fumes against you, and against your two friends: for you have not spoken of me the thing that is right, as has my servant Job.

⁸ Therefore, get yourselves seven bulls and seven rams, and go to my servant Job, and offer up for yourselves a burnt offering; and my servant Job shall pray for you. For I will bear his countenance in order not to deal with you after your folly, in that you have not spoken of me the thing that is right, as my servant Job has." ⁹ So Eliphaz the Temanite and Bildad the Shuhite and Zophar the Na'amathite went and did according as the LORD commanded them; the LORD also bore up the countenance of Job.

¹⁰ And the LORD restored the fortunes of Job when he had prayed for his friends; and the LORD returned all that Job had, twice over.

¹¹ Then all of his brothers and sisters and all of his friends came to his house and supped with him. They consoled him and showed him compassion for all the evils which the LORD had brought upon him. Each one gave a qesitah and each a golden ring; ¹² and the LORD blessed the last days of his life even more than he had its beginning. He had fourteen thousand sheep, six thousand camels, one thousand head of cattle, and one thousand she-asses; ¹³ he also had seven sons and three daughters. ¹⁴ The first he called by the name of Jemimah; the second Qeziah; and the third Qeren-Hapukh. ¹⁵ In all the land there could not be found any woman more beautiful than Job's daughters, and their father gave them an inheritance alongside their brothers. ¹⁶ And Job lived another one hundred and forty years after these events, and knew his sons and his son's sons, and theirs, four generations. ¹⁷ And so Job died, an old man contented with his days.

Discussion

Discussion of Chapter One

1:1–3 *A man there was from the land of Uz and his name was Job. He was a simple and straightforward man, a GOD-fearing man who turned away from evil. He had seven sons and three daughters. He owned seven thousand sheep, three thousand camels, ten thousand head of cattle, five hundred she-asses and was the head of a very large estate. He was the richest man in the East.*

It all sounds like the beginning of some wonderful fairy tale, full of noble and wealthy men from the mysterious land of the East. In the Hebrew language the word for *east* can also mean *ancient*, and conjures up the dream of a child's notion of wisdom and valor. "Seven sons and three daughters": whether it is because of some perfection felt in them, or because they are odd and somehow unbalanced, I do not know, but the numbers three and seven have always had a magic ring to them.

The language of Chapters 1 and 2 as well as that of Chapter 42 from verse 7 on differs markedly from that found in the central part of the book. Turning the page from Chapter 2 to Chapter 3 is like turning from Dick and Jane to Shakespeare, and I have tried to reflect that difference in the translation. Most scholars believe that Chapters 1 and 2 were written by another hand, and that may be the case. It is, however, not clear to what extent one can claim such historical knowledge. Much, on the other hand, can be said of its literary effect.

The childlike nature of the text, both with regard to
its diction and to its use of repetition, gives it a kind of
never-never feeling, especially when contrasted with the stark
reality felt in the rest of the text. The banter between God and
the Satan only adds to this feeling. If one includes the final
chapter, it is almost a classic comic situation in which bad
things happen to good people, but in the end everyone lives
more than happily ever after.

Whether it was an old folk tale which the poet used to
introduce his account, or whether a later thinker felt a need
to add a bit of comic relief after such trials; or even if it was
the poet himself who saw the last chapter as the true culmination of his story, is something we are not told. In the course
of this work, however, we shall try to show that Job's final
acceptance of the comic is part of the most serious intent of
the book.

Job is introduced to us as being a "simple" man. The
Hebrew word, תָּם (tam), carries with it that same duality one
finds in the English. It can mean either guileless or foolish.
The notion of the *tam* is central to the thoughts of most of the
actors in the Book of Job.[1]

 His sons used to make feasts in their homes, each man
1:4–5   *on his day, and send word to their three sisters to come*
         and eat and drink with them. Now when the days of
         feasting had gone full circle, Job sent word to them to
         sanctify themselves. He himself would get up early in
         the morning to make burnt offerings for each of his
         children; "For perhaps," Job said, "my children have
         sinned, and cursed GOD *in their hearts." Thus did Job*
         all of his days.

---

[1] For an account of the role played by the *tam*, see the discussion of 31:40
on page 215 below.

The first event we see is a round of family parties. Although the word used for feasting comes from the word meaning *to drink* and implies that wine was served, the fact that the sisters were invited would seem to indicate that they were wholesome and good-natured affairs. We all take it as part of the charm of the story that the sisters are merely invited and barely take any notice of the fact that they never host the parties themselves. We take it for granted that they have no independent wealth. It is not wrong of us to do so at this point, and in fact we would lose the spirit of the day should we assume otherwise.

The Hebrew text of verses 4 and 5 makes it clear that while these days were ample and full, there is no suggestion that the children of Job spent an undue amount of their time at such parties. Rather, these days marked a special time of the year. From every indication, they were in no sense religious holidays but merely days full of human good-naturedness. In verse 5, however, Job reveals that, while he trusts his children, he only partly trusts good-naturedness. He seems to have full trust in their actions, but he supposes that no one is in full control of the thoughts that can flit into and out of a human mind. The word he uses for *cursed* literally means *blessed*; but it is used euphemistically.

~   *One day the Sons of* God *came to present them-*
1:6   *selves before the* Lord, *and the Satan—that is, the Adversary—came along with them.*

At this point in the text we are introduced to a character who in Hebrew is called שָׂטָן (satan). Clearly the poet has some traditional usage in mind which he is either using or toying with. But so many traditions have grown up around the word that a longer route of explication will be required. It would be best, therefore, to look at each case in its own terms.

The term first comes up in the story of Balaam:

So Balaam rose in the morning, and saddled his ass, and went with the princes of Moab. But God's anger was kindled because he went; and the angel of the LORD *took his stand in the way as his* satan. *Now he was riding on the ass, and his two servants were with him.* [Num. 22:21–22]

And the angel of the LORD *said to him, "Why have you struck your ass these three times? Behold, I have come forth as a* satan, *because your way is perverse before me..."* [Num. 22:32]

The reader may wish to consult the entire story, Num. 21–24, 31. It is not clear that the angel is a being called *a satan*. Rather, *being a satan* seems to be an activity of the moment that any angel might be required to perform. Here, the angel's job seems to be to prevent Balaam from doing a wrongful act. It would not be easy to give a full articulation of that action because Balaam is a very complicated character.[2]

In the Book of Samuel, the term is used for a man whose original intention seems to be directed toward another's good, but whose actions nevertheless turn out otherwise.

Send the man back, that he may return to the place to which you have assigned him; he shall not go down with us to battle, lest in the battle he become a satan *to us. For how could this fellow reconcile himself to his lord? Would it not be with the heads of the men here?"* [I Sam. 29:4]

"What have I to do with you, you sons of Zeruiah, that you should this day be as a satan *to me? Shall anyone be put to death in Israel this day? For do I not know that I am this day king over Israel?"* [II Sam. 19:23]

In the Book of Kings, the term *satan* is used for the leaders of the nations who, unbeknownst to themselves, become God's way of chastening his people:

---

[2] On Balaam's character, see Robert D. Sacks, *A Commentary on the Book of Genesis* (Edwin Mellen Press, 1990).

But now the LORD *my God has given me rest on every side; there is neither* satan *nor misfortune.* [I Kings 5:18]

And the LORD *raised up a* satan *against Solomon, Hadad the Edomite; he was of the royal house in Edom...* [I Kings 11:14]

Strangely enough, it is only in the Book of Chronicles, the book that normally goes out of its way to avoid anything that tends to appear close to the mythic (such as the giants) that we see the Satan we know:

The Satan stood up against Israel, and incited David to number Israel. [I Chron. 21:1]

Throughout the Book of Psalms, the *satan* is the hated adversary (שָׂטָן) who accuses (שָׂטַן):

Those who are my foes without cause are mighty, and many are those who hate me wrongfully. Those who render me evil for good are my adversaries (יִשְׂטְנוּנִי, yis't'nuni) *because I follow after good.* [Ps. 38:20–21]

May my adversaries (שִׂטְנֵי נַפְשִׁי, sit'nei nafshi) *be put to shame and consumed; with scorn and disgrace may they be covered who seek my hurt.* [Ps. 71:13]

In return for my love they accuse me (יִשְׂטְנוּנִי, yis't'nuni), *even as I make prayer for them. So they reward me evil for good, and hatred for my love.* [Ps. 109:4]

Our *satan* is all of these, and he is none of them. As we shall see, he is convinced that man is radically incapable of being just. Deep underneath man's coat of decency lies a thick skin of self-interest; the rest is mere show. For him, God's high hopes for man are not well founded. Through the imagery of *skin* that runs throughout the book, the satan hopes to show God that if man were ever to face the unmediated nature of the world around him, man would show himself a bitter and vicious animal. By the end of the book we shall leave the

satan not because he arouses our hatred, but because we will
have seen a richer way.

When the satan says that he "just went down there to go for
a stroll" [1:7] he uses the verb הלך (halakh) in the reflexive
form, which normally means *a strolling about for its own sake
without any direct external goal*. When Genesis 3:8 speaks
of God "going for a stroll" in the Garden, there is a strong
implication that God has not come there intentionally for the
purpose of checking up on Adam. In the same way, when
God says to Abram, "Stroll about before me" (Gen. 17:1),
he wants to look at Abram's general way of being, rather
than at any particular goal or accomplishment. Even when
God invites Abram to "stroll about through the land ... for I
will give it to you" (Gen. 13:17), he means Abram to enjoy it
quietly without a sense of immediate possession. In a similar
way, when the satan speaks of a *stroll* he is claiming a certain
innocence of intention.

〰   *He said, "Naked I came out of my mother's belly and*
1:21   *naked I shall return there. The* LORD *gives, and the*
        LORD *takes; blessed be the name of the* LORD."

When Job speaks these words after the first round of
attacks, his perhaps almost thoughtless blurring of the distinction between his own mother and the great mother earth
may be seen as Job's first and rather naive glimpse into a
world larger than the world of man into which he was born.
Here the thought is almost thoughtless. We see it as only a
seed, yet we shall see it grow till its roots are sturdy enough
to crack the strongest city wall.

Discussion of Chapter Two

~   *Then the Satan answered the* LORD *and said: "Well,*
2:4   *skin beneath skin! Everything a man has he will give*
     for his life."

When the Satan now appears for the second time before
the LORD, he taunts him for the trust he puts in man, using
the words עוֹר בְּעַד־עוֹר. The Hebrew word עוֹר means *skin*,
while בְּעַד means *away from* or *out through*, as in the phrase
to look out through a lattice:

> *Out of the window she peered, the mother of Sisera gazed*
> *through the lattice: "Why is his chariot so long in coming?*
> *Why tarry the hoofbeats of his chariots?"* [Judges 5:28]

בְּעַד can also mean *beyond, under*; and hence *in place of*, or
on behalf of.

No one seems to know what the Hebrew expression means.
Most have translated it as "skin for skin" on the assumption that it was a saying current among traders in furs and
hides, though it is not clear to any of these translators what
may have been meant by the expression or how it may have
applied to this situation.

For reasons cited above, we have taken the Satan to mean
that, while Job may have the superficial look of a God-fearing
man, once that surface has been scratched one finds another,
more protective, layer behind it—one based on self-interest
alone.

The imagery of skin will gain great importance throughout the main body of the text. In light of this, it is tempting
to suppose that this phrase, "skin beneath skin," at least, was
crafted by the same hand as the main body of Job, even if the

preponderance of Chapters 1 and 2 was not. But such specu-
lation is not the object of this work.

It is interesting to note that in verse 7, the Satan did not
in fact try to "...get to his bones and his flesh," as he said he
would, but attacked Job's skin, the surface of his being. Job had
said "Naked I came out of my mother's belly and naked I shall
return there" [1:21]. In verse 5, the Satan had implied that Job
was not as naked as he had pretended to be, but had an inner,
thicker coat of self-protection; and now he is out to prove it.

At the end of the chapter we are introduced to three more
players in the drama. This introduction is presented in the
poet's own voice. It is written neither in the high prose style of
what follows nor in the folk—one might even say, childish—
style of what preceded it. Yet it makes no sense without them,
nor do they make much sense without it. Thus there seem to
be fairly solid grounds for assuming that the Book of Job was
written by an author who, like Shakespeare, could speak in
many voices. It is, of course, totally unclear how much one
can know about such matters.

> *Now when Job's three friends heard about all the evils*
> 2:11   *that had come upon him, they came each man from*
> *his own place—Eliphaz the Temanite, Bildad the*
> *Shuhite, and Zophar the Na'amatite.*

So far as one can tell, the genealogies of the characters
seem to be as shown in the chart opposite.

As we can see, the Book of Job presents itself as being tangentially aware of the book that tells the tale of the genesis
of the Sons of Israel. It also presents most of the characters
involved as being tangentially related to that people. This
aspect of the book will not change even when, in Chapter 32,
we meet the next character, Elihu—although the question of
his identity will complicate the matter somewhat. This book,

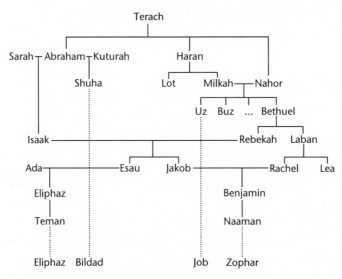

Genealogies of Job and his three friends

then, insofar as it speaks of a human world, has as its principal subject matter a much wider world than the one which is spoken of in the bulk of the Torah.

Job is a descendent of the two non-chosen brothers of Abraham, Nahor and Haran. Bildad is a descendent of Abraham and the wife he had taken after our attention had been drawn away from him and to Isaak. Eliphaz is from the line of Esau, another non-chosen brother.

The last to join the discussion, Zophar, is, so far as one can tell, a descendant of Benjamin. All these men, however, come from Terach, and of him we read:

> *Terach took Abram his son and ... to go into the land of Canaan; but when they came to Haran, they settled there.* [Gen. 11:31]

Terach, the common grandfather, was the man who, on purely human grounds, saw or felt a need to leave his father's house and go to the land of Canaan; but he was not able fully to accomplish his goal. All of the men, then, seem to be heirs to such a tradition.

Discussion of Chapter Three

∿   *May the day of my birth be lost in oblivion...*
3:3

We are at a new beginning. With Job's first words the language has suddenly become somber, poetic and obscure.

The notion of *being lost* (אבד) has a double significance. It may imply something *not being at hand where it should be* ("my hat is lost, it is not here where it should be"), or it may suggest *being where nothing is*, and hence *being out of contact with every other person or thing* ("I am lost, I am in a strange place and do not recognize the place in which I find myself"). This side of things can best be seen by remembering that the word אבד is related to the word אֲבַדּוֹן, or Abaddon, the place of oblivion; and such ambiguity is often critical for the understanding of any given passage.

∿   *...and with it that night in which it was said: "A hero*
3:3   *has been conceived."*

Others offer that "a male" or "a man-child" has been conceived. But neither of those translations brings out the great feeling of joy which, the word גֶּבֶר implies, must have been felt that day by all the members of Job's family. My translation aims to bring out the irony of the verse: The very being of the Hero lies in his being remembered; but for Job, this day and everything in it is to be forgotten.

Sa'adiah,[3] with some justification, translates "born" instead of "conceived," and even cites some parallel texts. While there

_____

3 Saadia Ben Joseph, *The Book of Theodicy: Translation and Commentary on the Book of Job*, trans. L. E. Goodman (Yale University Press, 1988). The tenth-century Saadia Ben Joseph Al-Fayyumi (Saadia Gaon) was

can be little doubt that Job is indeed thinking of the day of his birth, it may be important to retain the fact that he speaks of it in terms of its more hidden causes.

> *May that day be a day of darkness. May God from*
> *on high not seek it out nor any brightness radiate*
> *upon it; but let darkness and the Shadow of Death*
> *redeem it....*

3:4–5

This sentence will echo and re-echo throughout the whole. The Book of Job, as we shall see, is a constant play between the way in which a lovely surface can obscure a darker center and the way in which our view of the deeper intent of things can often obscure our view of their simple surface.

Seven times during the course of these first ten verses we read the words "darkness" and "night." There are also words like "oblivion," and many others with the same intent—as if that day had contained a thing which no eye, human or divine, should ever have seen. Job's first reaction is to let it be abandoned in hopes that it, his own beginnings, would shrivel up and be gone from sight.

The Hebrew word צַלְמָוֶת (tzalmavet) is a compound word, coming from the two roots צל, shadow, and מות, death. Unlike English, Hebrew grammar does not allow for the possibility of compound nouns—except in the case of proper nouns, where compounds abound. This would argue for the notion that צַלְמָוֶת is the proper name of a place. On the other hand, it is possible that the name became generic, as we speak of "an Einstein." Perhaps the reader can get a better feeling for the problem by seeing how the word is used outside the Book of Job. At any rate, if it is a place, it does not seem to be identical with the Shadow of Death itself as we know it from verses like:

---

known for his philosophical, philological, grammatical and legal writings, biblical exegesis, and calendrical studies.

> *They did not say, "Where is the* LORD *who brought us up from the land of Egypt, who led us in the wilderness, in a land of deserts and pits, in a land of drought and the Shadow of Death in a land that none passes through, where no man dwells?"* [Jer. 2:6]

Rather, it seems to be a place here on Earth full of desolation and fear where no man dwells and death is ever near.

Although Job at one time will speak of it as a land to which he is going and from which he will "not return"—

> *Well, I will be going soon, going to a land of darkness and the Shadow of Death, and I will not return; to a land, a darkness of murk, the Shadow of Death and without order—a land whose light is murk* [10:21]

—at other times he thinks of it as a place which contains the hidden things that can be brought out into the light.

> *He unveils deep things from out of the darkness; he leads the Shadow of Death out into the light.* [12:22]

> *He [man] explores everything to its limit, even to this rock of murk and the Shadow of Death.* [28:3]

〜   *...let darkness and the Shadow of Death redeem it....*
3:5

These words are very curious. They are the first intimation of a thought which will grow and transform itself throughout the whole of the book. They imply that even at this early stage, Job dreams of a place, perhaps only in the gloom and the darkness, where there is room for the day which should not have been, a place where it can be itself; but for now, it is merely a passing thought and is quickly dropped.

〜   *...may a cloud dwell above it. May that which warms*
3:5   [כִּמְרִירֵי, *kim'riri*] *the day terrify it.*

It would be hard to find many works of which the Italian expression "*traduttore traditore*" (every translator is a traitor) is more true than of the Book of Job. It is obscure both in word and in grammatical form. Many words appear once and never again in the whole of the literature.

The word כְּמְרִיר (kim'rir) could come from the root מרר, *bitter*, but that is grammatically unlikely. The more likely root is כמר, which can mean either *to blacken* or *to warm*. Usually it is taken in the former sense, like a cloud or an eclipse. But since many men fear these things, it would also seem possible that Job is thinking of those creatures that fear the sunlight and crawl under rocks and dead tree stumps.

⟳
3:8
Those who despise the sea and those who are determined to lay Leviathan open will curse it.

Leviathan, who will be more fully described in Chapter 40, is mentioned in three other passages in the Bible:

> And on that day the LORD shall punish ... Leviathan. [Isaiah 27:1]

> You crushed the head of Leviathan and gave it as food to the people of the island. [Ps. 74:14]

> So is this the great and wide sea, wherein are creeping things innumerable, both small and great beasts. There go the ships: and there goes Leviathan whom you have made to play with. [Ps. 104:25]

As we can see, there is a certain ambivalence within the biblical tradition towards Leviathan. Isaiah considers it deserving of punishment, while for the Psalmist it is an innocent toy; and so at this point it is not yet clear what we are to make of these people who despise the sea, and who are determined to lay Leviathan open. Who are they? How do they look upon the swirlings of the sea? Are we to admire them or hold them in contempt? Perhaps we are to see them with compassion. More importantly, what does Job think of them now, and will it always be that way? While the poet forces us to raise these questions, he is clearly not yet ready to settle the issue. We may not yet even know what is at stake. In the Babylonian Talmud, Baba Batra 74b, Rav seems to suggest that he has seen the problem; and he speculates that there were actually two Leviathans, a male and a female.[4] But the text of Job does not appear to offer such a simple solution.

I would suggest, rather, that the Book of Job is an account of a man's attempt to face this ambivalence in order to discover under which welkin justice lies.

> *Let its morning stars darken. Let it hope for the light,*
> 3:9–10 *but let there be none. May it not see the eyelid of dawn open, for it closed not the doors of my mother's belly but hid my eyes from toil.*

As Job sees the world at this point, it is shrouded in a blind Promethean hope which has all been stripped away for him, and now he must lead a life which never should have been.

> *Why did I not come out of the womb and die, exit the*
> 3:11 *belly and perish?*

In a certain way the change—or we might even say the education—that we see taking place in Job throughout the book is reflected in his own and others' musings on the womb and the belly, in such passages as:

---

4 "Rav Judah said in the name of Rav: All that the Holy One, blessed be He, created in his world he created male and female. Likewise, Leviathan the slant serpent and Leviathan the tortuous serpent he created male and female; and had they mated with one another they would have destroyed the whole world."

Naked I came out of my mother's belly and naked I shall return there. The LORD gives, and the LORD takes; blessed be the name of the LORD. [1:21]

May it not see the eyelid of dawn open, for it closed not the gates of my mother's belly but hid my eyes from toil. Why did I not come out of the womb and die, exit the belly and perish? [3:9]

Why did you bring me out of the womb? Had I only perished without ever an eye to see me, I would be as though I had not been, as though I had been led from the belly to the grave. [10:18]

Job sees the womb as the gateway to a life of toil that never should have been. But Job's friends, except for Bildad, see the womb or belly as nothing but the container of empty rage. Here, for example, is Eliphaz:

Then Eliphaz the Temanite answered and said: Should a wise man even answer such blustery thoughts and fill his own belly with the east wind? [15:1]

Their belly brews deceit. [15:35]

And Zophar:

Since he knew no peace from his belly he cannot escape through his pleasure. [20:20]

As he is about to fill his belly, he will send out his burning anger upon him and rain it down upon him into his bread. [20:23]

And Elihu:

I am full of words, and the wind in my belly presses upon me. [32:18]

In Job's recollections and musings on the past, however, things were not so. Rather, the womb/belly was the beginning of all that was warm and near:

Did not he who made me in my mother's belly make him as well? Did he not form us in the same womb? [31:15]

From my mother's belly I was their mother's guide. [31:18]

By the end of the book, the womb or belly will have become for Job—and perhaps for the reader—that mighty, turbulent, and often ferocious, source out of which there has emerged a world full of life and living creatures; a world larger, stranger and more violent, but at times curiously more tender, than any man had ever seen. But at all times it is breathtakingly beautiful, and we stand in awe of that which does not know us.

> *From whose belly does ice emerge, and who gave birth to the frost of heaven?* [38:29]

> *But look now, here is Behemoth whom I made along with you. He eats fodder just like the cattle, but look at the strength in his loins. His might is in the muscles of his belly.* [40:15]

〰️ *Why were there knees to receive me, and what were*
3:12   *those breasts to me that I should have sucked?*

Mitchell's "Why were there knees to hold me, breasts to keep me alive?"[5] fails to capture the fact that Job is blaming himself for his own participation in the great lie of false hope. His first act was to cling on to life by allowing himself to be attracted to his mother's breast.

〰️ *Why does he give light to those whom toil has con-*
3:20–21 *sumed, or life to the bitter of soul? Or to those who wait for death when there is none? Or who dig for it more than for subterranean treasure?*

Man has a certain light, an innate sense of what is just and what is unjust. For Job, no man can ignore that light as long as

---

5 Stephen Mitchell, *Into the Whirlwind: A Translation of the Book of Job* (Doubleday, 1979).

he finds it within himself, and yet it is in constant opposition to the manifest will of God as seen in daily events. Would we not be better off without that light? The world makes too much sense to make no sense, and yet it makes no sense. If Job had no reason, the world would no longer look unreasonable, and he could sleep more soundly.

    I feared a fear and it came to pass, and what I dreaded
3:25   *has come upon me. I was not at ease, I was not quiet,*
     I had no rest, but rage came.

Here, ending the chapter, Job seems to admit that the beguiling character of the day of his birth was not total and absolute. Even when things were going well for him and the surface of the world made sense to him, he was uneasy. Perhaps it all looked too Hollywooden to him. Good things happened to good people, and bad things happened to bad people, so far as he could tell; yet he was not at ease. Seeing no reason for perfection, he was distrustful. He seemed to have known that if there were no reason behind it, it could not last, and that one day he and God would come to blows.

These thoughts had not come to Job in the form of thought, but in the form of unarticulated fear. Job's present discontent arises, as he sees it, from the sudden realization that the surface of the world, as it lay before him, had fallen out of harmony with the wisdom of the ages. But how sudden was that realization? Job had always felt—felt in the form of fear—that his commitment to the importance of the simple world of appearance, as it lay before man, would one day come into conflict with his understanding of that world as it had been formed by the wisdom of the fathers handed down from the ages.

Discussion of Chapter Four

Eliphaz speaks:

> ∽   *How can one speak without being more than weari-*
> 4:2–4   *some? But who can refrain from words? It was you*
>   *who always [taught] restraint and strengthened so*
>   *many frail hands, you who had the words to pick up*
>   *those that were stumbling and bolster the knees that*
>   *were about to bend.*

It is of utmost importance to note the genuine good will with which Eliphaz begins to speak. Only in that way can we catch a glimpse of what it was that made loving friends turn against Job so brutally.

> ∽   *But now it has come upon you, and it is indeed weari-*
> 4:5–6   *some. It has found you out and you are stunned. But*
>   *may not that dread itself be your surety; and your*
>   *hope, the simplicity of your ways?*

Eliphaz first tries to pull Job into being his old self. From Eliphaz's standpoint, Job's questioning indicates that he has forgotten his simplicity. He has taken awe and trepidation (ירא) for fear (פחד). For him the two actions seem to be almost identical; awe (ירא) of one who is no longer trusted readily turns into fear (פחד).

> ∽   *So far as I can see, those who plow evil and sow tribu-*
> 4:8–11   *lation reap them. One breath from God, and they are*
>   *lost, a puff of his nostrils and they are finished. An*

*old lion may roar and the savage lion give voice, but
the teeth of that spirited lion will be broken. The lioness is lost for lack of prey, and the young ones will be
scattered.*

At this point we can begin to see Eliphaz pulling away
from his friend. For Job's friends, and for Job as well, the
only proper home for man is the home of man—the home of
man as it has been defined by the wisdom of the fathers. The
only proper concern for man is his fellow man. Not to be at
home within that world is to be an outcast and a man of sin.
Throughout all of what follows we must constantly remind
ourselves that our daily lives depend upon such a world.
Only in that way can we begin to understand why good men
might turn brutal when that world is suddenly found to be
under attack. But for Job that world has begun to crack. Job
deeply believes in a just God, and yet he has seen the just in
meaningless pain. The wise men have assured him that all
will work out for the best, but it does not.

This moment, as we see, is not one of calm doubt and curi-
osity, but of belief, confusion, and indignation, a rage more
like the anger modern optometrists tell us about that men
feel when they have been fitted with a pair of glasses that
turns the world upside down, leaving the world of percep-
tion at odds with their understanding of the world they have
always known to call home; but this time there are no glasses.
Throughout the book, we shall see Job trying to find a home—
first in one of these worlds, the wisdom of the fathers, then
in the other, the world of the surface where the innocent die
in pain and suffering. But each world keeps blasting into the
other, inverting it and pulling it out of focus. When speech
cannot come together with the world, it gives way to anger,
rage, and madness.

◦

◐   *Shall a mortal be more just than his God?*
4:17

    These words, which Eliphaz hears spoken by a voice in a night vision, pose the central question of the book. But does the question even make sense? Is there any standard for justice apart from the will of God in the light of which his actions can be inquired into? Even if there is, what is its relation to what we humans feel to be just and unjust? And what if our human feelings are not in agreement with that standard? Job knows that all this is a question which must be faced one day, but he does not quite know in what terms it should be asked. He is not yet ready for the question, and makes no attempt to respond.

◐   *If he puts no trust in his servants and even to his*
4:18–21 *angels lays charge of folly, what of those who dwell in a house of clay, whose foundation is but dust? He will crush them like a moth. They are beaten from morning till evening. Forever they are lost and no note is taken. Their tent rope is pulled out from under them and they die without reason.*

With these words Eliphaz closes the chapter. He begins to face the question he has been implicitly raising since the beginning. In itself the world is totally indifferent, if not essentially hostile to human life. Human concerns for justice which remain within the plane of the human cannot be of cosmic concern. It is all no more than a tent which, by its outer surface, looks much like a solid structure, but which at the mere pull of a pin, can crumple out flat. It is unclear whether the phrase "without reason" refers to the thoughtless way in which the tent rope is pulled, or to the fact that men die without ever understanding why.

Discussion of Chapter Five

Eliphaz continues:

> ∼   *Cry out! Is there anyone to answer you? To which of*
> 5:1–2   *the holy ones will you turn now? For indignation can*
>   *kill a fool and jealousy murder a dunce.*

It is unclear exactly what Eliphaz means by "the holy ones," but the implication seems to be that nothing within the world as Job knows it can be holy. Within the limited world open to human comprehension there is nothing between man and unfriendly nature. Job's questions will go unanswered and his cries unheard.

Normally there is a distinction made between the אֱוִיל (eviyl), the fool who is considered morally guilty, and the פֶּתָה (poteh), the dupe or dunce; but for Eliphaz the difference is irrelevant. Well intentioned or not, the frustration which must arise out of daily defeat in the unfriendly world that lacks the holy must lead to destructive if not self-destructive anger.

> ∼   *Evil does not come out of the dust nor does tribu-*
> 5:6–9   *lation sprout from the ground: but a human is born*
>   *to tribulation sure as sparks fly upwards. Nonetheless*
>   *I would make my appeal to God and put my matter*
>   *before that GOD who accomplishes deeds great beyond*
>   *inquiry, marvels which have no number.*

Compare the verses "He will crush them like a moth" [4:19] and "Nonetheless I would make my appeal to God and put my matter before that GOD" [5:8]. Both Eliphaz and

Job accept these two statements; but for Eliphaz they live together snugly in the same world, while they rip Job's world in two. To Eliphaz there is always time for trust, and so for him all things make sense; but for Job, to "make an appeal" to one who can "crush them like a moth" leads only to madness.

〜   *He who gives out rain over the face of the earth and*
5:10–11   *sends water into the fields, he can raise the despondent on high, giving sanctuary to the mournful.*

Thus, says Eliphaz, as though in answer: Nature is not nature as it presents itself within the plane of human understanding. It is the same God who "gives out rain over the face of the earth and sends water into the fields" that "can raise the despondent on high, giving sanctuary to the mournful." But this can be seen only by those for whom rain is not looked upon as simply a part of the given, but as a daily marvel.

〜   *Have no dread of the beasts of the earth, for you have*
5:22–23   *a covenant with the rocks in the field, and the beasts of the fields will bring you peace.*

This is, in effect, Eliphaz's summing up of his argument. The word he uses here for *covenant* is בְּרִית (b'rit), the word used for Abraham's covenant with God. Peace in this most dreadful world is only achieved by a divine covenant with the rocks and the beasts. Threatening boulders are not held back in their places by any innate forces to be found within the rock itself, but by a divine covenant freely established by that same God who answers those who come to him.

But all of Job's arguments presuppose the relevance of the way things appear to naked man. They imply taking seriously what we have called the surface of things; that fire goes up, that dogs bark, and that innocent men sometimes seem to suffer. If arguments presuppose intelligibility then Job's arguments presuppose the relevance of the way things are in themselves. In other words, they presuppose either something like Nature in the ancient sense or Laws of Nature in the modern sense.

It is hard to know to what extent or in whatever vague way Eliphaz could have been aware of such an alternative. However, it is clear that he knows that the notion of rocks and beasts obeying a covenant is a notion that cuts deeply into Job's words.

Discussion of Chapter Six

Job, in answer, begins:

> ∾ *Oh, would that my indignation could truly be weighed,*
> 6:2 *my calamities all laid out together on the pan of a scale!*
> *Then would it raise up even the sands of the seas.*

But in fact, Job has almost no answer for Eliphaz. As we began to see in the reflection on verse 5 of the last chapter, the components of the world can be stated and agreed upon. But their relationships to one another, whether they lie together in peace or contend in anguish and in anger, or even what kinds of things can or cannot lie together, those are matters on which Job and Eliphaz may not be able to agree. Job's anguish, then, cannot be laid out on a common scale.

> ∾ *And thus I speak without care, for the arrows of the*
> 6:3–4 *Almighty are in me and my spirit drinks in their*
> *venom. The terrors of God are arrayed against me.*

The word Job uses for *venom* also means *fury*, and it will play an important role in the story. Job presents himself as "drinking in" the venom/fury. His thoughts and feelings are complicated and even contradictory, but they are still intelligible. At this point in his understanding, to come to terms with the surrounding world is to experience the world as it shows itself to him, to experience it as deeply as he can: and so he "drinks in their fury."

> ∾ *Will the wild ass bray when there is grass? Does the ox*
> 6:5 *bellow at his fodder?*

This verse gives a fairly good idea of how Job thinks about what we today, after the coming-to-be of Greek philosophy, would call the relationship of cause and effect. It is not so far from the thought lying behind the Latin *causa*, or the Greek αἰτία, both of which originally meant something like *to be responsible* or *to be guilty*; and one can see in Job's next statement the immediacy this concept has for him.

〰️   *Can what is tasteless be eaten without salt, or does*
6:6   *the slime of an egg white have any taste? My soul*
        refuses to touch them. They are like a contagion in
        my daily bread.

This represents the closest Job can come to telling the others what his world is like, this world whose parts do not fit together: it is like food that cannot be eaten. The rejection is immediate and total. For Job "the slime of an egg white" refers not just to a single dish but to his whole life. For him there is no world, whether this one or another, which is not filled with the contagion of disparity.

Thus even if the others, Eliphaz and the rest, cannot see the world as Job sees it, Job thinks they should be able to tell *just by looking at him* that something in Job's world has gone awry— but of course they cannot. But perhaps the surface is, after all, only the surface; and perhaps the others are right in pointing to a deeper wisdom underlying it. Even then, thinks Job, the surface should indicate the way, just as wisdom should give solidity to the surface. But here all seems to be at odds.

Through the immediacy of our response to taste (or tastelessness), one can see the power that exists in the concept of cause and effect to pull Job back into the surface plane, the world of growing corn and barking dogs, of temporary joys and of undeserved pain.

~   *Let me spring up in my writhing though he spare me*
6:10   *not; for never have I disavowed the words of the Holy*
          One.

In the preceding chapter Eliphaz had accused Job of having no contact with the holy; but from this statement it
becomes clear that whatever it was that Job saw, and which
cleaved his world in two, it did not have its origins in any
native antipathy towards the holy.

~   *Is my strength the strength of a rock? Do I have flesh*
6:12–13 *of bronze? No, I have no support within me and all*
          resourcefulness has been driven out.

Whatever it is, then, that Job has seen, it has *made him
weary*—to recall Eliphaz's plaint in 4:5. He can in his imagi-
nation envisage a being with the inner strength to maintain
itself in the midst of a crumbling world, but Job knows that
at this point he is no such being, and perhaps no man is.

~   *To those in despair the kindness of friends is due, but*
6:14–20 *trepidation and awe of the Almighty has forsaken*
          them all. My brothers have betrayed me like a wadi,
          a running brook that has gone dry. They crystal over
          with ice and invert to black. They hide themselves
          in snow. They thaw and disappear. In the heat they
          vanish from their place. Their beds twist and turn.
          They flow out into the vastness and are lost. The
          caravans of Tema look to them; the band from Sheba
          hopes for them but find themselves lost because they
          trusted. They arrived and were confounded.

These words of Job are specifically directed to Eliphaz. At
first the metaphor of the wadi seems dead, with no meaning
at all. What could it mean for a man to be like a wadi? And

yet, once the very simple and straightforward definition of
wadi—"a running brook that has gone dry"—is articulated
in speech, the metaphor begins to sing with life; and the
reader is even left with a slight feeling of shame for not having understood what Job was saying. Then, one after another,
the many disparate ways in which the metaphor holds begin
to pour out. Things known and trusted are not what they
are. Soft and skipping waters, which should flow with ease,
can turn hard and immobile. A surface of ice, which should
be crystal clear, can suddenly turn black, dark as the sea or
as Egypt's night, all depending upon how it is struck by the
light.

Job points specifically to the caravans of Tema and the
band of Sheba, men who knew the desert well, its every rock
and dune. If we, the readers, cannot feel their trust, we cannot feel their horror when they suddenly feel lost in a familiar
land. The reader must remember that Eliphaz, to whom this
speech is addressed, was himself a Temanite. Job is trying to
give Eliphaz some insight into his thoughts and feelings. He
has the almost self-contradictory task of making confusion
intelligible for him.

The moment we hear Job pronounce the word *trusted*, we
cannot help remembering that he, too, once had a whole
world he thought he could trust, a world he thought he knew
as well as the men of Sheba knew the desert.

> *So now you are as nothing, and at sight of terror you*
6:21–23 *have taken flight. But did I ever say to you, "Give me"?*
"Offer the bribe for me out of your wealth"? "Deliver
me from the hand of the foe"? or "Redeem me from the
hands of the Most Terrifying"?

The word we have translated as *foe* is צָר (tzar). Its root
meaning is *to be narrow*. The word itself has two quite

different meanings, both of which must always be kept in mind. On the one hand, it can be an inner feeling of being cramped, or of living within a narrow and constricting horizon. On the other hand, it can mean an outward foe. This duality wonderfully catches the ambivalence and wavering in Job's soul. Is this old foe pressing Job down from above? Or is Job straining to break out of what he perceives to be a narrow and fixed confinement?

Job, then, is also asking the question, "But did I ever say to you, 'Deliver me from the hand of narrowness'?"

> *Are you busy devising a proof in words while taking*
> 6:26 *the testimony of a despairing man to be no more than*
> *the wind?*

Job is beginning to see the double power of words—how words without vision can distort a world of pain into a vision—a vision of loveliness—without ever knowing that they have done so.

> *Stop, I beg you! Let there be no injustice. Give in! For*
> 6:29–30 *yet my stand smacks of what is right. There is no injustice on my tongue, and yet does not my palate know the taste of ruination?*

Notwithstanding the acknowledged power of words, Job seems to know that there is in every man a slight but uncomfortable feeling that perhaps Job is right after all.

Discussion of Chapter Seven

~
7:1–4

Does not a mortal have a term of duty to serve here on earth, and are not his days like the days of a hired servant? Like a slave he yearns for the shadows, like a hireling he hopes for his wages. So have I been allotted months of emptiness. Nights of toil have they apportioned me. I lie down and say, "When shall I arise?" and night drags on and I am sated with tossing till morning twilight.

There is a strange, eerie, almost Kafkaesque feeling to this set of verses. God is never mentioned in them and everything is stated in the indefinite third person plural or in the passive voice. Job presents man as feeling a horrible and meaningless but absolute and almost sacred duty to some nameless and totally unknown power.

This sense of duty—this sense that there is something to which, and to which alone, a man must devote his entire life—Job feels too. Some may try to name it or endow it with intent and love; and such individuals are at home with it. But for Job it has no name; it has no intent.

We moderns may want to call this feeling *compulsion*. We would begin to look for the causes of such feelings within man himself; but on all counts, the Book of Job suggests that there is something beyond man that Job has yet to see.

~
7:8

The eye that sees me takes no note of me; your eye is upon me, and I am not.

I was not able to capture the full force of verse 8. The Hebrew has a singularly chilling effect which I have not quite been able to achieve in English translation. The original simply reads עֵינֶיךָ בִּי וְאֵינֶנִּי (einikhah bi ve'eineni). Partly its force lies in the simplicity of the language: עֵינֶיךָ, your eyes, בִּי, are upon—or, more literally, *in*—me. The main force of the twist, however, is felt in the final word, וְאֵינֶנִּי.

While it is clearly felt as one simple word, וְאֵינֶנִּי is composed of three parts. The first part, וְ, when it first hits the ear, simply means *and*; but what follows it can suddenly and retroactively twist it into *but*, or *nonetheless*, or can even place *in spite of the fact that...* in front of the first word. Thus thoughts that are set up to go together smoothly may be suddenly found to go awry. (For further remarks on this problem, see the Discussion of 8:2 below.)

The second part, אַיִן—or, as we find it here, אֵ—means *nought*, or *nothing*, or *non-being*.

The third part, נִי, is a suffix formed from the first person singular pronoun אֲנִי and, as a suffix, it means *my*. The literal meaning of the word as a whole, then, would be *and my non-being* (*is*).

Actually the word אֵינֶנִּי is not all that uncommon. It often occurs in such phrases as אֵינֶנִּי נֹתֵן לָכֶם תֶּבֶן, *I am not giving you straw* (Ex. 5:10) and כִּי אֵינֶנִּי בְּקִרְבְּכֶם, *for I am not in your midst* (Deut. 1:42). But when it stands bare and alone, it suddenly dissolves the world into nothingness.

༄   *No, I cannot restrain speech, but will speak out of the*
7:11   *narrowness constricting my spirit.*

That feeling of being cramped and crushed by his old enemy, narrowness [6:23], itself persuades him again that he *is*. This is an important turning point for Job. From his last considerations, he knows that to take his own existence seriously will require a return to the surface. That superficial world which he had rejected for the sake of human companionship must be reconsidered.

❧ *Am I the sea or some monster that you set watch over*
7:12 *me?*

This is a revealing question. For Job the idea central to human society, that man is ever under the care and watchful eye of his maker, is crippling and ultimately fatal to the human spirit.

Job's question leads him to this conclusion:

❧ *When I said that my bed will show me compassion*
7:13–16 *and my couch bear my complaint, you frightened me with dreams and terrified me with visions; and I preferred strangulation and death to my own substance. I have contempt; I will not live forever. Then just let me be, for my days are but the mist of a breath.*

The feeling of contempt which Job has for himself and for his life is to be understood in contrast to the compassion of which he speaks in verse 13. These two passions, contempt and compassion, which are presented here as polar opposites, will continue to play that role until Job's final speech; then their opposition will lead Job to a new and strange kind of harmony.

Bed and the pleasure of self-contained sleep should carve out a world for Job, a three-dimensional world which is all his own and which should reflect and support that surface world Job had thought to see about him. But it does not. The feeling of being watched, and therefore of being some kind of monster in need of being watched, has so completely overwhelmed Job's inner world that even in his dreams he is tortured by an amorphous sense of guilt that arises out of the sense of being watched. Job's need to contact the outside world of his three friends is so great that their world's watching God has become the author of his dreams. These thoughts culminate in the great statement of verses 17 and 18.

〜 *What is a mortal that thou shouldst magnify him?*
7:17–20 *And that thou shouldst set thine heart upon him? Yes, and inspect him every morning and test him every minute. When will you let me be? You'll not even let me alone to swallow my own spit. Supposing I have sinned, what have I done to you, O thou Great Watcher Of Man?*

Verse 17 is meant to ring as a psalm, while what follows in the text is Job's ironic commentary. For Job, one need only think the tradition through to see its horrors; but that was a thing which no thoughtful and caring man had ever done before, so far as he knew.

> *What is man, that thou art mindful of him? and the son of man, that thou visitest him?* [Ps. 8:5]

or, as Job might have rendered it,

> *What is man that you are always watching him, or the son of man that you are always checking up on him?*

Job's disdain continues in verses 18–20. Again he seems to have in mind a variety of psalm-like lines which must have been on everybody's lips, such as:

> *He will not let your foot be moved, he who keeps you will not slumber. Behold, he who keeps Israel will neither slumber*

nor sleep. The LORD *is your keeper; the* LORD *is your shade*
on your right hand.... The LORD *will keep you from all evil;*
he will keep your life. The LORD *will keep your going out*
and your coming in from this time forth and for evermore.
[Ps. 121:3–5, 7–8]

But for Job they take on the cast of ironic horror. Verses
11 through 21 then turn out to be Job's great discourse on
the relationship between privacy and human dignity. To be
constantly watched, and hence never to be oneself for oneself alone, is, for Job, to be less than human. Even the act of
complaining is itself a subhuman act, and Job must exhort
himself actually to do it. To be watched as a thing out of its
place is already to be out of place, or to be like a thing that
cannot know its own place but must be watched and kept in,
like the sea.

And so Job turns to his bed. Sleep is the one place that he
had expected to be *his* place, but even there the outside can
enter inside in the form of dreams and terrible night visions,
making his place not his place; and for Job, a thing without a
place is a contemptible thing.

Perhaps the one conscious act that, because of its totally
internal nature, a man thinks he can perform in total privacy, is the act of swallowing his own spit. Job feels that if the
traditional understanding of God is true, even this has been
denied him. Being permeated by God both in mind and in
body, he feels untrusted, and hence untrustworthy.

When Job utters his psalm-like quote, we can see how
those words which must have meant so much to him in the
past, have suddenly become full of sardonic terror.

If there is anything to this understanding of the passage,
then in contrast to the word *contempt*, the compassion spoken of in verse 13 must mean *leaving room for*, or *recognizing*
the place of, another. Much of the remainder of the book will

be devoted to an attempt to understand what it means to have compassion for another being. The fundamental problem is to learn to recognize the full existence of the other as other, and its relation to the recognition of self as self.

Discussion of Chapter Eight

〜 *Then Bildad the Shuhite answered and said: How long*
8:1–3 *will you continue to recite these things with words of*
such mighty wind? Will God pervert judgment?

The Hebrew which I translated as *with* is simply the particle ו. This particle is a general connective, and is usually
translated as *and*. To have some understanding of the problem facing the translator, the reader need only note that the
word *and* in the sentence "You mean you were in town and
you didn't call?" is by no means the simple *and* that appears
in phrases like "bread and butter." As I noted in the discussion of 7:8, it can mean *but*, or *when*, or a thousand other
renditions.

In the Book of Job the problem is particularly acute. Well-
connected arguments can so easily turn into nothing more
than a mass of sentences all lying in a heap. The reader is
hereby warned that we have translated the particle ו in a
thousand different ways. Otherwise the sentence would have
read: "How long will you continue to recite these things and
your words are such a mighty wind?"

The Hebrew I here rendered as *judgment* is מִשְׁפָּט (mishpat). I was not able to find a single English word to serve as a
consistent translation. מִשְׁפָּט can mean *judgment*, both in the
sense of a general law and in the sense of a specific judgment
made by a given judge. It can also mean a *trial*, or the *argument* or *case* prepared by either side. Other translators, with
some justification, have translated it as *right*. Unless otherwise noted, I use either *judgment* or *case*.

Bildad will start his argument proper only in verse 8, and it will have a great deal to do with the relation of fathers to sons and of sons to fathers. Before beginning that argument, however, he wanted to make it clear in the first seven verses that he thought that, as far as any actual punishment for any actual individual sin is concerned, each man must suffer for his own.

❦   *Only ask of the first generations. Seat yourself firmly*
8:8–10   *upon what their fathers had searched out; for we are only of a yesterday and know nothing, our days are but a shadow passing over the land. Will they not teach you and speak to you as the words come tumbling out of their heart?*

This is Bildad's main argument. Wisdom is not available to the human mind outside the context of a human and hence a political tradition reaching back to the fathers. The span of a single lifetime is too short to gather the experience or the insight which would be needed even to begin an approach to a way of life dedicated to an autonomous inquiry into the surface of things, even such a life that someone like Socrates might one day lead.

The combined wisdom of the fathers who, over many ages, have slowly planted our roots by living through life, is to be trusted beyond the inquiries of a single man who must have held himself back from life in order to question it; and such is the case no matter how thoughtful that attempt may have been.

Although these roots can become obscured or lost through adversity and doubt, any search to discover wisdom must be a search to rediscover it. Wisdom can only be found within the confines of a long established, well nurtured home.

❦   *Can papyrus flourish where there is no marsh? Or can*
8:11–14 *reed flourish without water? While yet in their tender*

days, they wither before any grass, still unpicked. Such is the course for all those who forget God. For him all hope will vanish. The profane man is lost, for he who feels a loathing for his own sense of trust will come to rely upon a spider web.

Bildad even seems to have compassion and a kind of love for the tender reed who goes it alone, the man who does not seat himself firmly in the ways of fathers or nourish himself in the waters of tradition, but tries to search out wisdom for himself. But much as he may love such a reed, he sees it as a thing that cannot last. Other plants may be out there that can stand without the marsh, but not man, the tender reed. Such men have forgotten God, and are lost.

As we have seen in the footnote to 8:14, there is some controversy over the meaning of the line "The profane man is lost, for he who feels a loathing for his own sense of trust will come to rely upon a spider web."

If this reading is correct, however, Bildad may have in mind something like the rather sycophantic way in which that arch Machiavellian, Joab, fawns upon God's altar at the end of his life (I Kings 2:28).

🔗
8:15–18   *He will lean upon his house but it will not hold; he will hold fast to it but it will not stand. It may sit fresh under the sun and shoots may spring up in his garden, with roots twining round a knoll and clinging to the house of stone. Yet his own habitat will devour him and deny him, saying, "I have never seen you!"*

For Bildad, even a lonely reed like Job needs a context within which to inquire—a home that sits fresh under the sun, and a garden with roots twining round a knoll. The language Job speaks and even the content of his questions presuppose, and are in good part derived from, the very path

Job has disowned. The world in which Job grew up may have been a comfortable home, a house on which Job still must lean, but it will not hold; it can no longer bear Job's weight. Ultimately, Job's rejection of the wisdom of his home will cause his home to reject him; and for Bildad, a man without a home is a man who has no place on which to stand.

         ⚬   *Such are the delights of his ways, and out of the dust*
8:19   *another will spring,*

When Bildad speaks these words with an irony somewhere between pity and sarcasm, he seems to know that Job's problem is an eternal problem and that there will always be men like him.

         ⚬   *But surely God will neither have contempt for a simple*
8:20   *man nor strengthen the hand of the evildoer.*

Bildad's alternative to the man of inquiry is the simple man, as he understands it. *Simple*, תָּם, was the word used for Job so often in the first chapters. In fact, except for Zophar, the Satan, and the Voice of the tempest, all the characters in the drama in one way or another think of simplicity as a high, if not the highest, human virtue—though they do not all agree on what the simple is. For Bildad, the word is to be understood in contradistinction to the man of inquiry. The views of the other characters will be considered in the discussion of Chapter 31.

Discussion of Chapter Nine

∾   *Yes, all that I know; but then what can make a mortal's*
9:2   *justice apparent to God?*

When Job says this, he is beginning to think that there
may be a critical sense in which Bildad is right. The distinction between the thoughtful and the thoughtless may not be
visible from the highest point of view. He begins to fear that
from such a perspective the surface of things may completely
disappear. On the one hand, this conclusion leaves Job confused and perhaps a bit frightened. On the other hand, that
confusion will ultimately force him to peer into a world well
beyond the narrowness of his own native borders.

From the first ten verses of Chapter 9 one can get a wonderful sense of the duality contained in the word ירא (yara),
awe and trepidation, on which I remarked in a footnote to 1:9.
In them Job is constantly pulled from terror to awe and back
to terror. He is both drawn to and repelled by a world that is
too large to contain him. It is awesome, but he can find no
place in it for himself or for his simple surface understanding
of human justice.

∾   *He passes by me, but I cannot see him. He moves on,*
9:11–13   *but I do not comprehend him. He snatches up, and who*
           can stop him? Who can say to him, "What is it you
           are about to do?" But God will not turn back his anger.
           Under his rule even the ministers of Rahab bend low.

In verse 2 Job showed that he had recognized Bildad's good
will and realized the truth of what he had said, but he also

knew that he had not yet addressed himself to the question raised by Eliphaz in 4:17: "Shall a mortal be more just than his God? or a hero more pure than his maker?"

For the moment, at least, he is content to raise the question in its enormity without trying to answer it. God seems to live in a world so far above the cares of mortal justice that even to raise the question now seems meaningless. The motions in that world are so large that to him it seemed unavoidable that the little things would be crushed; and those who are small enough to see the things that fall through the cracks are too small to be heard. Nevertheless he says:

~   *...even though I am in the right, still I cannot do it. Yet*
9:15   *I must plead for what seems to me just.*

Job must not only come to terms with two conflicting worlds, he must act in them as well; and what each world commands the other has forbidden.

Actions cannot be performed in *a* world. They are forever performed in *the* world, and their consequences reverberate throughout all worlds. Either way, Job cannot do what he knows he must do.

In the first verses of Chapter 9 Job presented the fundamental problem of the book. Job is caught by a divided duty. God is God, and yet what seems just cannot seem unjust. Justice demands articulation, yet the act of articulation points back to the speaker who feels perverse when he considers the enormity of the distinction between himself and his notion of God; and he falls silent. But in his silence he again becomes aware of his own innocence, and justice again begins to raise her demands. This constant, unresolvable cycle leads him only to pain and confusion.

~   *Though I am just, my own mouth would condemn*
9:20–21   *me. I am simple but he will show me perverse. I am*

simple but I no longer care and have only contempt
for my life.

By the time of verse 21, Job's sociality, his need for human
companions and fellowship, is so great that when others
condemn and reject him, he takes the only course left
open to him. He rejoins society by joining them in his own
self-condemnation.

When facing the world around him and the conditions it
has placed upon his being, Job feels out of place, contorted,
and perverse; and yet, since he knows of no crime or guilt, he
knows of no way of expiation. He even begins to feel guilty
of the sin of having seen his own innocence. Divine wisdom
and everyday justice—each seems to mock and jeer at the
other till the whole turns meaningless.

〰   *The earth has been placed into the hands of the guilty.*
9:24   *He has covered the eyes of its judges. If it be not he,*
      then where is that one?

When Job, thinking of the source of all that has taken place,
asks this question it is, of course, intended to be rhetorical.
For Job there can be no second God who is Lord over the
surface: no one else who could be guilty. If the tart is gone,
some knave must have stolen it.

〰   *Even if I should say "Let me forget my complaint,*
9:27–28 *abandon my long visage, and put on a cheerful look,"*
      even then would I yet feel the dread of all my grief,
      since I know that you will never find me pure.

Even at this point Job could put a false face over the surface
and go on back to his friends—let it all rest in oblivion as he
had once thought to do. "Sometimes," thinks Job, "the Old
Trick works. Smile at the day, and the day smiles right back
at you." But not this time. That ugly surface world, and the

feelings of fear and guilt which come from having seen it, will not go away. Once the surface has been seen, it cannot be unseen.

The end of the chapter lies near the heart of things as they have been ever since the world began to fall out of focus. Job knows that he is guilty in the only world that he has ever known, and yet he knows that he is not guilty.

Job had grown up with his friends in a comfortable world with its demands and its proscriptions. It all made sense to him, and in the main, things turned out for the best. By all the standards of that world, a world which he knew and had always lived by, he, Job, is a guilty man; and yet when he honestly tries to look into himself to find something that would make sense out of what has happened, he finds an innocent man.

Words like *inside* and *outside* begin to lose their meaning. Is his innocence out there on a surface that deeper wisdom cannot comprehend? Or is it to be found only within himself?

Discussion of Chapter Ten

~ *My spirits feel a loathing towards life. I will unleash*
10:1–2 *my complaint and speak in the bitterness of my soul.
To God I say: Do not condemn me, but let me know
the cause of this struggle against me.*

In Chapter 4, Job had said: "I would answer him, choosing
my words against him with care." Now the process has begun,
although he knows that there will be no court and no judge.
Despite the bitterness and confusion in his soul, Job is beginning his brief in the ordinary way, asking for the grounds of
God's complaint.

~ *Does it seem good to you that you oppress, that you*
10:3 *have contempt for the toil of your own hand, but radiate upon the counsel of the guilty?*

Job intends this statement as an answer to what Bildad had
said in his last speech:

> *But surely God will neither have contempt for a simple
> man nor strengthen the hand of the evildoer. He will fill
> your mouth with laughter, and your lips with shouts of joy.*
> [8:20][6]

~ *Do you have eyes of flesh? Can you see as mortals see?*
10:4–7 *Can time mean to you what time means to a mortal? Do your years pass by as the years of a human,
that you probe back into my perversions and track*

---

[6] On the relation between contempt and laughter see also the discussion
of 30:1 on page 203 below.

> *down my every sin? Somewhere in your mind I am*
> *not guilty, and yet there is none to save me from your*
> *hand.*

With this passage, Job is beginning to see more deeply why there can be no court of decision. If God can feel neither the dragging nor the rushing of time, he can understand neither punishment nor human suffering. Hope and fear are both meaningless apart from the human sense of time. If God cannot feel them, he cannot understand his own judgments.

In verse 6 Job is saying that if, as the Psalmist says, "A thousand years in his sight are as but yesterday when they are past" (Ps. 90:4), God cannot understand the sins of Job's youth as being just that—sins of youth, acts of a long dead past.

∿   *Your dealings with me were full of life and loving care.*
10:12–14 *Your guardianship watched over my spirit, and you*
          treasured all these things up in your heart. But I know
          what you have in mind; if I sin you will be watching
          and you will not clear me from my perversion.

God had seemed to make each thing in nature, including Job himself, with perfection, love, and care. For the most part everything seemed to be full of love and life, and yet in this case everything has gone so wrong.

∿   *Well, if I have been guilty, the grief is mine; but even*
10:15   *when I am innocent I have been so sated with reproach*
        that no feeling of honor is left in me and I see only my
        own feebleness.

This is, perhaps, Job's deepest insight into the nature of his own feelings and thoughts. Job knows that, like all men, he has surely made some mistakes in his life; and perhaps more than most men, he knows that he has always been the one to suffer on account of them. But the present situation is different and falls well beyond reasonable bounds.

Job feels that he is beginning to lose his struggle with the outside world, the world of Eliphaz and the rest of mankind, as well as with the world of pain. In order to come to terms with the noise of all those accusations, and yet remain part of that outer world—his only source of human relationship— he finds himself beginning to believe in his own guilt even though he knows that he is not guilty. He can live with this contradiction only by taking his mind away from that which is best in him, and seeing only his own frailties.

Discussion of Chapter Eleven

Zophar says to Job:

∽ *You say "My tenets are spotless. I am pure in Thy sight."*
11:4–6 *Oh, if only God himself would open his lips and speak*
to you, tell you the secrets of wisdom; for discernment
is many-sided...

Zophar thinks in terms of God's "secret wisdom." The force—and hence the deceptive force—of human speech is its ability to speak of a part, even a random part, as if it were an intelligible whole. Job's arguments presuppose that there is a single surface view of things, and that it is sufficiently open to human comprehension to serve as an adequate foundation for human existence. But "discernment is many-sided." There may be many such surfaces, no one of which fails to obscure some vital part of the whole. The things within our ken, though they seem to hold together in a beguiling sort of way, may require so much modification by what is beyond them as to render all human judgment inadequate, even to the point of meaninglessness. The spotless, seen within a larger context, may seem spotless no longer.

∽ *...and you must know that God will bear some of*
Job 11:6 *your perversions for you.*

The word עָוֹן (avon) which has traditionally been translated *iniquity*, and which I have rendered as *perversion*, tends to be used in the Torah in a rather specific way; and it is not impossible that Zophar has in mind a distinction which the Torah makes between עָוֹן, perversion, and חֵטְא

(chet), sin. חֵטְא means *to miss the mark*, while עָוֹן comes from a root meaning *to twist*, or *to distort* or *pervert*. It is something that can happen to a path, to a right, or to a mind, and hence it implies an effect on all future growth. חֵטְא refers to an act, עָוֹן to a way of being. If one has missed one's mark, the only thing to do is to try again; but if something has been twisted, that is to say perverted, trying again will not help.

Consider:

> ...*visiting the perversion of the fathers upon the children to the third and forth generation of those that hate me.* [Deut. 5:9]

Contrast this verse with

> *Fathers shall not be put to death for their children nor shall children be put to death for their fathers, but each man shall die for his own sin.* [Deut. 24:16]

From Deut. 24:16 it is clear that no one can be held responsible for the sins of his or her own particular parent; but with perversion it is a different matter. In the Torah there is a general tendency to use the word *perversion* to refer to those acts of the fathers which have a lasting and devastating effect on the whole of the nation. An example of *perversion* in our own era would be black slavery in early America. For another, even an immigrant who has newly become a citizen of this country—innocent, like all others, of any *crime* his father may have committed—has, by virtue of becoming part of us, inherited a debt to the Native American peoples, a debt which can never be paid in full.

❧ *The deepest things of God, can you find them out?*
11:7–10 *Would you discover the utmost things of the Almighty? It is higher than heaven—what can you do? Deeper*

> *than the Pit—what can you know? Longer than the*
> *earth is its measure and broader than the sea. If he*
> *should pass by and separate or close up, who can turn*
> *him back?*

For Zophar, the incommensurability which has been perplexing Job finds its origins in the fact that the workings out of human justice take place in a realm far beyond its own ken. No view except God's view is large enough to make sense of itself. The problem, according to Zophar, is not merely one of having a large enough horizon. It is the myriad of little separate worlds each of which might suddenly come into contact with any other, or claim a being apart from any other. No world can perceive its effect on any other world till God brings them together—and then it is too late.

⮑   *But if you direct your heart firmly and spread out*
11:13,   *your hands to him.... You will be secure because*
11:18–19 *there will be hope. You will burrow in and lie at ease.*
         You will be in repose and none shall make you afraid.

According to Zophar, then, the incommensurability is only apparent and is due to the limited character of man's superficial view of his own world. If man were to clean his own heart of all injustice and trust in God, all would be well, and man would emerge as the center of all that is visible.

Discussion of Chapter Twelve

⁓ *You are indeed of the people, and with you learning*
12:2–3 *will die; but like you, I too have some understanding*
which does not fall short of yours.

Job's friends live in a world which they share with a whole people, while Job is alone in his. Perhaps they understand their world as well as any that live in it, yet each world is only one, and all must be heard.

⁓ *But now I have become a joke to my friends, one who*
12:4 *would "call on God and have him answer"; simple and*
just, yet still a joke!

While Job has a certain kind of respect for Zophar's wisdom of the ages—that which comes only with time, reflection, and belief—he cannot totally ignore the surface of things, the plain look of things as they reveal themselves to anyone who is immediately involved. But the surface is all too easily forgotten, and its uncomfortable remnants can be escaped by turning them into a joke. At this point in his thought, this notion of immediate involvement is of prime importance for Job. Without it things are merely the way they are said to be.

⁓ *For those who can think at their ease there is always*
12:5 *scorn for calamity. But it's out there waiting for any-*
one whose foot should happen to slip.

When Job says this, he implies that there is an unintended irony lying behind the great psalms like Psalm 19. For, despite that psalm's opening words—"The heavens are telling the glory of God"—the story actually told by the heavens is one of great horror.

⤳
12:10–12 *In his hand is the soul of every living thing and the breath of each bodily man. Does not the ear try words as the palate tastes food? Is wisdom with the old, or does length of days make for understanding?*

Although the Book of Job often concerns itself with the contention between *hearing* and *seeing* for the true image of knowledge, the imagery of taste (טַעַם, ta'am) and of the palate (חֵךְ, cheikh) is of some help in our attempt to understand what Job means by *knowing*. The subject first came up in Chapter 6:

> *Can what is tasteless be eaten without salt, or does the slime of an egg white have any taste? My soul refuses to touch them. They are like a contagion in my daily bread.* [6:6–7]

Taste is what makes knowledge worthwhile. The taste of a world is what makes that world liveable. Unlike seeing, taste includes the most important aspects of an object, its beauties and its uglinesses. Knowledge is not a passive act. It presents itself to us in such a way that we cannot but react. At this stage, to know is not to comprehend the whole as an object outside of the knower but to ingest a part of the object, either to make it part of oneself or to spit it out.

⤳
12:13–14, *With him are wisdom and valor. His are counsel and*
16–18 *understanding, and what he tears down can never be rebuilt.... Both the one who errs and the one who causes the error are his. He makes counselors to go about ravaged, and even the judges he drives into madness. He undoes the restraint of kings and restrains by a strip about their loins.*

The kaleidoscopic melange of order and disarray which Job sees in the world about him throughout the remainder of the chapter is wonderfully captured by the language of the text. The word מוּסָר (musar), which we have translated as *restraint,* comes from the root אסר, meaning *to bind.* It can also mean *discipline* both in the noble and in the harsh sense. Moreover, the word for *strip* or *belt,* though it comes from a different root—אזר, *to gird, encompass or equip*—sounds as if it came from the same root. We almost have:

> *"He undoes the discipline of kings and disciplines them by a discipline about their loins."*

The surface world, to which Job has committed himself to taking seriously, is a crazy, contradictory world, full of wisdom, valor, and madness; full of roads to glory that lead nowhere. The simple world of growing corn and barking dogs has become more like a Picasso still life which, when it first comes to sight, seems to be no more than a blue bottle and a bowl of fruit lying on a country table; yet as one looks on, order begins to evaporate—and one begins to wonder how, if Heisenberg with his uncertainty principle is right, Ptolemy could ever have even *seemed* to be right. The world is too orderly, too revelatory, to be a chaos; and yet chaos is where it always seems to find itself.

∼   *He obliterates the speech of the trustworthy and takes*
12:20   *taste from the elders.*

Job repeatedly plays with the fact that the palate is an organ of both taste and speech, as if the knowing coming in and the speech going out were the same thing. We saw an earlier example in Chapter 6:

> *There is no injustice on my tongue, and yet does not my palate know the taste of ruination?* [6:30]

And in Chapter 29 Job will recount:

> *The voice of the nobles was hushed, and their tongue stuck to their palate, for an ear had heard and it blessed me; an eye had seen and it approved, because I had saved a poor man when he cried out, and an orphan when there was no one else to help him.* [29:10–12]

But later, Elihu will declare:

> *Behold, I open my lips and the tongue in my palate begins to speak.* [33:2]

From these two statements, it is hard to infer exactly what is meant by the word *palate*. The least one can say is that it is an organ of taste and of speech: that it is not the tongue itself, but something which, in some way or another, can contain the tongue.

When Job says:

> *Could I have rejoiced when hardship struck at those that hate me or come to life because evil had found them, without giving my palate over to sin by asking for his life with a curse?* [31:29–30]

he means that his speech is not merely "on the tip of his tongue," as we sometimes say, but that it comes from within and hence implies room inside, out of which speech comes. He also implies that speech is necessarily accompanied by pleasure or pain, anger or delight: he would have tasted the sinfulness in his curse even as he spoke it. This adds to the notion that, for the moment at least, there is for Job an immediate interrelationship bordering on unity between an object, human awareness of it, human speech concerning it, and human reaction to it. Job is suggesting that this near-unity is possible precisely because, and only because, the speech in question is speech about a *world*.

Discussion of Chapter Thirteen

~ *All this my eye has seen; my ear has heard and*
13:1 *understood.*

Job begins this part of his argument with the assertion that he has heard and fully understood the tradition. The implication here is that the tradition, as such, is not capable of defending itself. This leads to a new turn of things when he says:

~ *I would speak with The Almighty! I wish to argue with*
13:3–4, *God. But you are a bunch of worthless doctors who*
7–12 *plaster over with lies. Would you speak unjustly for God's sake? For his sake would you speak words of treachery? Would you show him favor, or even argue his case for him? Will it turn out to be good when he comes to examine you? Do you think you can deceive him as you can deceive a mortal? Certainly he himself would argue against you. If you were to show him even hidden favor, would his preference not be to terrify and let his fear fall upon you? Your aphorisms are proverbs of ash, your bulwarks, bulwarks of clay.*

To uphold the tradition by denying the surface, or as Job thinks of it, by "plastering over with lies," that is, by calling things just when they seem not to be just, is ultimately destructive of the tradition itself. The true foundation of the tradition must ultimately lie at ease with the surface, and any foundation which must smooth over the surface and, by implication, cannot meet it on its own terms, is a "bulwark of clay."

⁓   *It may be that he will slay me. I have no higher expec-*
13:15–16 *tations. Nonetheless I will defend my ways before*
        him. That too has become for me salvation, for the
        impious do not approach him.

Here Job is once again playing with the psalmic literature.
What must have been a well-known saying—

> *My strength and the music of the Lord, and he has become*
> *for me salvation.*

—occurs in Ex. 15:2, Is. 12:2, and Ps. 118:14. It is also remi-
niscent of the phrase in Ps. 118:21:

> *I thank thee that thou hast answered and thou hast become*
> *for me salvation.*

Nor is Job the only biblical character to play with the line.
Joab once said to his brother Abishai:

> *If the Syrians are too strong for me, then thou shalt become*
> *for me salvation.* [II Sam. 10:11]

Job has been caught between the two worlds. The surface
and human care for the surface have demanded what wisdom has forbidden. As in the case of Socrates, Job's courage
has no existence in its own right but is an integral part of his
grasp of the importance of the question in front of him. Job
must act in accordance with those human concerns, while
feeling the full weight of wisdom's prohibition.

When in 13:16 he rehearses the phrase "has become for
me salvation," Job adds the critical words, "That too"—as
though to suggest that he may have glimpsed some new kind
of salvation, though searching it out may be dangerous and
may require great courage. In light of the first verses of the
chapter, we can see that Job, like Socrates, implicitly suggests
a need to reconsider our notion of true piety. It may con-
sist in the attempt to understand the words of the God—in

Socrates' case the Delphic Oracle—by taking them seriously, while at the same time facing the claims of the surface.

We must also remember that in verse 9, Job had implied that it was a lack of courage that led Zophar to his false piety.

〜 *Why do you hide your face from me and think of me*
13:24–26 *as your enemy? Would you terrorize me like a driven leaf? Or put me to flight like a piece of dry straw, that you write bitter things against me and bring up the perversions of my youth?*

The trial has begun; and Job commences by associating perversion with the past; but for him it is a long distant, even dead, past. Nor was this the first time he had uttered such thoughts. In Chapter 10 he had said:

> *Do you have eyes of flesh? Can you see as mortals see? Can time mean to you what time means to a mortal? Do your years pass by as the years of a human, that you probe back into my perversions and track down my every sin? Somewhere in your mind I am not guilty, and yet there is none to save me from your hand.* [10:4–7]

Not perversion but the *charge* of perversion is the true source of human suffering. Told in writings that he is heir to a long forgotten perversion, man is denied a past on which to build a firm foundation. He becomes the "...piece of dry straw blowing in every wind."

Twice before Job had connected the question of perversion with the problem of being watched. First in Chapter 7:

> *Yes, and inspect him every morning and test him every minute. When will you let me be? You'll not even let me alone to swallow my own spit. Supposing I have sinned, what have I done to you, O thou Great Watcher Of Man? Why have you set me on course against you so that I have*

become a burden even to myself? Why can you not pardon my transgressions or bear my perversions? For now I shall lie down in the dust. You will seek for me, but I am not. [7:18–21]

Again in Chapter 10:

Your dealings with me were full of life and loving care. Your guardianship watched over my spirit, and you treasured all these things up in your heart. But I know what you have in mind; if I sin, you will be watching and you will not clear me from my perversion. Well, if I have been guilty, the grief is mine; but even when I am innocent I have been so sated with reproach that no feeling of honor is left in me and I see only my own feebleness. [10:12–15]

He will do so still again in Chapter 14:

Then no longer would you keep track of my every step and scrutinize my sin. My transgression would be sealed up in a pouch and you would plaster over my perversions. [14:16–17]

It is this sense of being watched, not because of anything he has done, but because of what he is, because of his inherited perversion, that has reduced Job to nonbeing . People do indeed suffer for the actions of past generations, but to regard that as some form of poetic or even divine justice rather than a horrible necessity is to undermine that sense of honor required to right the effects of those ancient actions.

In the ten closing verses of the chapter, we get a closer look at Job's first view of the clash. He can lay out his case and it can be made solid. He can demand to know the exact nature of the charges laid up against him and their precise number. Such is the nature of all the evidence, but it is not clear that there is any way of presenting such evidence in the other court. Like Socrates, Job can only speak by means of human speech; unless room can be left for that, nothing that Job has, or sees, or knows can ever be worth any more than that "piece of cloth that the moths have eaten" [13:28].

Discussion of Chapter Fourteen

⌁   *A human is born of woman, short-lived and full of*
14:1–3   *rage. He sprouts up as a fresh bud and withers. He*
         flits by as a shadow and cannot endure. Can you
         open your eyes even to one such as that, and yet come
         along with him to proceedings raised against you?

Note the change to the third person throughout the chapter. Job will defend not himself alone, but mankind in his own person. Man is not the best of all conceivable creatures. He is, in fact, "...born of woman, short-lived and full of rage"; yet such is the man whom Job has chosen to defend. Is God willing to judge mankind in terms of the highest goals of which they are capable, or will he insist upon the highest standards absolutely? It is one thing to strive toward impossible goals from within; but to feel constantly judged by them from without—and so to be made ever to feel want—is, for Job, to render all those strivings meaningless.

⌁   *Who can bring a clean thing out of an unclean thing?*
14:4

Justice must expect from each thing the highest possible; to demand more of a man, or of a tree, would be unjust. One wonders if the thoughts Job is thinking at this juncture might not be part of what led men to the concept of "the nature of a thing" as something that must be accepted essentially as is.

⌁   *Then turn your gaze from him and let him be, so long*
14:6   *as his days as a hireling are acceptable.*

If man's nature is limited, a way must be found for him to be.

∽   *For a tree there is hope. If it is cut down, it renews*
14:7–12 *itself and its sprouting never wanes. When its roots*
become old in the land and its stump is left in the
dust to die, then even at the mere scent of water it
bursts into bloom and sends out branches like a young
sapling. But when a hero dies, he perishes and is no
more. A human expires, and where is he? The waters
are gone from the sea. The river becomes a wasteland
and is dried up. A man lies down and rises not. Till
the heavens are no more they shall not wake nor be
roused from their slumber.

The compelling mood of this passage lies in the capacity of
a man, with thoughts so laden with death, to give such full
articulation to a world bursting with life. From it we learn
much about Job.

∽   *You would call, I would answer, and you would have*
14:15–17 *love for the work of your hands. Then no longer would*
you keep track of my every step and scrutinize my sin.
My transgression would be sealed up in a pouch and
you would plaster over my perversions.

Thoughts of the finality of death have tired Job, and now
he is slowly drifting off into a wonderful daydream in which
the two worlds begin to blur over and merge into a single
world. All the contradictions are gone. There is calling and
answering. The hands that made Job no longer devour him,
but instead love him. It is a wide world full of room for man
and room for God.

In verse 17 Job's daydream culminates with an end to the
watching and the cessation of all charges of perversion. But
verse 18 brings and end to the dream:

～ *A mountain has fallen and crumbled away, a rock*
14:18 *dislodged from its place.*

Job suddenly wakes, and the din of the clashing worlds
has been magnified a thousandfold. The surface world has
been washed away. There is nothing left but the pain of a lost
dream.

～ *The waters have worn the stones away and its tor-*
14:19–22 *rents have washed away the dust of the land. So you*
have trashed all mortal hope. You have overpowered
man, and he has resigned. You have mangled his
face and sent him off. His sons were honored but he
never knew of it. They were in disgrace, but he was
unaware. His body surrounds him with pain, and his
spirit is eaten away.

These last verses seem critical, though I have not been able
to understand them as I should wish. The best I can do is
to point out that when Job suddenly wakes from his dream
and finds himself back in the clashing worlds, feeling gruffly
awakened, his first thoughts concern not the problem of perversion but its inverse. The problem has shifted—from an
over-burdensome awareness of the acts of the father on the
part of the son, to an agonizing lack of awareness of the acts
of the son on the part of the father; but I do not pretend to
see the full implications of that shift.

Discussion of Chapter Fifteen

~ *Then Eliphaz the Temanite answered and said: Should*
15:1–4 *a wise man even answer such blustery thoughts and fill his own belly with the east wind? Should he argue with such barren words and idle talk that goes nowhere? You have abandoned awe and deserted the grounds of all discourse with God.*

For Eliphaz human speech on such matters is nothing but a bellyful of the East Wind. He accuses Job of having "...abandoned awe and deserted the grounds of all discourse with God."

For Eliphaz, awe (ירא) of God is the ground of all discourse with God. Earlier [4:6] he had in fact called it "your surety and your hope, the simplicity of your ways." How are we to understand the relation between awe and speech? Had not Job claimed the very opposite? "Remove your hand from me, and let not your terror frighten me. Then summon me up and I will reply, or let me speak and you shall give answer" [13:21–22].

Job wishes to speak with God in terms of the highest human goals. To Eliphaz this means, in effect, abandoning the concept of perversion in favor of notions of right and wrong, of the just and the unjust. Job, then, wants human discourse, a discourse in which the human voice can be heard. If another voice is to be heard, it must be heard in another way. It must be held in awe rather than followed by thought. Eliphaz therefore challenges Job:

~ *Were you the first human to be born? Did you come*
15:7 *writhing into being before the hills?*

Eliphaz is accusing Job of believing that, in anguish and pain, he pulled himself into being and thus owes no debt to the past because he has received nothing from the past. He is older than the mountains, stands on his own feet, and the baseness of his origins is his pride rather than his shame. Eliphaz's sarcastic use of the phrase "before the hills" recalls these verses:

> *I, wisdom, dwell in prudence, and I find knowledge and discretion.... The* LORD *created me at the beginning of his work, the first of his acts of old.... When there were no depths I was brought forth, when there were no springs abounding with water. Before the mountains had been shaped, before the hills, I was brought forth.* [Prov. 8:12, 22, 24–25]

> *Before the mountains were brought forth, or ever thou hadst formed the earth and the world, from everlasting to everlasting thou art God.* [Ps. 90:2]

To Eliphaz, Job is in effect claiming to be wisdom, or even to be God himself.

~ *What has taken hold of your heart and so dazzled*
15:12–13 *your eyes that you have turned your spirit on God and dredged up such words out of your mouth?*

Eliphaz admits here that Job has not simply and negatively turned himself from God, but that something of deep human concern has "dazzled his eyes." In verse 6 Eliphaz had said: "Your own mouth condemns you, not I, and your own lips have testified against you"; and now it is clear what he meant. For Eliphaz, the surface world—the world to which Job has committed himself—is not merely a superficial world, as the other friends had thought. It is an unclean and deeply corrupted world precisely because it looks so real that it can dazzle the eyes. To take it otherwise, as "grounds of discourse" [15:4], is nothing more than, as he said at the outset, to fill one's belly with the east wind [15:2]. A twisted view and a crafty tongue can build Job's arguments, but they can only distract the mind and turn it from realizing its true position.

    ∾   *What is a mortal that he should be clean, or one born*
15:14   *of woman that he should consider himself just?*

In many ways this is Eliphaz's most cutting argument. Underlying Job's commitment to the surface world is his assumption that, no matter how narrowly limited the horizons of that world may be, such scraps of truth as they may contain are sufficiently connected to things presently unseen that by pursuing them and the questions they give rise to in their own inadequacy, they can lead beyond themselves to a wider and more complete understanding of ourselves and the world in which we live.

    ∾   *If he puts no trust in his holy ones and even the*
15:15–16   *heavens are not clean in his sight, what of man—*
             that abhorred and corrupted one—who drinks up
             injustice like water!

All men are guilty, even his holy ones, but Job more than all because of his denial of that guilt.

    ∾   *Listen to me! This thing have I surely seen and will*
15:17–19   *relate, a thing which the wise have reported from*
             their fathers and have not withheld. To them alone
             has the land been given, and no stranger has gone
             among them.

Eliphaz has somehow vaguely seen that each man is always caught up within one horizon or another. What men see or do not see is a function of its scope. Wisdom inhabits a land that has been given. As a thing to be preserved, it requires a proper place. For Eliphaz there is a peculiar unity between speech and place. The stories, which wise men have told and retold, reverberate through the rocks and trees till they become part of the place of telling.

    〰️　　*The guilty man writhes in pain all his days and the*
15:20–23　*number of his years lies hidden from those who can terrorize.... He can have no trust that he will return from the darkness, and he is ever on guard against a sword. He wanders for bread, not knowing where. He knows only that the day of darkness is ready at hand....*

Eliphaz is thinking of what he had said in verse 7. Man's struggle is not his glory, but his shame. Guilt makes man a stranger to the world and turns his world into a battlefield. Since he has no home, there is nothing for him to defend with dignity. There is, in fact, nothing heroic in that struggle to ennoble it, and it transforms him into a beast.

    〰️　　*He dwells in cities of desolation, in houses not fit to*
15:28, 31　*be lived in and bound for the trash heap.... Let him not trust in deceitful nothing, for his compensation will be nothing.*

To consider man as a beginning in himself, with nothing behind him, is to "trust in a deceitful nothing." Any gains achieved purely on the basis of man's struggle are open to being lost in that very struggle, since no other claim for legitimacy can be made for them.

The self-made man, as such, has no goal *except* self-making; but since there is nothing definite about this goal, he can have no sense of fulfillment. His sense of struggle as being at the foundation of existence, Eliphaz argues, prevents man from thinking in terms of a goal towards which the struggle is aiming. It therefore degenerates into struggle for its own sake.

Discussion of Chapter Sixteen

〜 *I have heard too much of this rot. Bringers of a toil-*
16:2–3 *some compassion, the whole lot of you! Is there no end*
to such blustery talk? What ails you that you answer
me so?

Job's first words are spoken directly to his friends in full
awareness of context. His friends were, indeed, to have
brought him compassion.

> *Now when Job's three friends had heard about all the evils*
> *that had come upon him, they came each from his own*
> *place—Eliphaz the Temanite, Bildad the Shuhite, and*
> *Zophar the Na'amathite. They conferred with one another*
> *and planned to come together to console him and to show*
> *him compassion.* [2:11]

But the compassion was to have helped him over the sight
of toil:

> *For it closed not the gates of my mother's belly but hid my*
> *eyes from toil.* [3:10]

> *Why does he give light to those whom toil has consumed, or*
> *life to the bitter of soul?* [3:20]

Verse 3, "What ails you that you answer me so?" is Job's
answer to Eliphaz's statement:

> *Should a wise man even answer such blustery thoughts and*
> *fill his own belly with the east wind?* [15:2]

It is their blindness that has driven Job mad. His friends
are part of the surface world. They see the innocent suffer
every day, and yet they do not see that they see. Job sees a
world that cannot see itself.

To Job, Eliphaz has become a man who cannot allow himself to be human, raising himself up by bringing all men, including himself, down. His contempt for the surface has rendered him insensitive to innocent suffering.

The sight of a man from the surface who has condemned the surface so that it seems to condemn itself has forced Job to testify against the world for the sake of the world. Job is lost, confused, and angry. He believed in a world that did not believe in itself and that had attacked him for doing so. Job has been broken. Indicative of his madness throughout this chapter is the jagged and abrupt way in which he constantly switches persons from third to second and back to the third, and when he uses the second person, it is not always clear whether he is addressing his friends or God. God, his effects, and the effect that belief in him have, come all of a jumble into Job's mind.

〜 *I too could speak as you do if it were you instead of*
16:4–6 *me! I could heap words upon you and shake my head; strengthen you with my words or hold you in check by the motion of my lips. But when I speak, my own pain is not held in check, nor does it subside when I am quiet.*

This is a wonderful comment on words, what powers they have, and what powers they do not have. They have a power both over the one spoken to and over the speaker himself. Words have the power to take away pain. Eliphaz knows more than most that what Job says of himself is true:

It was you who always [taught] restraint and strengthened so many frail hands, you who had the words to pick up those that were stumbling and bolster the knees that were about to bend. [4:3–4]

but for those who have peered behind the curtain, the magic is gone, and words no longer have their power.

~,   *Oh, how he has worn me out! You have wiped out*
16:7–8 *my whole community. You have shriveled me up as*
        a witness, and this distortion has risen up to testify
        against me.

His defense would stand him well in any court, human or
divine, working under rules intelligible to man. Job knows
that, but has been worn out. There is that infinite wheel of
suffering that brings feelings of guilt—and feelings of guilt
that bring suffering. In defending himself against a world
of charges, Job finds himself having to accept the terms in
which those charges are made. As he does so, he feels himself being sucked more and more into the world that makes
those charges. Once he is captured by that world, his defense
begins to melt.

~   *My foe hones his eyes against me.*
16:9

What a telling expression of the way in which an angry eye
can sharpen itself by its own act of cutting!
    As we know from the discussion of 6:23, the verse may also
be translated: "My narrow constraint hones its eyes against
me." This ambiguity is key to understanding the kind of madness one sees in Job throughout the remainder of the chapter.
Job feels an angry world pressing down upon him, constricting his view till he himself begins to feel small, petty, and
guilty of believing that his world could be other.

~   *Let not the earth cover over my blood or find a place*
16:18–22 *for my outcry. For now my witness must be in heaven.*
        The one who can testify for me must be on high. Oh,
        my advocates, my friends, my eyes weep before God.
        Will no one argue for a hero before God as a human

should do for a friend? For but a few years will pass
by, and then I shall go the way that I shall not return.

Job's anger is gone now, but not his madness. Rejected now by both earth and heaven, but still convinced of his own innocence, he makes an appeal to both, expecting help from neither. Somewhere God must have the evidence; and man, as a solid friend trusting both in Job and in himself, must find it out.

Discussion of Chapter Seventeen

〜 *My spirit has been destroyed and my days snuffed*
17:1–3 *out. The grave is ready for me now. Mocking men are*
always about me and my eye lives under their discon-
tent. Put up now, go my surety. Who will be the one to
take my hand on it?

Chapter 17 is a continuation of the scene which began around verse 18 of the last chapter. Job had asked for a man, one of his friends, to be his advocate. Their answer, and Job's initial reaction to it, become clear from verses 1 and 2. He is rejected. Then, in verse 3, we are to imagine Job, a smile slowly brightening up his face, going over to each in turn with an outstretched hand.

〜 *So you have protected their hearts from insight, and*
17:4 *that is why even you no longer have any respect for*
them.

But in verse 4 it becomes clear that no one had moved a muscle or returned his smile. Then Job must have raised a half-angry, half-knowing eye toward heaven. God, according to Job, has misjudged man. The wisdom that he has passed down to them through the fathers has so closed them off from the surface that even the wisdom he had once given them has become useless.

〜 *My eyes are blind from indignation and all form*
17:7–9 *appears to me but as shadows. The upright are*

appalled by that. The pure rise up against such impiety. The righteous hold tight to their ways and the man of clean hands adds to his strength.

Job must have been thinking: "The others, Eliphaz and Zophar and the rest of mankind, they all live in what seems to them to be a single world. It has its ways and its forms. They share an outward cast of sanity which they maintain by clutching onto it tightly lest it shatter; but for me the molds have already cracked and when outward form begins to melt inner sanity cannot hold."

∽ *Then let them all pass by in review. No, I find no wise*
17:10 *man among you.*

Job, in a crazed vision, sees himself as a general, with the whole world marching past him in uniform and on review. But he soon returns to his former thoughts about those who can "hold tight to their ways":

∽ *My days have passed by. My ambitions have been*
17:11–12 *snapped, all that my heart possesses. They claim it is day when it is night, and in the face of darkness they say that light is near.*

"They" (Eliphaz, Zophar, and the bulk of mankind) preserve the singleness of their world—their molds are never cracked—because their outlook undergoes constant transmutation and deformation till it fits their world exactly. Night is called day, innocent is called guilty, and pains which should be faced are eternally called temporary.

Job's next speech will turn out to be a critical one in the development of the book as a whole.

⁓   *If then I must take the Pit to be my home, and spread*
17:13–16 *out my couch in darkness, call out to the muck, "Thou*
          art my Father," and call out "Mother" and "Sister" to
          the maggots, where then is my hope? O my hopes,
          who will ever take note of them? They have all sunk
          down into the Pit and together they lie in the dust.

False hopes drive out the true. We do not know yet exactly
what Job's hopes for himself and perhaps for the whole of
mankind were. We only know that they are incompatible
with the notion that man is a maggot. The best one can do
for now is to say that the notion of man as a maggot seems to
be equivalent to the total denial of the ultimate relevance of
the surface as it appears to man.

Discussion of Chapter Eighteen

Bildad begins:

〰 *How long will you continue to set these traps in speech?*
18:2–4 *Try to understand and then we will speak. Why are*
we considered beasts and made unclean in your eyes?
You, you who tear yourself apart in anger, is the earth
to be abandoned for your sake? Or the rock dislodged
from its place?

We remember that it was Bildad who showed a certain kind of genuine compassion for the tender reed which he ultimately had to condemn. Here again we see the same patience and understanding in his dealings with Job. These verses should be sufficient to assure us that Bildad, at least, is neither a beast nor unclean. We must take his implicit advice to Job with great seriousness.

Let us suppose that there is something to what Job is saying. Is it worth all the anger? Can he achieve anything beyond tearing himself apart? What does Bildad mean when he says, "Is the earth to be abandoned for your sake? Or the rock dislodged from its place?" There are so many things he could have meant.

Did he mean: "Job, you are too quick and have not sufficiently considered the thing you are asking for. If God were suddenly to change the whole world and make it conform exactly to your admittedly just deserts, how many others would have to suffer undeservedly because of that change?"

Or he may have had in mind the time back in 14:18 when Job had said: "A mountain has fallen and crumbled away, a rock dislodged from its place." That was the moment when

Job woke from his false dream and was suddenly confronted by the surface again, as though for the first time. Perhaps Bildad is saying that wisdom does not come in a flash. A sudden confrontation with the surface could itself turn out to be as deceptive as any old wives' tale. Horrors loom out in great disproportion; goods may be taken for granted and overlooked. Time, generations of time, may indeed be required for a tradition to pull our perceptions back to reality.

Or Bildad's question may have been a response to Job's last thoughts. If so, what are we to think of all Job's hopes? Even supposing that Job and all men were free to work towards them on their own, could they actually accomplish such ends? Would things in fact be better? In the remainder of his speech, Bildad will go on to articulate his reasons for believing that such a thing is not likely.

It is critical for an understanding of the argument to note that the word *God* does not occur in Bildad's speech until the very end [18:21]. It is, in fact, the final word of the last verse; and therein lies the whole of its rhetorical value. But even there, God does not appear as an actor. Instead we have lines like "The light of the wicked will be smothered and there will be no glow around his fire" [18:5], in which no direct cause is given.

Even more indicative of the tenor of the passage as a whole are lines like "The stride of his perversion will be hobbled. His plans will trip him up, for his own feet will lead him into a net, and he will stroll right into the trap" [18:7–8]. Such repeated use of the passive voice, and the presentation of a causeless world, lets us know that Job's high hopes for man will all go awry in—as the chapter's final words put it—"a place that knows not God."

Discussion of Chapter Nineteen

Job begins:

> ∿ How long will you torment my spirit and crush me
> 19:2–6 with words? These ten times you have humiliated me!
> Do you feel no shame to be so harsh towards me? Even
> if I have erred, that error must lodge within me; but if
> you must place yourselves above me to prove my dis-
> grace, know that it is God himself who has perverted
> me.

In the last chapter, Bildad had said: "The stride of his perversion will be hobbled" [18:7]; and later in this chapter, Job
will admit that "indignation is a perversion meet for the
sword." Job is angry because he knows that Bildad is right,
and he knows that Bildad is right because he, Job himself,
has already tasted that anger. Behind Bildad's thinking is the
sober notion that angry men cannot be free men. For Job,
however, men who are not free cannot help but be angry. By
perverting error into perversion, God has perverted man.

> ∿ He has barred the road and I cannot pass through. He
> 19:8–9 has covered my path with darkness, stripped all glory
> from me, and removed the crown from my head.

The anger that arises out of finding oneself living in two
worlds is closely related to the problem of freedom. Roads
that are open and beckon in the one are closed and forbidden
or make no sense in the other. Motion that cannot move turns
into anger. Each world has its rightful claim, and yet there
is no neutral ground for judgment. To Job, he and perhaps

all men almost seem to have been born into a bright and glorious path, with a crown on their heads; but all that has been stripped from him. Man was born into a single world, a bright and unveiled surface in which the paths were open and action was possible in spite of the random harshness of disease and famine.

Now we can begin to get a somewhat clearer picture of what Job meant in his first speech [3:3–10] when he said: "May the day of my birth rest in oblivion ... for it closed not the gates of my mother's womb but hid my eyes from toil." It was not an ugly day. Job had cursed it because, in its beauties, it gave rise to all those hopes which were soon to be dashed.

〜   *He made my brothers withdraw from me, and of my*
19:13–20 *friends he has made strangers. Those who were close to me have left; ... My breath is repulsive to my wife, and to the sons of my own belly I am loathsome. Even children have contempt for me. When I rise, they speak against me.... My bones stick to my skin and to my flesh. Only the skin of my teeth ceases to hold.*

Job is now more estranged from the outside than at any other point in the poem. He is left within himself. Disease has drawn closer, and those whom he loved have gone further away. Even the breath that escapes the self has become other, and makes others of others. The distinction between self and other has all but replaced the distinction between the surface and the wisdom of the ages. The world of the surface, which no longer believes in itself, also no longer believes in Job—partly because he is a part of that surface, but primarily because he was the one who believed in the surface. The harshness of the surface, the disease, has pushed the surface farther from him, his own skin pulls tighter round him, and his gums begin to lose their grip.

〰   *Who will find a place that my words may be written*
19:23–25 *down? Who will see to it that they are inscribed in the Book: with stylus of iron and with lead incised in rock forever? Yet I know that my vindicator lives and that one day he will stand up upon the dust.*

When one reads this verse, it is hard not to be aware of the fact that there was at least one poet who did in fact provide that place; for the Book of Job lies open before us.

Job's statement "I know that my vindicator lives" appears to come in answer to his question: "Who will find a place that my words may be written down? Who will see to it that they are inscribed in the Book: with stylus of iron and with lead incised in rock forever?"

Job sees the one he calls "his vindicator" as the one who will appear one day and understand deeply enough to write down his tale for others to read. He regards his words as something to be set down for all time, though he can have no assurance that they will ever be read. It is implied, however, that whatever Job has seen will always be there to be seen. It is further implied that even if someone, after having read the book, should see what Job has seen, nevertheless that person will not have experienced what Job has experienced. The mere awareness that there once was another who was not *other* will change all that radically. For him there will be no place for anger. The first seer is a lonely seer with no one to confirm or sanction.

〰   *Even after my skin has been stripped away, yet from*
19:26–27 *out of my raw flesh shall I behold God. It is I myself*

who shall see. My own eyes must behold, and not those of a stranger, although the vitals within my bosom are finished.

We must examine more closely the role that *skin* has been playing, and will continue to play, throughout the book as a whole. In his dream of the past it was one of the things for which Job remembered God most fondly.

With skin and flesh you clothed me, and knit me all together with bones and sinews. [10:11]

But in the proem the Satan had attacked his skin with boils, and throughout the remainder the skin appears as the seat of Job's bodily illness:

My skin has become hard and begins to ooze. [7:5]

My bones stick to my skin and to my flesh. Only the skin of my teeth ceases to hold. [19:20]

My skin turned black and is now peeling off; my bones are scorched by the heat. [30:30]

It was also Bildad's prime example:

His skin will be eaten away; death's firstborn will consume his members. [18:13]

We have yet to meet Leviathan; but as we can see, he has a hide—that is, skin—impenetrable by man:

Can you fill his hide with harpoons, or his head with fishing spears? [40:31]

"Skin" is that thin film of protection between self and other. When it is gone, even the most gentle and pleasant breeze is the source of measureless pain; and for Job at this point, every other is *other*. In opening himself up to the surface world, Job exposed himself and left himself even more naked than when he "came out of his mother's belly" [1:20].

In doing so, he showed that courage which he had accused Zophar of lacking.

The Satan had said "skin beneath skin!" [2:4]. According to him, Job had a thick skin of self-interest under his soft skin of openness. If Job does live up to the present verse, the Satan will have lost his bet because Job will have proved that he has no such skin behind his skin.

For the first time in the book we are also beginning to see the importance that seeing, and especially seeing for oneself, has for Job. For the moment at least, he has started to feel that all his anger and confusion might stem from the fact that, while he has seen the surface with his own eyes, he has only "heard ... as ears can hear" [42:5].

Discussion of Chapter Twenty

〰 Then Zophar the Na'amathite answered and said: It
20:1–3   is my disquietude that would have me answer; all for
a feeling that lies within me, for I seem to hear the
admonition of my own shame; a spirit out of my own
understanding would have me reply.

Zophar makes no attempt to refute Job nor even to disagree
with or blame him. Instead, he gently suggests an alternative
to seeing for oneself which he has found within himself. It's
more like hearing than it is like seeing. Yet it is not the hearing the others spoke of—hearing the wisdom of the fathers.
One might call it a kind of hearing for oneself. It does not
arise from the surface of an external world but comes from a
deeply internal sense of shame that breaks down the distinction between admonition and understanding. For Zophar,
this new understanding reshapes and gives meaning to the
surface.

〰 the joy of the guilty has been quick, and the delight of
20:5–9   the defiled but of a moment.... The eyes that observed
him have given o'er; they no longer even take note of
him in his place.

The superficial world does not bring along with it an
understanding of itself. Although it takes place in time, it can
reveal neither its own past nor its own future. As we remember from Zophar's first speech, the daily events, which take
place on the simple plane of the surface world, are in fact
so complicated that their interconnections are well beyond
the realm of human ken. Only by searching out a deeper

understanding of wickedness and of joy in themselves do we come to realize that they cannot live together for long. It may be true that no lightning bolt will strike at the guilty man from out of heaven. He continues to breathe and take up space but, great as he may be, he ceases to be part of any man's world. They no longer treat him or recognize him as a human being. As he loses connection with others, he loses all sense of connection with himself. Even a surface world, in order to exist, must be recognized as such.

~ *His sons find favor with the poor; their hands return*
20:10 *his wealth.*

If whatever he has done is inevitably to be undone by his own, he must live knowing that all will be as if he had not been.

~ *His bones are full of vigor, yet they lie with him in the*
20:11–14 *dust....the bread in his bowels will become the gall of an asp within him.*

The world must be a world for someone. For bread to be bread, it must be digested well. The world is not merely a given, it must also be a received. To be, it must be received by a soul capable of receiving it. Job's allegedly surface world has been ill-digested and has turned into the gall of an asp.

~ *He shall not see the streams, the rivers, or brooks*
20:17–18 *of honey and butter. The fruit of his labors he shall return and never consume. Oh, he will receive the full compensation of his labors but it will bring no joy.*

Zophar, of course, means that he will look right past much of the world without ever noticing it or its beauty. The world of listening says that what Job or any man can see for himself, with his own eyes—this surface world—radically depends upon that self and upon those eyes. The streams, the rivers, and brooks of honey and butter have all faded out of his vision so that he scarcely sees them and will never remember them. In short, they are as little a part of his world as he is a part of the world of other men.

Zophar's speech reveals and even exemplifies itself. The words of verses 16 and 18 could have been said by someone in anger, but no one while steeped in anger would have noticed the things he points out in verse 17.

⁓   *Drawn, and through his body it goes, lightning swift*
20:25–26   *into the gall, and terror strikes at him. The whole of*
       darkness has been stored up to be his treasure. He
       will be consumed by an unblown fire and all shall go
       ill with the remnant left in his tent.

To appreciate the imagery of the "unblown fire," imagine a fire that has suddenly flared up as though blown by some gigantic bellows—although no bellows is seen and no wind is felt. Where cause is silent, there terror reigns.

⁓   *The heavens will expose his perversion, and the earth*
20:27–29   *shall rise up against him. The harvest of his land will*
       be exposed, trickled away on the day of his wrath.
       Such is the portion of the wicked human; an inheri-
       tance left him by the word of God.

With these words, Zophar is acknowledging that Job is right, in a way. Perversion does not reveal itself in a surface world in its own terms. We cannot see it or feel its effects upon us as such. If the heavens do not lay it bare for Job, the rising of the earth will appear to be as uncaused as an unblown fire. Job's anger has its roots in his view of the world. But loneliness and fear will ultimately drive him to actions such that, even on the surface, "The heavens will expose his perversion, and the earth ... rise up against him."

Discussion of Chapter Twenty-One

Job speaks:

〰️ *Listen well to my words; let that be your compassion.*
21:2–4 *Bear with me while I speak, and after I have spoken,*
then you may mock. Is my complaint against human-
kind? If it were, why has my spirit not worn itself out?

For Job, Zophar is right. He asks: "Is my complaint against man? If it were, why has my spirit not worn itself out?" A man cannot live on hatred for his fellow man. His spirit would wear itself out. But Zophar was wrong in one respect. Job *can* see beauty in man and in the world. We know that, for he saw it on the day he was born. Job's complaint is against that beauty which obscures all that is unpleasant by contorting the surface to make it fit a plan—rather than allowing each man, standing on his own two feet, to meet that world as it is.

In Job's mind, the true misanthrope is not one who is angry with man for believing himself to be a maggot; the true misanthrope is the one who loves man even while believing that man is in fact a maggot.

〰️ *Why do the wicked live on, ancient, yet heroic in*
21:7 *power, their seed firmly established by their side...?*

The wicked do not disappear or fade from the minds of men, as Zophar had contended. On the contrary, they become the main subject of the historian and are glorified by the poets; think, for example, of Romulus. When the founder of a great nation commits a horrible crime, it is the deed and not the man that is forgotten.

For Job, Zophar's remarks—perceptive as they are—have not fully faced the question, because Zophar has not fully faced the world. The depth of Zophar's understanding of a part has obscured his vision of the whole. To that extent, he has contorted the surface in order to allow himself to look at it. There may exist some small voice, as Zophar had said; but it is the better, not the worse among men, who listen to it.

~
21:19–21
God, you say, will treasure up all his wickedness to lay upon his sons. Why then, let him complete the bargain now and then shall he learn. Let his eyes see his own ruin and let him drink of the Almighty's cruet of fury: for what does he care for his house after he has gone, and the number of his months has been cut off?

Verses 19 through 21, the culmination of the first part of Job's speech, are intended to be Job's answer to what Zophar had said to him in his last speech:

> *The whole of darkness has been stored up to be his treasure. He will be consumed by an unblown fire and all shall go ill with the remnant left in his tent. The heavens will expose his perversion, and the earth shall rise up against him.* [20:26–27]

Zophar's notion that divine justice works in unseen ways and by unblown fires is both unwise and unjust. If the punishment is not related to the crime, it will not seem to be related to the crime; and then, however much our demands for justice may have been met, the one who is punished will have learned nothing. This roundabout justice is also unjust because too often it is the innocent who suffer in the process. It may have been enough for the guilty one to see his offspring "strike up with timbrel and with lute and rejoice to the strains of a pipe" [21:12] when they were children and under his care; but when in later life God treasures up all his wickedness to lay upon the sons it is they who are left to pick up the pieces, while the father may neither know nor care.

〜
21:28–33   *For you say, "Where is the house of this prince? Where is this tent, this dwelling place of the evil ones?" Have you not inquired of every passer by, and did you not recognize his sign that the wicked man is spared on the day of calamity, rescued from the frenzy? And who can make him face his ways? Well, his deeds are done now, and who will repay him? When he is brought to the grave, they will set a vigil over his tomb. The clods of the wadi will fall sweetly upon him. Every human will march along after him, and those who precede him will be without number.*

The end of this chapter introduces a somewhat eerie feeling that is not easy to interpret. So far as I understand it, Job is thinking about a case in which everyone somehow knows that somewhere, sometime in the past, something horrible has happened; but in order to live with the surface, they have so transformed the past that no one remembers who, or what, or when; and so all has returned to peace and tranquility.

Discussion of Chapter Twenty-Two

∼ *Oh, you are evil. Are there no bounds to your perver-*
22:5–7 *sions? You have impounded your brothers on a whim,*
and whatever clothed the naked you have stripped
away. You have given no water for the weary to drink,
and bread you have withheld from the hungry.

Eliphaz's opening verses in this chapter are particularly harsh. Job has been attacked for his anger, his thoughts, and his opinions; but up to now no one has accused him of such acts as those named here. From what we have seen so far of Job's character, this sudden torrent of accusations appears to be quite undeserved. Not only is it inconsistent with the picture we have of Job from Chapter 1, but in Chapter 29, Job will declare:

> *...for an ear had heard and it blessed me; an eye had seen and it approved, because I had saved a poor man when he cried out, and an orphan when there was no one else to help him. The blessings of those who had been lost came to me, and I made the widow's heart sing. I put on judgment, and it covered me. A just cause fit like a coat or a hat. I became eyes to the blind, and feet to the lame. I was a father to the needy, and often I would search out a case for a man whom I did not know. I would break the jaw of the unjust and wrest the prey from his teeth.* [29:11–17]

It hardly seems as if Eliphaz can be speaking of the same man. Perhaps one should discount God's praise of Job at the beginning of the book as belonging to a very different strain of the story. Or perhaps Job's claim to have "put on judgment" is an outright lie; or perhaps he deludes himself about what really happens in the surface world. We have no way of knowing. We can only say that if Job really is as despicable as verses 5–7 allege, he deserves everything that has happened to him; the whole book becomes trivial, and the tempest merely a tempest in a teapot.

Another possibility is that Eliphaz is simply afraid to acknowledge that innocents indeed suffer. Such thoughts may so threaten to pull his world apart that he must call the just man unjust, and thus manage to maintain his ease.

Or perhaps Eliphaz is right, but in a way that Job could not have understood. Even if Job should climb a hundred hills, and in each valley clothe a hundred naked men—in the surface world there is always another hill not climbed, and another unclothed man. Justice, for Eliphaz, may require what no human can perform. No matter how much good a man may do, it is never enough; he is still guilty.

〜 *Have you kept to that primordial path which the men*
22:15–16 *of wickedness have trod, men who were snatched up*
before their time?

Eliphaz believes that Job's insistence on taking the surface world seriously would in fact amount to nothing more than a return to pagan times, when the sun was thought to be a god and the bringer of all warmth and sustenance, but no relationship was seen or felt then between divinity and morality.

In verses 12 through 18, Eliphaz seems to be trying to prod Job into seeing that the finitude of his surface world implies that there can be no universal standard for justice beyond the surface world itself. The only thing in the visible world above man is the sun, which, as far as concerns itself, shines on good and bad alike.

〜 *Please, come close to him and be at peace. All good*
22:21–26 *things will come your way. Receive guidance from*

his mouth and keep his saying in your heart. If you will return to the Almighty and be rebuilt, if you keep injustice far from your tent, take gold dust for sand and nuggets as mere rocks in a stream, the Almighty will be your gold and most precious silver; for then you shall have taken delight in the Almighty and raised your countenance up unto God.

In Eliphaz's last words, he pleads with Job to give up his claim to the critical significance of the surface. The surface world is a world in which each thing is only what it is. Gold dust is gold dust, nuggets are nuggets, and the guilty are guilty. But if a man is "rebuilt," he may proclaim his words and thus it shall be. The surface world, the world of nature, can be rebuilt—radically changed—by Job's return to closeness to God.

Discussion of Chapter Twenty-Three

〰   *My musings are bitter again today. My hand is heavy*
23:2   *from all my groaning.*

When Chapter 23 begins it is the morning of the next day.
Job may have thought that after a good night's sleep his world
might look different, that confusion and frustration might
vanish like a mist or like some bad dream. But the problems
did not just go away. They were real and he was bitter. But in
verses 3 through 7 he begins to imagine what it might be like
if he and God were in fact to come to trial.

〰   *Who can tell me how to find him! How I might come*
23:3–7 *to his appointed place! I would lay out my case before*
         him, and fill my mouth with arguments. I would
         know with what words he would answer me! I want
         to understand what he would have to say to me.
         Would he strive against me with his great power? No,
         surely he would place his confidence in me. There an
         upright man can reason with him, and there would I
         be released from my judge forever.

"No," thinks Job, "things cannot be as Eliphaz says. If things
are in no way what they are, then the just is not just, and all
becomes meaningless. If this slender bit of the surface before
me has no place within God's whole, how could it even *seem*
to stand before me?"

〰   *So, onward I went, but he was naught; to the rear, but I*
23:8–9 *discerned him not. To the left among his works I could*
         not grasp hold. He enveloped the right, but I saw not.

Job suddenly finds himself in a totally empty universe. Nonetheless he composes his defense as if God and the world were present and fully attentive.

❧ *But he knows the way I have taken. He has tried me*
23:10–12 *and I have come through as gold. My foot held tight to his track; I kept to his ways and did not swerve. Nor have I departed from the commandments of his lips. From within my breast I have treasured up the words of his mouth.*

Job's spirit is not innately that of a rebel. He accepted the world he grew up in, and he loved it. It filled his breast; and the human horizon, as it was defined by "the words of his mouth," he held as a treasure. Still, there was a kind of emptiness. He looked around him for the source of those things that he treasured most, but all was veiled. He believed only that the one he could not see could see him.

❧ *But he is of but one purpose, and who can dissuade*
23:13–15 *him? His soul need only desire, and it is done. He will fulfil what has been prescribed for me, and he has many such things about him. It is because of all this that his presence leads me into confusion. When I reflect, I fear him.*

But God's law in speech was belied by God's law in action. The first filled Job's breast and seemed the only thing of value in the world; the second seemed a nest of meaningless chaos. Such was the presence that led Job into confusion.

❧ *God has softened my heart, the Almighty has led me*
23:16 *into confusion.*

To see what Job means and the irony implied in his words, one must consider the duality of having a soft, that is, vulnerable, heart. To have a soft heart may be laudable:

> *Because your heart was soft and you humbled yourself before God when you heard his words against this place and its inhabitants, and you have humbled yourself before me, and have rent your clothes and wept before me, I also have heard you, says the* Lord. [II Chron. 34:27]

But it may also be experienced as a fearful affliction:

> *...and shall say to them: Hear, O Israel, you draw near this day to battle against your enemies: let not your heart be soft; be not in awe of them, or tremble, or have any trepidation.* [Deut. 20:3]

It was God's talk of justice that first softened Job's heart and laid it bare to be buffeted by his actions. The soft heart which came to be out of a love of justice is another way of speaking of Job's lack of an underskin. It was this openness that left him open to so much pain.

Discussion of Chapter Twenty-Four

 ⌒   Why has not the Almighty set aside specific times for
24:1   judgment?

The word צָפַן, translated here as *set aside*, is a rather complicated one. We have considered it already, but not in much
depth. The full range of its meaning can only be seen by
looking at how it is used throughout the Book of Job:

> But you **treasured** all these things up in your heart. (10:13)

> Who can move you to hide me in the Pit and **conceal** me till your
> anger passes? [14:13]

> The guilty man writhes in pain all his days and the number of his
> years lies **hidden** from the ruthless. [15:20]

> So, you have **protected** their hearts from insight, and that is why
> even you no longer have any respect for them. [17:04]

> The whole of darkness has been stored up to be his **treasures**.
> [20:26]

> God, you say, will **treasure** up all his wickedness to lay upon his
> sons? Why then, let him complete the bargain now, and then shall
> he learn. [21:19]

> From within my breast I have **treasured** up the words of his
> mouth. [23:12]

> Why has not the Almighty **set aside** specific times for judgment?
> [24:1]

 ⌒   ...Now, even those who know him cannot recognize his
24:1   timing [literally, "his days"].

The all-too-often-praised unintelligibility of divine order
and justice leaves men no imitative models, models without
which all law is quick to disappear. Punishments that do not
clearly appear as punishments, rewards that do not clearly

appear as rewards—such things do no good, and it is the innocent who suffer.

        🙠   *Boundary-stones are carried off, flocks seized and*
24:2   *peacefully sent to pasture.*

The collapse of civilization, according to Job, begins with the destruction the most tangible sign of that act which first brought it into being: the distinction between *mine* and *thine* as marked by a simple boundary-stone.

        🙠   *The poor of the land hide themselves together. They*
24:4b–10 *are wild asses in the desert, going off about their labors*
            of snatching up at dawn. They have only the waste-
            land to provide food for the young men.... Naked,
            they pass the night without clothing; and shelter from
            the cold there is none. Drenched by torrents in the
            hills, they cling to a rock for want of shelter. Without
            clothing, they go about naked.

The picture that Job paints here is that of a world reverted back to primitive, almost animal-like days. The times that Eliphaz had warned of are already around us, but they were none of Job's doing. The true cause is God's justice, which lacks the kind of order and timing that man can grasp.

        🙠   *From out of the city the dead groan, wounded souls*
24:12 *cry out; yet in all that God sees nothing unsavory.*

Whatever remains of civilization serves only to increase the sense of degradation.

        🙠   *They were rebels against the light who could neither*
24:13 *recognize its path nor remain within its course.*

It is not immediately clear to whom the word *they* refers; but by his use of the emphatic pronoun, I take it that the poet has not switched subjects but is still speaking of the poor. If this is the correct interpretation, Job is not talking about sin at this point, but of the depravity that can only arise out of the total hopelessness described in verses 7 through 12.

Translations vary greatly from verse 18 through the end of the chapter. Some translate verse 18 in the indicative while others put the whole passage in the hortatory: "May he be held in discredit ... and may his lot be accursed.... May he not turn down the path."

The essential problem is that, taken in the indicative, the passage would seem to be in direct contradiction to everything Job has been saying so far. Some even solve the problem by attributing the speech to one of the other speakers. None of these solutions is absurd or impossible.

However, if we take the poet still to be speaking about those of the poor who were first drawn into degradation and then into crime, the passage begins to make a bit more sense. Job would then be saying that they, and not the truly unjust, are the ones who are in fact more likely to suffer ill effects from their actions.

This interpretation should not be overlooked, though it is far from certain. The main argument in its favor is that while verse 25 does not sit very well with the hortatory interpretation, the rest of the passage, if taken to refer to all wrongdoers, does not sit well with the book as a whole.

Discussion of Chapter Twenty-Five

In order to understand this, the shortest chapter of Job, we must begin by looking at the plan of the book's central section, which contains Chapters 3 through 25. The following table gives the order of the speeches and the number of verses each contains.

Chapter	Job	Eliphaz	Bildad	Zophar
3	26			
4–5		48		
6–7	51			
8			22	
9–10	56			
11				20
12–14	75			
15		35		
16–17	38			
18			21	
19	29			
20				29
21	34			
22		30		
23–24	42			
25			6	

As we can see, the original plan called for three rounds of three sets of two speeches each. We can also see that the dialogue was cut off in the middle of Bildad's last speech and that Zophar's final speech was never given. However, we are never told whether it was Bildad who terminated the conversation, or whether Job cut him off. In any case Bildad ends with these words:

◌⌇ *And now what of these mortals, the maggots; or the*
25:6   *son of man, the worm.*

We remember them well. In Chapter 17, Job had said, "If
then I must ... call out "Mother" and "Sister" to the maggots,
where then is my hope?"

Job had always known that the claim that man is a maggot
would end conversation, because it denies the relevance of
what, for Job, is the ultimate grounds of any human conversation. For Job there is an equation between the notion that
man is a maggot and the claim that the surface view of things,
as it reveals itself to human thought as such, is of no ultimate
relevance. Since the surface *is* the surface precisely because
it is a surface *for man*, it has no other being than to be the
beginning for man. In spite of the constant strife within Job's
soul caused by the contradictory claims of the surface world
on the one hand and awe of the Lord on the other to be the
beginning of wisdom, what is first for man as such must be
the beginning of human conversation.

Conversation, then, must come to an end precisely because
Job has no proof that he is not a maggot. If the surface world
made perfect sense, he would know that he was not a maggot; but it does not make perfect sense. It is full of enigmas
and contradictions, and yet for Job it makes too much sense
to be simply forgotten.

Bildad was always the most understanding of the three,
but now he is the one to make the final break. We ask ourselves why. Perhaps the first thing to notice is that while he
has totally abandoned any attempt to come to terms with Job,
Bildad was the only one of Job's friends who had never condemned him personally.

He seems to have learned from Job that any attempt to find
a compromise on the question of the status of the surface
world would be meaningless.

"Look high as the moon, nothing shines. Even the stars are not pure in his sight" [25:5]. Bildad has taken the other path: nothing shines and man is a maggot! Bildad has seen that the only viable counterposition to Job requires diminishing the status of both man and the visible universe.

To put it otherwise, Bildad began in Chapter 8 with the position that no single man, by himself, has a sufficiently large horizon to carry out the project Job has proposed. Only the wider horizon supplied by the wisdom of the ages will do as the foundation of human thought. He now sees that position as untenable. If a single man's horizon is necessarily too confined, it can only mean that the human horizon as such, including that of the fathers, is defective. Man is a worm and has only a worm's-eye view.

Nonetheless, he has not condemned Job. Why? Is it because he too knows that he cannot prove that he is right and hence that Job is wrong?

Thus, two old friends part.

Discussion of Chapter Twenty-Six

〰️ *Then Job answered and said: Oh, why must you try to*
26:1–2 *help when you are so powerless? You would save me*
with a mighty arm, but you have not the strength!

These are Job's last words to his friends. He has come
to terms with them in his own mind now. They are all
well-meaning men; Job knows that, but each must go his
own way. They all want to help, but without having faced the
surface of things in the way in which Job has faced it, they
cannot share his question and so are powerless to be of any
help.

We may not find an answer to the question, "Does seeing
come from having the strength to look, or does the strength
to look come from the having seen?" We may not find an
answer because there may be no answer; there may only be
the going back and forth, each time deeper and deeper, each
time richer and richer. To ask, as children sometimes do,
"Who started it?" may be to be carried off into an infinite
regress. Is it that we do not see because we have not looked,
or have we not looked because nothing has caught our eye?
Or is it that something else has caught the eyes or the ears of
Eliphaz and the others?

〰️ *Whose spirit is it that has been coming out of you?*
26:4

This question is critical to our understanding of why the
dialogue has ceased. Job implies that it is not their own
spirit that has been coming out of them. Their voice is not
home-grown because it did not arise from within their own

horizons. Our own voice, for Job, is the only voice able to articulate all those blurred and obscured thoughts which are first stirred up from within our own particular partial awareness of the surface of things as it lies within our own particular shaggy and ill-defined horizon. Other thoughts may have a brilliant central focus, but when they have been poured from one mind into another, they lose that unique periphery which once connected them to the land in which those particular thoughts were born. For that reason there are no pathways which could lead one back to his own horizons and beyond. Too often what was once a living thought in the teacher becomes a hardened dogma for the student—precisely because he cannot reach out to a horizon that is no longer available to him. He is then continually forced to return to the center, which he can only voice in comfortable repetition.

Job is alone now. He says:

∽   *Ancient specters writhe beneath the waters and those*
26:5   *who dwell in them.*

Job is finally free, free to settle down and live in his surface world. But something—some ancient specter, older by far than he—begins to writhe, or dance, or to give birth (for the Hebrew word means all of those things) beneath it. Job is beginning to reflect upon the fact that his surface world is nothing more than just that, a surface—a thing in need of support from within. The question is whether this surface is just a veneer, only competent to support human existence at its most minimal level, or whether it is an integral external appearance through which whatever lies beneath it can reveal itself. At question is not the absolute truth of the surface, but its relevance as a beginning point in the search for the truth.

For the present, Job has only focused on the surface, but he is beginning to feel disturbed and to wonder how his world can be more than "a northern land stretched out over the chaos or an earth suspended above the nothingness" (compare 26:7).

One suspects that Eliphaz might have looked at things in just that way. For him, the human view of the surface has been so contorted by man's perversion that nothing behind it can be recovered. A new heaven and a new earth must be revealed to him before he can proceed.

Of God, Job says:

⮑   *The Pit stands naked before him and there is no*
26:6–7 *cover for Abaddon. He stretches the northern lands*
       out over the chaos and suspends the earth above the
       nothingness.

Not only does Job have no account of the existence of his world, he also sees it as a fragile realm, constantly under the threat of all those forces that could, and yet do not, destroy it. Job can neither account for, nor doubt the relevance of, his surface world.

⮑   *Oh the thunder of his mighty deeds, who can reflect*
26:14 *upon it!*

The shaggy limit of Job's clarity ebbs its way into darkness and obscurity. God has shrouded from man the source of his own existence, and he cannot tell what gives his little world its solidity.

Discussion of Chapter Twenty-Seven

> 27:2
>
> *By the life of that God who has merely thrown aside the whole of my case, the Almighty has embittered my soul!*

Job has seen a great deal; but when he returns to his own immediate world, the claims of justice still loom above him. There is great poignancy when Job in effect swears by all that is holy that all that is holy is also unjust. This is the conflict that has given rise to the bitterness in Job's soul.

> 27:3–6
>
> *Yet so long as there is breath within me, or the spirit of God in my nostrils, never will my lips speak any injustice, or my tongue utter deceit. No, I'll not pretend that you have been just. Even till I perish, I shall not turn my simplicity from me. I shall not disavow my integrity, but cling tight to my righteousness and not let go; for my heart has never felt pangs of reproach.*

Gratitude is forced to manifest itself as ingratitude. The spirit of God, as it manifests itself in Job's nostrils, can show gratitude for its value and integrity only by clinging to that integrity—in spite of the fact that the result of that act appears as ingratitude.

It is difficult to know how we are to understand the verses of the rest of the chapter. If, however, one takes them to be Job's account of how the world once looked to him, they begin to come into focus. There was a time when Job was an integral part of the human world around him. He shared its views and he shared its trust. Because his own ways were simple, he could sense mock-piety in others. In verse 5 Job maintains that there has been no essential change in his simplicity, although it has suddenly found itself under an alien horizon.

Discussion of Chapter Twenty-Eight

〰️
28:1–4
There is a mine for silver and a place where gold is made pure. Iron is taken from the earth, and the rock is made to flow with copper. Man brings an end to the darkness. He explores everything to its limit, even to this rock of murk and the Shadow of Death. Far from any habitation, he blasts out channels. Abandoned by every passer by, destitute of all humanity, they wander.

This whole chapter, one of the most beautiful passages in the book, could be read as the first Ode to Man. Few works in literature have praised in such elegant speech the Baconian ideals of the conquest of nature. Job sees this apparent greatness as an image of his own quest. Men have looked beneath the surface. It is their glory. They too have left the land of human habitation as Job has left his friends, and with them all of human society. By their own powers they have dug down under the surface and found a world of riches which they have conquered and made their own; but what of Job?

〰️
28:5
There is a land which gives us our daily bread, but underneath it churns like fire.

According to this view, the surface of nature—to which Job has committed himself—gives little indication of the true nature of the world that supports it. The "land which gives us our daily bread," and on which we live our daily lives, is a much too meager horizon to form the basis of meaningful human conversation. Its inner churnings must first be searched out.

〰️
28:7–10
No bird of prey knows the trails. The eye of the falcon has never caught sight of it, nor have the sons of pride

ever trampled it over. The lion can bear it no witness,
but man has put his hand to the flint and overturned
mountains by the root. He rips open channels through
the rocks. His eye sees every precious thing.

Man can force nature to reveal itself in ways it cannot do
on its own. Man can overcome nature, and hence he can
overcome the paltriness of his own nature. In this sense, man
is not a part of nature—not because of any perversion in his
nature but because he can conquer and rule over nature.
Even man's scheme to reveal nature is not supplied by nature.
There are no veins in the rock to guide his way. He must rip
open a path by his own might.

〜   *He binds up the flowing rivers and the hidden things*
28:11   *come to light.*

From Job's time to Faust's, containing the inundation of
chaotic waters has been the symbol of man's understanding
of and control over the world in which he lives.

〜   *Yet wisdom, where can she be found?*
28:12

Perhaps the most impressive aspect of Chapter 28 lies in
the care which Job has taken in thinking through and articu-
lating both sides of this question. One cannot but be moved
by verses 1 through 11, but the bare mention of the word "yet"
in the present verse is sufficient to turn things quite around.
Verses 12–18 are magnificent in their ability to reveal simul-
taneously both the richness and the poverty of the project of
conquering nature.

〜   *She [wisdom] is concealed even from the birds of*
28:21   *heaven.*

Man can only dig beneath the surface; but even if, like birds, they could fly above it, it would do them no good.

⁓   *But GOD understands the way to it; he knows the*
28:23–24 *place, for he can look to the ends of the earth and see*
          all things that are under the sky.

In this and the following passages, Job seems to be trying to restate for himself the arguments of the others in terms that fit the world as he has been able to see it up till now.

⁓   *When he established the weight of the wind, and set*
28:25–27 *out the waters according to its measure, when he gave*
          a law for the rain and a passageway for the voice of
          the thunderbolt, then it was that he saw it, counted
          it, measured it, and delved into it.

Unlike man, God has a complete view of an all-encompassing horizon. Man's horizons, by contrast, are limited, and their edges hazy. Rumors from beyond seep in, and obscure pathways lead out. What we see implies what— or that—we have not seen. The ambiguity of whether it is a *what* or merely a *that* is central to the reading of the book. Job's question is whether a man of care can rummage through his shrouded way and begin to pierce beyond his own horizon, or if man is faced with a gulf beyond which he cannot pass.

⁓   *And then he said unto humankind, "Behold, awe of*
28:28   *the Lord, that is Wisdom, and to turn away from evil*
          is understanding."

The structure and sense of this verse give it the ring of a quote from psalmic literature. If this suspicion is true, it would add to the notion that this chapter is not to be read as a simple recantation on the part of Job, but rather as his attempt to restate the thoughts of others in terms that make sense to him, in order to come to grips with his awareness of the partial nature of his own grasp of the whole.

Discussion of Chapter Twenty-Nine

∽   *And again Job took up his proverb and said...*
29:1

The only other chapter that began with this formula was Chapter 27. There it followed a chapter that included the verse "Ancient specters writhe beneath the waters and those who dwell in them." Here it follows a chapter that began: "There is a mine for silver and a place where gold is made pure."

The two verses seem to be radical statements of the two alternatives facing Job. They are polar opposites, one being ruled by mighty God, the other by mighty man. Yet in both of them the placid world we call home rests upon, or is suspended over, another world, rich and turbulent. In both cases, the surface world can only be understood or appreciated in terms of that underworld. Both are presented in the form of an excursus from Job's proverb.

∽   *Who can return to the months gone by, to the days*
29:2–6 *when God watched over me, when his lamp shone over my head and I walked in the darkness by his light; back to my autumnal days when God was at home inside my tent, when the Almighty was yet with me, and I with my lads all about me; when my feet were bathed in cream, and the rock poured out its streams of oil for me?*

Perhaps Job made a mistake when he wished to banish the deceptive beauty of the day of his birth. Job was already in his autumnal days, retired, and ready to curl up by the fire.

Spring and summer had come and gone. He had raised a good crop of fellow citizens, manuring them well with justice and kindness. The seeming was good.

Verses 7 through 17 present us with the most complete picture we shall have of what life had been for Job before his world began to fall apart. A just cause fit like an old coat or an old hat. Being just was natural and comfortable for Job, and the world he knew fit around it.

〜   *I thought to myself: "I shall perish in my own little*
29:18   *nest, my days having multiplied as sand."*

This verse in its context, together with verse 4, is, as it were, one of Job's main credentials for being who he is. The implication is that the ability to rule men well, and the love of doing so—plus the willingness to relinquish that rule when the time comes—is what both forces and allows Job to face the surface of things with dignity and concern.

Discussion of Chapter Thirty

∾
30:1
> *But now they have turned me into the joke, those younger than I, whose fathers I would have felt contempt to put with my sheep dogs.*

Job's words are intended as a reference back to verses in the last chapter:

> *They waited for me in expectation as for the rain; their mouths opened wide as if to catch the spring rain. I joked with them a bit, so that my kindness would not overwhelm them since they had no self-confidence.* [29:23–24]

Job's friendly laughter, intended to relieve others of the burden of that crippling kind of gratitude which leaves them with only a feeling of debilitating dependance, has been answered by a derisive laughter.

∾
30:2–8
> *What is the strength of their hands to me, those men from whom all vigor has been lost, a wasteland in want and starvation? They gnaw at a parched land and destroy as they are destroyed. They gather mallow and leaves from the bushes. Broom root has become their food. Driven from the heart of things, they are cried upon like thieves. They find their quarter in river beds, in holes in the dust and the rock. Braying in the bushes, they huddle together under a weed. Sons of Fools and Sons of Nobodies! They have been whipped from the land.*

In turning laughter into scorn they have lost all humanity without even gaining true animality. Their needs remain human, but the contempt implied by their jest makes it impossible for them to join with others except in the most direct sense of huddling together under a weed, sharing only their inability to share. They are human without the means to be human.

◇   *And now they have made a ditty of me and I have*
30:9–10 *become a byword to them. Oh how they abhor me and keep their distance; they do not even refrain from spitting in my face.*

In saying this, Job acknowledges that he is no longer able to maintain the fiction that these men are powerless and can do no harm. The mass effect of those who cannot see the surface has, for Job, overwhelmed the surface. The land of laughter, joking, playing, of scoffing, and of scorn—all the same word in the Hebrew text—has become confused for Job and intertwined with the problem of contempt and compassion. His good-natured jest which stemmed from his compassion has become his companions' gibes and contempt.

◇   *They come in a great burst, wave after wave of*
30:14–15 *destruction. Terror turns upon me; it pursues my gentility like the wind, and my salvation passes me by like a cloud.*

The confusion of his feelings of contempt and compassion then works upon his received notion of being watched to produce a deep sense of guilt which terrifies his inner sense of gentility. Verse 17 and what follows is to be taken in a completely literal way. It reads:

◇   *By night my bones are whittled away, and the gnaw-*
30:17–19 *ing never ceases. My clothing envelops me in great*

constraint and the collar of my tunic chokes at me.
It throws me into the mire and I become as dust and
ashes.

It is not uncommon for people to be told by their dentist
that their gums are in poor condition because they clench
their teeth at night. It is hard to imagine how much pain
we can both inflict upon ourselves and withstand in sleep
by twisting and turning, feeling without waking. But why
should Job feel this guilt so deeply in his being, and punish
himself so harshly for a crime which he knows he had not
committed? This is perhaps the most fundamental question
raised by the book. It is a question that has been peering at us
from behind every page, an enigma too vital to be evaded by
speaking of two Jobs or of multiple authorship.

In facing this problem in a day when the works of Freud
have become so much a part of the air we breathe, I feel much
like a five-year-old boy dressed in his Little Lord Fauntleroy
suit, trudging home from the pond with a tiny sailboat under
his arm: how shall he relate the great saga of his day's adven-
tures at the dinner table when the list of guests includes such
men as Darwin and Melville? Yet even in our little pond the
question still looms at us large: why should a man like Job
feel the weight of guilt for a crime which he knows he did not
commit, or feel that his soul has been perverted by an original and all-encompassing act of the fathers, that for him has
no such power over the human spirit?

As Eliphaz, and in fact as the whole of human society
known to Job, sees it, Job is too perverted to recognize his
own perversion with any clarity, and his view of the world
is too narrow to see his own sin. He must learn to forego the
limited view of man and listen to the voice of God as it reveals
itself to him in his own night visions. Job's nightly twistings
and turnings are caused by his own guilt. Conscience is the

means of divine retribution. But doubts have been raised concerning this way of looking at the world, both in terms of itself and in terms of the injustice that it may be causing with regard to Job.

Is it, then, by considering himself guilty and by causing himself such pain in order to prove to himself the existence of his guilt that he can come to terms with other pains, ones which have no cause? Our guilt, confirmed to us by our own self-punishment, then becomes the reason for our otherwise reasonless pain.

Or does the feeling of guilt, of being punished by an all-seeing, all-loving God, act as our only immediate guarantor of the cosmic significance of our actions?

Or do we, by condemning ourselves on the charge of sin, wish to place ourselves in a rank beyond ourselves, by becoming the condemner as well as the condemned? If this is the case, what does it imply? Is it some strange kind of Kantian freedom that we feel in that we, and no other (such as the deposed father), have become Lord and Master over ourselves? Or is it a way we have of silently and subliminally feeling the joys of tyranny, even at the expense of living our daily life under the pain and fear of that tyranny?

Compelling as these ideas may be in general, they do not seem to be quite adequate in the case of Job. They presuppose, and gain their force from, the cognitive power of human thought. They intend to give a thoughtful and reasoned account of the workings of the human psyche, which touches the heart of the matter as it is, apart from the needs and drives of the investigator himself. That may not, of course, always happen, but the science assumes that at least in theory it is possible. That would suggest that the human psyche can only be understood if it is fundamentally conceived as something capable of understanding, and hence of misunderstanding, itself.

⌒   *I walked in gloom with no sun above. I stood up*
30:28–29 *in the assembly and cried out; and thus I became a*
brother to the Jackal and friend to the Ostrich.

The Hebrew word תַן (tan) has several meanings and each, as we shall see, constantly rings of the others. It can mean *sea monster,* or *serpent;* or, as in our case, it can mean the *jackal.* Even when תַן is used with a singular verb, it (in this respect resembling the name of God) normally takes a plural ending—either the regular Hebrew ending תַנִים (tanim), or the somewhat more foreign, and hence somewhat more mystical sounding תַנִין (tanin).

Job's great complaint, that Man is ever watched rather than trusted, began in Chapter 7 with the words:

> *Am I the sea or some monster* (tan) *that you set watch over me?* [7:12]

But now his awareness of being watched and the failure of his brothers to recognize his brotherhood have left him feeling strangely pulled by a sense of brotherhood towards that same *tan,* but this time it has come in the form of the Jackal.

The Jackal, wild cousin of the domestic dog, and constant companion to the Ostrich, is pictured throughout the Bible as roaming through the land of desolation just beyond the world of man.

> *I went out by night by the Valley Gate to the Jackal's Well and to the Dung Gate, and I inspected the walls of Jerusalem which were broken down and its gates which had been destroyed by fire.* [Neh. 2:1]

Like Job, the *tan* lives on the edge of the desolate city, in a wasteland devoid of human habitation:

> *Hazor shall become a haunt of jackals, an everlasting waste; no man shall dwell there, no man shall sojourn in her.* [Jer. 49:33]

*And Babylon, the glory of kingdoms, the splendor and pride
of the Chaldeans, will be like Sodom and Gomorrah when
God overthrew them. It will never be inhabited or dwelt in
for all generations; no Arab will pitch his tent there, no shepherds will make their flocks lie down there. But wild beasts
will lie down there, and its houses will be full of howling
creatures; there ostriches will dwell, and there satyrs will
dance. Hyenas will cry in its towers, and jackals in the
pleasant palaces; its time is close at hand and its days will
not be prolonged.* [Isaiah 13:19]

Job has acted as a man, and yet no man sees him as a
man. Perhaps he has no choice now, other than to abandon
both society and his own sociality and meld into the world
that knows no human eye or human tongue. For him it is a
frightening thought, but the reader knows that it is into just
such a world that the Voice of the tempest will soon beckon
him.

Discussion of Chapter Thirty-One

∽ *I have made a covenant with my eyes, for how could I*
31:1   *gaze upon a maiden?*

Job adopts here a much more formal and legalistic turn of
phrase than Eliphaz had used in Chapter 5:

> *Have no dread of the beasts of the earth, for you have a cov-*
> *enant with the rocks in the field, and the beasts of the fields*
> *will bring you peace.* [5:22–23]

Job's formulation can even be used to refer to the legal
forms of a marriage. The verse holds within it the full tension and contradictory interweaving felt at the end of the
last chapter between sociality and the need for autonomous
understanding. As the tension in this verse implies, sexuality
is claimed both by nature and by convention. What seems
natural and direct for the one requires law and ceremony for
the other. This inner conflict is also part of what is felt as
guilt.

Job, by the preeminently socio-political act of entering into
a covenant, is cutting himself off from the most primal form
of sociality. Human sexuality, in its ambiguities, is central,
then, to all this disarray. In giving us a kind of immortality, it
is another key to our autonomy, but in so doing, it reminds us
of our lack of immortality, our weakness and need for others.
It is, then, also key to our sociality. Again the two are linked,
and in their opposition give rise to shame and guilt.

∽ *Let him weigh me on the scales of justice, and then*
31:6   *God will know of my simplicity.*

In spite of all the rift between Job and his friends, or between Job and God, or between Job and Job, one thing seems to be held in common; not wealth (or what is sometimes called manliness), but Justice is seen to be the highest human virtue among all involved. There is also, at least on Job's part, the feeling that there is some common understanding concerning what things are just and what things are unjust, regardless of however rough-and-ready that understanding might be for Job.

The disagreement, however, seems to center itself around a question concerning the guarantor of that justice. Job believes in that guarantor, but with his own eyes he can see nothing guaranteed.

〰 *If ever I felt contempt for the cause of one of my ser-*
31:13–15 *vants, man or maid, when they brought case against me—what would I do when God rose up? How would I answer him if he should call me to account? Did not he who made me in my mother's belly make him as well? Did he not form us in the same womb?*

These are Job's last words before entering the whirlwind. They are, so far as one can tell, an honest attempt to recount his way of life, and they are intended to make clear that his actions have always been in accordance with justice, as that term is understood by the tradition, the fathers, and the law.

For the tradition, it is God who is the guarantor who stands behind this understanding. Job's position, however, seems more nearly expressed by the words

> *Did not he who made me in my mother's belly make him as well? Did he not form us in the same womb?* [31:15]

In Chapter 3, there was a brief discussion of the importance of the words *womb* and *belly*. I noted there the importance which these two words have for each of the three speakers.

But now we must take a second look at Job.

Even at the very beginning of the book, Job had said:

> *Naked I came out of my mother's belly and naked I shall return there.* [1:21]

In Verse 15, Job implied that what supports his understanding of justice differs from the foundation as understood by the tradition. For each, the foundations are closely connected to what we have called sociality, the forces which bring men together. As hitherto understood, sociality stood in opposition to autonomy. For Job, the world of sociality had become a painful world. It concealed the human need for autonomy in very brutal ways.

In his former understanding, the womb, which was often related to death, was a place of quietness where each could rest wholly undisturbed and wholly unsubservient to any other.

> *Small and great, all are there, and the slave is free of his lord.* [3:19]

We are beginning to see a different Job, one who is beginning to spell out to himself the implications of what the Job of Chapter 1 had said when he equated his mother's womb with the earth. Verse 15 indicates that sociality may have a more cosmic origin and have its roots in an original unity rather than in a later coming together.

Such thoughts are not wholly foreign to the Bible, but they must be understood within their proper context.

The first ten chapters of the Book of Genesis do indeed give an account of the coming-to-be of the whole of the human race from one original human being, and they tell the story of the development of that world up until the time of the Flood. However, it must be noted that after the episode of Noah's drunkenness (Gen. 9:20–27), not one of these incidents or characters is ever mentioned again either in the Torah or in the Earlier Prophets. The names Adam, Eve, the Garden of

Eden, Cain, and Abel, Noah and his ark, are totally dropped
from the text. Once a covenant has been made between God
and the animate world, the one made after the Flood, it and
only it is to be relied upon, and nothing is to be established
on a more primitive foundation. All is forgotten in Noah's
drunken spree. Only Ham, who saw his father naked, was
excluded and cursed. The sight of his antediluvial origins,
even though it may have been accidental, so fascinated Ham
that he was unable to take part in the new covenant and was
therefore cursed.[7]

   If Job, as seems here to be the case, sees sociality as having
its justification not in a Guarantor who ensures that each will
receive his just rewards, but in some form of original unity,
the distinction between autonomy and sociality begins to
evaporate. Perhaps these things are not very clear to Job, but
they do indicate his need to raise those difficulties which will
eventually send him into the tempest. Making clear to himself the implications of this way of understanding what lies
beyond his horizon will imply that he must face that world
which he so feared when he spoke of becoming "a brother to
the Jackal" [30:29]—that world which the prophets and the
Psalmist call "the land of jackals."

   For the present, however, Job wishes to make clear to his
friends that they are all in fundamental agreement concerning the place of justice in human action, no matter how much
they may disagree about the nature of its foundations.

~   *if ever I have seen the radiance of the light or the*
31:26–28 *moon walking in splendor, and with my heart secretly*
          attracted, placed my fingers to my lips to kiss them,

---

[7] For further discussion see Robert D. Sacks, *A Commentary on the
Book of Genesis* (Edwin Mellen Press, 1990).

even that would have been a juristic perversion, for I
would have forsaken God the most high.

This at least, Job and his friends share: that neither wealth
nor beauty, but justice, is of ultimate importance—though
the verse shows that this is not due to any lack of sensitivity
to beauty on Job's part.

Later in the chapter one can get a glimpse of at least a part
of what Job means by justice:

∾   *Could I have rejoiced when hardship struck at those*
31:29–31 *that hate me or come to life because evil had found*
        them, without giving my palate over to sin by asking
        for his life with a curse? Even the men of my own tent
        would have said, "Who will let us at his flesh? We
        will not be satisfied."

Job seems pleased, confident that his followers honor justice more than they honor their leader. For him it is indeed a
sign of his virtue as a leader.

∾   *I left no stranger sleeping out-of-doors but opened*
31:32–34 *my doors to the traveler. Would I have covered over*
        my transgressions like [some] human or concealed
        perversion in my bosom through terror of the great
        multitude? or was I so shattered by family disgrace
        that I would stand petrified, not daring to go out the
        opening way?

We are now quite close to the culmination of Job's speech.
The beginning of his final argument is based on his way of
being. His willingness to stand at the opening of his world
and to risk going beyond it indicates a man not shattered by
family disgrace—here equated with the concept of perversion.
If I understand the grammar correctly, Job is arguing that the

feelings of guilt and perversion, which stem from the respon-
sibility we have had to bear for the acts of the fathers, lead, if
concealed, to a terror of all that is around us. We therefore
stand petrified and cannot allow ourselves to peer beyond the
city—even as Job now stands at the opening, "not daring to go
out."

⌒ *Who will find someone to listen? Well, here is my*
31:35–37 *writ: Let the Almighty answer, or let the man who*
has a quarrel against me write it down in a book.
I'll hoist it up on my shoulders, or wear it round me
like a crown. But I will also give him an account of
my every step and I will present it to him as a prince.

And now we have such a book in our hands. It contains
the speeches of Eliphaz, Bildad and the rest of those who
have a quarrel against Job. In Chapter 19, Job had said:

> *Who will find a place that my words may be written down?*
> *Who will see to it that they are inscribed in the Book:*
> *with stylus of iron and with lead incised in rock forever?*
> [19:23–24]

The two books Job longed for have become one book. It is
a dialogue in which each has tried to articulate the ground
upon which he stands, and, if only by implication, the horizon under which he stands.

By the end of this speech Job seems to be clear that a complete articulation of his own position is not possible except
in the context of a complete articulation of the thought and
hence the accusations of those who oppose him.

⌒ *But if my own land cries out against me, its furrows*
31:38–40 *weeping together, and claims that I have eaten its*
produce without payment and snuffed out the life of

its owners, then may thorns grow in that place for wheat, and foul weeds for barley.

As we have seen, there is a disagreement between Job and his friends concerning the true foundations of justice. From the point of view of his friends, Job's understanding of justice has no foundation. He is, therefore, an unjust man. Job understands their position. He has no proof with regard to the ultimate value of the purely human perspective concerning the just and the unjust. Such things must still be open. Verses 38–40, Job's last words, are a counterpart to Bildad's last speech at the end of Chapter 25. They state the parameters within which mutual existence is possible.

It is understandable that the friends should proclaim Job unjust; and, indeed, perhaps it would be wrong of them not to do so. But if their understanding of the world and man's place in it should lead them so to misinterpret any definite act of Job's as to unfairly accuse him of some specific act of injustice, then, regardless of how that complaint may have been voiced, there can no longer be any grounds for mutual respect.

❧ *The words of Job are* tam.
31:40

The word תָּם (tam), which for the sake of unity I have consistently rendered as *simple* throughout the whole of the translation, must now be faced in all its complexity. First, it must be pointed out that the *tam* is of critical importance for nearly every voice heard in the Book of Job. In that sense, at least, it binds the proem (Chapters 1 and 2) to the rest of the book. For each speaker it is a virtue, if not the highest virtue. This remains true no matter how much they may disagree about other matters. Even Job's wife knows that the central issue is his *tam*. Only the Satan, Zophar, and the Voice of the tempest never mention it.

God:

> *He was a* tam *and straightforward man, a* GOD-*fearing man who turned away from evil.* [1:1; compare also 1:8 and 2:3]

Job's wife:

> *And his wife said to him, "You are still holding tight to your* tam*."* [2:9]

Eliphaz:

> *But may not that dread itself be your surety and your hope, the* tam *of your ways? Think back now, who being innocent was ever lost?* [4:6–7]

Bildad:

> *But surely God will neither have contempt for a* tam *man nor strengthen the hand of the evildoer.* [8:20]

Job:

> *Even till I perish, I shall not turn my* tam *from me.* [27:5]

Elihu:

> *One who has* tam *knowledge is among you.* [36:4]

Although each praises the *tam* in his own way, it is not clear that they would totally agree on which things are *tam* and which are not.

Even the beginnings of the word are somewhat unclear. Its most rudimentary meaning seems to be *finished*:

> *On the tops of the pillars was lily-work. Thus the work of the pillars was* tam. [I Kings 7:22]

However, the word "finished" has a certain duality to it. A new car, just off the assembly line, is said to be "finished"; but after a bad wreck, it can also be said to be "finished." This antithesis is felt more strongly in Hebrew than in English because the English word "finish" is felt to mean the end of a process in either case, no matter whether that process leads to excellence or to destruction. The word *tam*, on the other hand does not quite contain the notion of process to hold it together.

> *When that year was* tam, *they came to him the following year, and said to him, "We cannot hide from my lord that our money is* tam; *and the herds of cattle are my lord's. There is nothing left in the sight of my lord but our bodies and our lands."* [Gen. 47:18]

From there the word acquires that special meaning which implies a kind of excellence. Think of the word "finish" as it is applied to fine furniture:

> *Next he overlaid the whole house with gold, in order that the whole house might be* tam; *even the whole altar that belonged to the inner sanctuary he overlaid with gold.* [I Kings 6:22]

In that sense, it came to be used of a "perfect" lamb, one that was worthy of being offered in sacrifice:

> *Your lamb shall be* tam, *a year-old male; you may take it from the sheep or from the goats.* [Ex. 12:5]

In his final song, David sings:

> *The God who has girded me with strength has set free my path to be* tam [II Sam. 22:33],

as if men were in fetters which prevent them from being *tam*; as though *tam* were somehow man's natural state.

This man, the man who is *tam*, is neither the man of the city, nor the man of the field, but the man living in tents:

> *When the boys grew up, Esau was a skillful hunter, a man of the field; while Jacob was a* tam *man, living in tents.* [Gen. 25:27]

Tam can also mean *innocent*—either in the sense of having committed a crime while being unaware of certain critical facts, as, for example:

> *But a certain man drew his bow and in his* tam *struck the king of Israel* [I Kings 22:34],

or because one is not capable of suspicion:

> *Did he not himself say to me, "She is my sister"? And she herself said, "He is my brother." I did this in the* tam *of my heart and the innocence of my hands." Then God said to him in the dream, "Yes, I know that you did this in the* tam *of your heart; furthermore it was I who kept you from sinning against me. Therefore, I did not let you touch her."* [Gen. 20:5–6]

Tam is also used to describe the individual virtue of an individual man, apart from any excellence as a founder or leader:

> *These are the descendants of Noah. Noah was a righteous man,* tam *in his generation; Noah walked with God.* [Gen. 6:9]

> *When Abram was ninety-nine years old, the* LORD *appeared to Abram, and said to him, "I am God Almighty; stroll before me, and be* tam." [Gen. 17:1]

In answer to Bildad's statement that

> *surely God will neither have contempt for a* tam *man nor strengthen the hand of the evildoer* [8:20]

Job replies:

> *I am* tam *but he will show me twisted. I am* tam *but I no longer care and have only contempt for my life.... Therefore I say that,* tam *or guilty, he destroys all.* [9:20–22]

For Job, the *twisted* (עקש, 'aqash) emerges as the prime opposite of the *tam*. This is the only time *'aqash* occurs in the text; it seems to be a more forceful substitute for the term עָוֹן, *bent*, the word we have been translating as *perverse*:

> *Whoever walks in* tam *walks securely, but whoever follows twisted (*'aqash*) ways will be found out.* [Prov. 10:9]

Discussion of Chapter Thirty-Two

At the beginning of this chapter we are introduced to a new character, Elihu the son of Barachel the Buzite, of the house of Ram. There is something mysterious about the sudden appearance of this man, and the mystery will only increase as we read on. We do not know when he arrived or how long he had been listening. Nor do we know how much he knows of Job and of his concerns. As we shall see, there are too many strange and intriguing internal problems to account for them by merely assuming, as some do, that the passage was added as a whole without much regard for the greater context.

There is even something dark and confusing about his genealogy, conjecturally represented in the chart on the facing page. Although the name Barachel is otherwise unfamiliar, in light of the other cases the reader is naturally led to assume that Elihu is a descendant of Ram the son of Hezron, the eighth-generation progenitor of King David. This would make him a part of, or at least close to, the royal line and perhaps even a long-awaited descendent of David himself. On the other hand he is said to be a Buzite, a descendant of Buz the younger brother of Uz. That would make him a cousin to Job; but whether he is a first cousin or a tenth cousin we do not know because we are never told when all these events occurred. Elihu either is or is not part of the royal line, and each reader must decide.

〰 *Elihu ... was angry at Job, fuming because he con-*
32:2 *sidered himself more just than God.*

At first we are a bit uneasy because the text does not make clear who the antecedent of the word "he" is. Is it Job? or is it Elihu himself? This feeling is enhanced by the fact that the

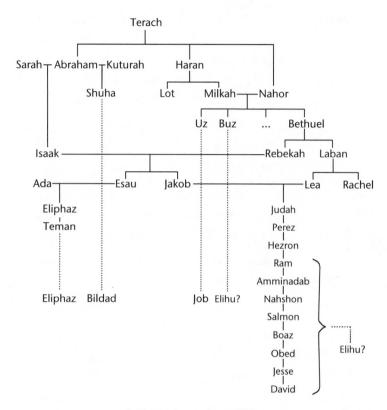

Conjectural genealogy of Elihu

word used for "fuming" (אף) is commonly, though not exclu-
sively, used of God.

∽ *I am but young in years, and you are most venerable;*
32:6–7 *and so I shrank back and was in awe to declare my*
thoughts in front of you. I said to myself "Let the genera-
tions speak, and the fullness of years proclaim wisdom."

Our suspicions soon begin to melt. One cannot help but be
moved initially by this young man. He seems respectful and
mild, but he also seems to speak with an air of understanding
and authority. Several times he speaks of the deference he is
wont to pay to his elders and the awe (ירא) he feels in rising

to speak among them. Nonetheless, he feels strongly that he must speak out. When he begins to speak, he presents himself as a patient young man who is willing to listen to others and who implies that Job's arguments deserved to be heard before they can be answered.

~
32:13   *Beware of saying we have found wisdom; God will defeat him, not man.*

The verse, Elihu's first reprimand to Job's friends, is critical in our attempt to understand Elihu and who he is; but the grammar is ambiguous. Greenberg translates:

> *I fear that you will say, "we have found the wise course; God will defeat him, not man."*

In contrast, the International Standard Version reads:

> *So that you cannot claim, "We have found wisdom!"; let God do the rebuking, not man.*

The two differ in a critical respect. Since Hebrew does not employ quotation marks, it is uncertain whether the phrases "We have found wisdom" and "God will defeat him" belong to the same voice, or if Elihu is speaking the second phrase in his own voice.

It is difficult, if not impossible, to know which alternative the poet intended—or if what was intended is the very ambiguity itself. The first reading would imply that the others wrongfully claim to have found a certain wisdom, and that their wisdom consists of the knowledge that "God will defeat him, not man." Elihu would then be accusing the other three of believing that no answer to Job or his questions is available within the realm of human understanding—which would imply that the remainder of Elihu's speech will be that purely human attempt to answer Job.

On the second reading, Elihu would be accusing the friends of believing that they have found a certain wisdom with which they can defeat Job; whereas in fact only God can defeat him, not man. If this is how the verse is to be understood, we can only take Elihu to be asserting that the remainder of his speech will carry more than human authority. In fact, in verse 12 of the next chapter Elihu will go so far as to say: "I will answer you, for God is greater than any mortal."

As we began to see in verse 9, Elihu, despite his piety, resembles Job in not completely sharing the horizon of the Fathers.

> *It is not the great who are wise, nor is it the elders who understand judgment.* [32:9]

As a whole, Elihu's speech seems to imply that for him, too, an older world has been shattered; but as yet we do not know the cause.

Discussion of Chapter Thirty-Three

Elihu challenges Job by saying:

∽ *Answer me, if you can. Lay your case out before me*
33:5–6   *and take your stand. Here I am, just as you wished,*
standing in for God.

It is clear that this is a critical passage in our attempt to understand who Elihu is, or at least who he claims to be and perhaps even believes himself to be. It is also a very difficult passage to interpret.

Translators vastly disagree about verse 6, *Here I am, just as you wished, standing in for God* (הֶן־אֲנִי כְפִיךָ לָאֵל, hen 'ani kefikha le'el). Greenberg translates: "You and I are the same before God." Alter: "Why, I am like you to God." RSV translates: "Behold, I am towards God as you are." KJV: "Behold, I am according to thy wish in God's stead."

The problem lies in the meaning of the word כְפִיךָ (kefikha). It comes from the root פה, meaning *mouth*. The initial כ (sounded *ke*) primarily means *like* or *as*, but its effect can vary greatly in individual cases. For example, אֲשֶׁר (asher) means *which* or *that*; but כַּאֲשֶׁר (ka'asher) means *when*. The final ךָ (sounded *kha*) ending is a second personal ending. When attached to verbs or prepositions it is objective; when attached to nouns it is possessive. The problem is what they mean when strung together. The word כְפִי usually means something like *according to*, as in these examples:

*Each morning let each man gather **according to** his eating.* [Ex. 16:21]

*...woven work **like/after the fashion of** a coat of mail.* [Ex. 28:32]

In accordance with *his years let him repay.* [Lev. 25:53]

Each man **according to** *his work.* [Num. 7:5]

Each man **according to** *his share.* [Num. 35:8]

These are the horns which scattered Judah, **so that** *no man could lift his head.* [Zech. 2:4]

Therefore I also have made you contemptible and base before all the people **inasmuch as** (כְּפִי אֲשֶׁר) *you have not kept my ways.* [Mal. 2:9]

And these are the number of the bands of the armed troops who came to David in Hebron to turn the kingdom of Saul over to him **according to** *the word of the Lord.* [I Chron. 12:23]

Each man **according to** *his work.* [II Chron. 31:2]

As we can see, the expression never means *the same as.* The closest it ever comes to having that meaning is in Ex. 28:32, the second of the examples given above; but even there, one thing (a coat of mail) only provides a pattern for a totally different kind of thing (woven work). In all other appearances in Tanakh it means *in proportion to* or *according to.* Unfortunately, there is only one other instance in which the object is a thinking, speaking being. That instance is in I Chron. 12:23, the penultimate of the examples just given; and there the expression clearly means *according to his word.*

The next item to look at is the first ל in לָאֵל. In general, it is equivalent to the English word *to.* Strictly speaking, Hebrew has no independent word for *become.* Thus הָיִיתִי מֶלֶךְ means *I was king*; but הָיִיתִי לְמֶלֶךְ means *I was to king* or, more simply, *I became king.*

The first words of the verse הֶן־אֲנִי, usually collapsed into one word, הִנֶּנִי, mean *here am I.* When put together with the ל, one finds expressions such as הִנֶּנוּ לַעֲבָדִים, *we have become slaves to you* (Gen. 50:18). Thus, Elihu's expression הֶן־אֲנִי כְּפִיךָ לָאֵל might be understood to carry the echo of a far stronger declaration: "I am become God."

For Elihu, Job is right about one thing, at least: the anguished perplexities that arise within the sphere of human cognition can find for themselves no solution from within the borders of that sphere. For him too, there is a great world beyond the human realm which is full of terror. Elihu has already rejected Bildad's wisdom of the Fathers:

> It is not the great who are wise, nor is it the elders who understand judgment. [32:9]

And he has seen the inadequacy of the human horizon:

> Now he has set out no words against me; and I shall not reply using your reasonings, for they have been shattered and can no longer reply. All meaning has left them. [32:14–15]

At the heart of Elihu's understanding of man is the notion that Job's request cannot be fulfilled. Man has not the stamina to face what lies beyond his own horizons. Instead, Elihu offers himself as one who, knowing of the terrors that lie beyond the human sphere, can listen to Job's case from within the human sphere. Job cannot go beyond the human, but neither is there any need to go beyond it if Elihu is standing in for God.

~ 33:8–11   *Oh, you have spoken it into my ear, and I still hear the sound of each word. "I am pure, free of transgression." "I am clean." "There is no perversion about me." "He finds ways to oppose me," and "He thinks of me as his enemy." "He puts my feet in the stocks." "He scrutinizes my every wandering."*

Surprisingly, Elihu suddenly turns on Job. There is something curious about these verses. Elihu insists that Job had spoken directly to him; yet there is little textual indication that Job was even aware of Elihu's existence. We are not told when Elihu arrived, so we do not know whether he had been there from the beginning or not. Elihu seems to know the gist of what Job has been saying; yet his quotations are never quite exact.

⮑   *Why do you vie with him? He is not obliged to answer*
33:13–14   *on every count. Yet God speaks once, even twice, but*
          none take note.

It might be wise to remind ourselves of how the poet has used the word שָׁמַר, which we have translated *to take note of* up to this point. In general, to take note of a person or thing is to allow it to become part of one's world; hence, *not* to take note of a person or thing is *not* to allow it to become part of one's world. For example:

> *The eye that sees me takes no note of me; your eye is upon me, and I am not.* [7:8]

⮑   *It may be in a dream, or in a vision of the night,*
33:15–18   *when heavy sleep falls upon mortals as they slum-*
          ber in their beds. He unveils the ears of mortals and
          places his seal upon their conduct to turn a human
          away from action and conceal pride from the hero.
          He will bring his soul back from the Pit, and his life
          from perishing by the sword.

At this point, Elihu is trying to address the feeling Job had expressed earlier:

> *When I said that my bed will show me compassion and my couch bear my complaint, you frightened me with dreams and terrified me with visions; and I preferred strangulation and death to my own substance.* [7:13–15]

Man, for Elihu, has only one contact with the realm beyond man. That contact is sleep. In sleep we can see, and yet not take note. In sleep we can allow ourselves to perceive all that we would keep distant from our daily lives. Man, for Elihu, has only vague intimations of the frightful pit that lies beyond the realm of human ken. Irrational fear is God's signpost, meant not to punish but to warn. It is our only way of knowing that our own conceit has brought us to the edge of the pit we do not see. Job has already been where he wishes to go in the only way in which he can, and he has seen for himself that it is no place for waking man.

But for Job, the land of dreams has been so contorted by civil needs—particularly his need of the friendship of his accusers—that the compassionate has become the terrifying. Job's three friends, and even civil society as a whole, consider Job to be an outcast. His suffering is so great that it would terrify them to suspect that such suffering was not caused by some deep guilt.

Job's frightening dreams come from his need to be part of the civilization which has condemned him. But to Elihu, Job is judging in terms of his own world things that can only be judged fairly in terms of a world into which Job can never enter.

~ 33:19   *He is tried by pain in his bed, and his bones ceaselessly twist in strife.*

Elihu is describing man's condition, which Job knows only too well:

> *When I said that my bed will show me compassion and my couch bear my complaint, you frightened me with dreams and terrified me with visions; and I preferred strangulation and death to my own substance.* [7:13–15]

~ 33:20   *His life renders his bread loathsome, and his soul takes no delight in fine food.*

Job anticipated this verse in Elihu's speech when he said:

> *They are like a contagion in my daily bread.* [6:7]

〜 *His flesh is devoured, no longer to be seen, and his*
33:21 *bones are ground away and disappear.*

Job knows this as well:

> *By night my bones are whittled away, and the gnawing
> never ceases.* [30:17]

And yet, for Job, the world is more complicated; feelings of
guilt do not of themselves imply guilt:

> *Though I am just, my own mouth would condemn me.* [9:20]

〜 *His soul draws near to the muck and his life is*
33:22 *[attracted] to [all that] brings death.*

With this speech, Elihu concludes this part of his argument. His speech as a whole seems to be grounded upon his
conviction that man must be kept from peering beyond his
own horizon. The human fear of what is beyond the human
is a divine gift. The fear of death is a divine rectification of
the fascination that the human soul feels for death. So much
Elihu says, but he does not elaborate. However, in what may
be the final crux of his tenets, Elihu goes on to say:

〜 *If there only were a messenger, an interpreter—one in*
33:23 *a thousand, to tell man what is right for him.*

The word here translated as *messenger* is מַלְאָךְ (malakh).
Malakh often implies a divine messenger, and it is the normal
word used for an angel. The next word, מֵלִיץ (melitz), can
mean *an interpreter*, in the simple sense of one who stands
between two people who speak two different languages:

*They did not know that Joseph understood them, since he
spoke with them through an interpreter.* [Gen. 42:23]

An interpreter's function is to make the thoughts of each
person intelligible to the other; thus an interpreter must feel
at home under both horizons, and to that extent he must
live beyond either one of them taken singly. Job had already
sought a go-between who could make his case intelligible:

*Will no one argue for a hero before God as a human should
do for a friend?* [16:21]

∼   *He would have mercy on him and say: "Redeem him
33:24   from descending into the muck, for I have found his
           ransom."*

For Elihu, the human voice cannot make itself heard in
the highest court. Job's desired advocate, his friend, cannot
be merely a man like himself. He must be an interpreter, one
who can stand between God and man. Again Elihu seems to
claim or to imply that he himself is that one.

Man does not own the surface world. It is not his to inquire
into and to enlarge its borders. If the surface world is not
ransomed by one who is richer than man, it will all turn itself
into muck.

∼   *Let his flesh become brighter than youth, and let him
33:25–26   return to his springtime days. Let him but supplicate
           unto God and he shall be accepted and see his face
           with shouts of joy, for he shall return to mortal man
           his sense of righteousness.*

This interpreter would conquer all the frightful things
that live in the world beyond the world of man. The terrible
face of God would now become the home of joyous man.

Job would stand where he could not stand before and laugh where there was only horror, because the horror would have been banished.

> ↪ *Let him only stand squarely in front of mortals and*
> 33:27–28 *say I have sinned; I have dealt perversely with what was right, and my accounts have not been settled. Thus he shall redeem his soul from passing into the muck; and his life shall see in the light.*

Job, for his part, has only to confess to a sin which, by its nature, he does not and cannot know that he has committed. Primarily, as Elihu points out, this means accepting the notion of perversion as fundamental to human existence. Job's old hopes, that the human perspective has a legitimate place in any ultimate account of things, will still "be all heaped together in the muck," but his soul will be redeemed and pass beyond.

> ↪ *Pay heed, Job, and hear me; be silent now and I will*
> 33:31–33 *speak. If you have the words, respond to me. Well, speak! For I wish to justify you. But, if you have nothing, then listen to me. Be silent and I will teach you wisdom.*

In a strange way, we have returned to the end of Chapter 26, where we left Bildad; and Job still has no answer but remains silent.

Discussion of Chapter Thirty-Four

◞   *Then Elihu answered and said: Hear my words, ye*
34:1–2 *wise men; give ear to me, all you who know...*

In Chapter 34 Elihu speaks not to Job, but to those whom
he addresses as "ye wise men" at one point or as "ye men
of heart" later in the text. They, it is to be understood, are
the wisest men of the city. Before them he makes a number
of accusations which are, as we shall see, intended to define
the boundaries of their understanding of justice and to prove
Job's guilt within those boundaries.

◞   *Now Job has said: "I am just" and "...that God who*
34:5–6 *has thrown aside the whole of my case"; "I declare*
       false the judgment made against me" and "The arrow
       was mortal, though I was without transgression."

Elihu's first accusation is that Job had said "I am just."
While it is indeed true that Job has said those words, Elihu
has ignored their context:

> *I would now answer him, choosing my words against him*
> *with care, but even though I am in the right, still I cannot*
> *do it. Yet I must plead for what seems to me just.* [9:14–15]

> *Though I am just, my own mouth would condemn me.* [9:20]

> *Well, if I have been guilty, the grief is mine; but even when*
> *I am innocent I have been so sated with reproach that no*
> *feeling of honor is left in me and I see only my own feeble-*
> *ness.* [10:15]

> *But now I have become a joke to my friends, one who would*
> *"call on God and have him answer"; simple and just, yet still*
> *a joke!* [12:4]

I have laid out my case and I know I shall be vindicated.
[13:18]

Elihu's next accusation is that Job said, "...that God who has thrown aside the whole of my case" and "I declare false the case made against me."

While there clearly is adequate substantiation for these accusations, they do not tell the whole tale. Job's main argument is much less personal than would appear from Elihu's account. For Job, it is more a matter of the position of human thought as such—as a number of passages attest:

If trial be by strength, he is the mighty one; and if by court of law, who will plead my case? [9:19]

He is not a man as I am, that I can answer him, that we can come together under judgment. [9:32]

I have laid out my case and I know I shall be vindicated. [13:18]

Can you open your eyes even to one such as that, and yet come along with him to proceedings raised against you? [14:3]

He has encircled me with his net. I scream "Violence" but I get no answer. I cry out, but there is no place of judgment. [19:7]

I would lay out my case before him, and fill my mouth with arguments. I would know with what words he would answer me! I want to understand what he would have to say to me. Would he strive against me with his great power? No, surely he would place his confidence in me. There an upright man can reason with him, and there would I be released from my judge forever. [23:4–7]

By the life of that God who has merely thrown aside the whole of my case, the Almighty has embittered my soul! [27:2]

Elihu next accuses Job of having claimed to be "without transgression." In fact what Job said was:

> *Why can you not pardon my transgressions or bear my per-*
> *versions? For now I shall lie down in the dust. You will seek*
> *for me, but I am not.* [7:21]
>
> *Let me know my transgression and my vices.* [13:23]
>
> *My transgression would be sealed up in a pouch and you*
> *would plaster over my perversions.* [14:17]
>
> *Would I have covered over my transgressions like [some]*
> *human or concealed perversion in my bosom through terror*
> *of the great multitude?* [31:33]

⁓
34:7–9   *What hero is there like unto Job who drinks up mock-*
         ery as if it were water, joins company with those who
         deal in wickedness, and walks with men of evil? For
         he has said: "It is of no use to a hero that he be in
         GOD's favor."

The significance of the word *drinks*, as it has been used
from the time Job's friends appear till the end of Elihu's
speech, is markedly different from the connotations of the
word *tasting* that we discussed in Chapter 12.

The complete list of its appearances is:

> *Oh, would that my indignation could truly be weighed, my*
> *calamities all laid out together on the pan of a scale! Then*
> *would it raise up even the sands of the seas. And thus I speak*
> *without care, for the arrows of the Almighty are upon me,*
> *and my spirit drinks in their venom.* [6:2–4]
>
> *...what of man—that abhorred and corrupted one—who*
> *drinks up injustice like water!* [15:16]
>
> *Let his eyes see his own ruin and let him drink of the*
> *Almighty's cruet of fury.* [21:20]
>
> *What hero is there like unto Job who drinks up mockery as*
> *if it were water?* [34:7]

In this section of the book, *drinking* implies a taking into
oneself, even greedily, the uglinesses of the outside world.

For Job it is the first step in coming to terms with them. But for Eliphaz and for Elihu it is only the final step in succumbing to them.

> *Who laid charge upon him to care for the earth?*
> 34:13–15 *Or who placed upon him the whole of this fruitful ground? If he cared to, he could gather his spirit and his breath back into himself. Then all flesh would perish and mankind would return to dust.*

Job's view of man, Elihu argues, presupposes an independent world having its own laws and ordinances of which God is the chief executor, and to which he therefore has certain duties and obligations. But there is no such world. The whole structure of the world is an expression of his spirit. For man to demand justice from God would be as if an author had found himself drawn into court by a character in one of his own novels. With respect to God, man has no being apart from the role assigned to him by the hand of God.

> *Shall he that hates judgment bind up?*
> 34:17

One can best see what Elihu means with these words by considering other passages in which "bind up" (root חבשׁ) has been used:

> *For he causes pain, but he **binds up**; he wounds, but his hands heal.* [5:18]

> *He **binds up** the flowing rivers and the hidden things come to light.* [28:11]

Elihu purposely uses a word that can have either a gentle meaning, as in the first of the above examples, or a violent one, as in the second.

〰 *Would you condemn the Magnificent Just One, he*
34:17–19 *who can say to a king, "You are worthless," or to the*
nobles, "You are guilty men"? Who shows no favor to
any liege, or recognizes the prince above the pauper,
since they are the works of his hand, every one?

With this verse Elihu reminds his hearers of what he understands to be the foundation of political life. Job, he argues,
does ill to base his understanding of justice purely on the
human perspective. This is true for two reasons. First, true
justice requires the notion of equality before the law; but that
equality only becomes visible when all men are seen as being
equally derivative from that which is beyond man. Men are
equal because they are all equally the work of the hand of
God, and God is equally above all. Further, this implies a
mutual recognition of the limitations of the human sphere
which apply to all men as such. For Elihu, both the judge and
the standard of judgment must come from beyond. Equality
before the law is compatible with structured political life
only if that equality has a pre-political foundation. But that
foundation rests upon a world closed to man.

〰 *They can die in a moment; the people tremble at mid-*
34:20–23 *night, and pass on. The mighty are turned aside, but*
by no [human] hand, for his eyes are upon the ways of
man, and he watches his every step. There is no dark-
ness and there is no Shadow of Death for the worker
of wickedness to hide in, nor has he ever yet accorded
it to man that he go with God into judgment.

Here, it seems evident, Elihu is trying to address himself to
what Job sees as the most serious of his charges, which are:

Am I the sea or some monster that you set watch over me?
[7:12]

Who can move you to hide me in the Pit and conceal me till your anger passes? Set me a fixed limit and remember me. [14:13]

Then no longer would you keep track of my every step and scrutinize my sin. [14:16]

Elihu praises God precisely where Job had questioned. If divine justice were to model itself after human justice, as Job implies, it would leave itself open to all the wrangling, loopholes, and ambiguities that mark human justice. Its whole force resides in its unknown, and hence unquestionable, character.

~   *He shatters the magnificent, no knowing how many,*
34:24–29 *and sets others up in their place. Surely he can recognize their deeds. Everything turns to night, and they are crushed. He slaps them down along with the guilty in full view of all because they turned away from him and do not comprehend his ways of bringing the cries of the poor unto himself; for he hears the cry of the needy. But when he is silent, who can condemn? If he should hide his face, who can even take note of him, be it a nation or be it a single human?*

Elihu argues that human justice is inadequate to deal with human misdoing because it cannot reveal to men the cosmic significance of their actions. It can at best show that one or more other human beings object to a certain kind of behavior. If they institute a law, it can only be because they have the power to do so—which would, of course ultimately imply nothing more than the rule of the strongest. If an act is to be seen as sinful it must be seen as violating an order beyond the sphere of merely human concern. Only in that way can it become clear that the weak, as weak, are heard.

Discussion of Chapter Thirty-Five

〜   *I will answer your words, and your friends along*
35:4–8 *with you. Look up into the heavens and see. Only*
        take note of the nebula, how high above you it is. If
        you have sinned, how could you perturb it; and even
        if you multiply your transgressions, how could you
        affect it? Or if you were righteous, what would you
        add to it? What could it gain from your hand? Your
        evils fall upon men like yourself, and your righteous-
        ness is for sons of man.

For Elihu, the cosmos, as distinguished from God, is wholly
indifferent to the fate of man and to human concerns. The
pull that Job felt into a realm larger than the human realm
is dangerously misdirected. In flirting with the land of the
jackal (30:29), Job is allowing himself to become enmeshed
in a world in which the word "justice" is a mute sound sym-
bolizing nothing. Job had said:

> *Does it seem good to you that you oppress, that you have*
> *contempt for the toil of your own hand, but radiate upon*
> *the counsel of the guilty? Do you have eyes of flesh?* [10:3–4]

But he cannot know what oppression is:

〜   *Under great oppression they cry out; they scream to*
35:9–11 *be saved from mighty arms; but none say, "Where*
         is God my maker, the one who makes songs in the
         night; who teaches us more than the beasts of the
         earth and makes us wiser than the birds of the sky?"

Those who wander beyond the human realm cannot marvel at the night songs of nature, or at man's preeminence among the creatures to be found there. To man it is a frightful place. He is crushed and can see nothing; he merely "cries out" and "screams to be saved." But for Elihu, to be attracted beyond the human sphere of understanding—for whatever reason—is to act with arrogance. This is what he had in mind when he said:

> *May Job's trials know no limit, because his answers are no different from those of the men of wickedness. He adds sin upon transgression, slaps us in the face, and continually speaks against God.* [34:36–37]

For Elihu, the world beyond the world of human concern is a world devoid of the concept of justice. There is nothing in terms of which man can speak so that God can listen. Among the Jackals, man is left in fear and total uncertainty.

Discussion of Chapter Thirty-Six

〰️   *But wait a bit for me, and I will show you. There is still*
36:2–3   *another word to be said for God.*

Elihu speaks here as if what he is about to say is but an
additional thought consequent to what he had said before.
What he goes on to say is, in fact, both new and also a bit
shocking. But it must be understood properly:

〰️   *As for kings about to ascend the throne, he seats them*
36:7   *forever and they are exalted.*

Taken in and by itself, this verse would seem to affirm the
doctrine we now call the Divine Right of Kings. However
much the statement may be qualified in the verses that are to
follow, and no matter how critical those qualifications turn
out to be, the verse must be faced in itself.

For Elihu, man's home is the *only* proper home for man.
Nothing in the visible universe beyond the realm of man can
support the human, that is to say, the political, sphere. In that
sense, there can be no such thing as Natural Right, nor can
there be any prepolitical Self-Evident Truths upon which the
political regime is to be founded, and therefore questioned.

Still speaking of kings, he states:

〰️   *If they can hear and obey, they will complete their*
36:11–12 *days in prosperity and their years in delight. But if*
              they cannot hear, they will perish by the sword and
              pass on without ever knowing why.

Monarchy, then, is limited not by the inalienable rights of man, but by divine providence. Even foreign tyrants who intend no good become tools in the unseen hands of God.

> And the LORD *sent against him bands of the Chaldees, and bands of the Syrians, and bands of the Moabites, and bands of the children of Ammon, and sent them against Judah to destroy it, according to the word of the* LORD, *which he spake by his servants the prophets.* [II Kings 24:2]

Having prefaced his remarks in this way, Elihu, because of his understanding of divine providence, is forced to conclude that Job's own behavior is the true source of all his pain. In light of this he turns back to Job and, among other things, he declares:

∼   *Beware, do not turn to wickedness, for that is what*
36:21 *you have chosen rather than poverty.*

Job, like a guilty man—or so Elihu believes—has strayed beyond the realm of human society. Job has, in that sense, become an outlaw among other outlaws. What tempted him to stray may be of little importance; once having passed the civil borders, he must find himself to be as one of the pariahs. He may even have been fully determined to find justice and order; but he will find nothing of either justice or order there. His cries will go unheard, and nothing there will remind him of justice. For Elihu, no son of Adam can remain just in a world in which there is no foundation for the concept of justice.

Therefore, insofar as the human horizons point beyond themselves, they point not to nature and its laws, but to God and his guiding providence. It is not a time for inquiry, but a time for song and exaltation:

∽   *Remember then to exalt his works of which mortals*
36:24–25 *sing. All humans have beheld him. Mortals have*
         looked upon him from afar.

Elihu continues:

∽   *Behold, God is exalted but we cannot know. The*
36:26–28 *number of his years cannot be unearthed. He draws*
         up droplets of water, and the moisture refines itself
         into his mist that flows together into the nebula and
         trickles back down upon mankind.

According to Elihu, the visible universe beyond man is
directed by the hand of God solely towards the good of man
and his concerns:

∽   *Who can comprehend the expanse of the clouds, the*
36:29–33 *roarings under his canopy? He spreads out his light*
         over it, and covers over the roots of the sea; for with
         them he pronounces judgment upon the nations and
         provides food in abundance. He covers over the light-
         ning in his hand and commands it to strike at its
         mark. But the roarings tell of him, amassing anger
         against injustice.

However, if Job is tempted into that world, he will be faced
only by the nebula and the constant roaring. To man, God's
labyrinthine complex of delicately interwoven ends will seem
no more than a roaring mass of anger, an incoherent nebula.
Throughout the passage Elihu speaks of the way in which
God *covers over* or hides from mankind their frightful origins as they manifest themselves in the roots of the sea, and
in the lightning that strikes. We have already seen something
of Elihu's argument that Job, by his demand to question,

threatens to break through the barrier that God has placed between man and his own destruction:

> *He unveils the ears of mortals and places his seal upon their conduct to turn a human away from action and conceal [cover over] pride from the hero. He will bring his soul back from the Pit, and his life from perishing by the sword.* [33:16–18]

Job, too, at one time had such thoughts:

> *I was not destroyed by the darkness only because he had concealed [covered over] its thick murk from me.* [23:17]

Even now it is a struggle for Job, but for him the need to see for oneself, with one's own human eyes, keeps reasserting itself at each turn.

Discussion of Chapter Thirty-Seven

〜 *At this too, my heart trembles and leaps from its*
37:1–2 *place. Listen, listen well to the rage in his voice and*
the groaning that comes up out of his mouth.

Rage (רֹגֶז, rogez) is a passion that Job has seen in God, in
the earth, and in man:

> *There the guilty cast off their **rage** and there rest those whose*
> *power is spent.* [3:17]

> *I was not at ease, I was not quiet, I had no rest, but **rage***
> *came.* [3:26]

> *...who can cause the earth to reel from its place till its pillars*
> ***rage**.* [9:6]

> *Oh, there is peace enough in the tents of robbers and security*
> *for those who **enrage** God, which God himself has placed in*
> *their hand.* [12:6]

> *A human is born of woman, short-lived and full of **rage**.*
> [14:1]

With his warning words, "Listen, listen well to the rage,"
Elihu is trying to give Job a picture in sound of what he will
see if he wanders off into the land of the jackal, crossing over
beyond the world of man with human eyes and human ears.
Should that happen, the divine would appear as bestial.

〜 *Straight down it comes, under the whole of heaven.*
37:3–4 *His light goes out to the ends of the earth, and then, a*
roaring voice. He thunders with the voice of his majes-
tic pride, and when they are heard he does not hold
them back.

Most translate *his lightning*, rather than *his light*; and, clearly enough, that is what Elihu means. However, the word he uses is the simple everyday word for light, which is indeed the way the word first hits the ear. This way of speech gives one a much better sense of Elihu's feeling that the fearful lies close behind the mundane. What can be more peaceful, more of an airy nothing than *light*? And yet in a moment it can become a roaring lion.

The root of the word I have translated *majestic pride* is גאה, which denotes something wholly indifferent to human concerns, good or bad. It is either superhuman or subhuman—if indeed that distinction can still be said to hold.

> *Can papyrus flourish [show its* **majestic pride***] where there is no marsh?* [8:11]

> *You must feel the* **majestic pride** *of a lion in hunting me.* [10:16]

> *There they cry out, but he gives no answer to the* **majestic pride** *of evil men.* [35:12]

> *Here your* **majestically proud** *waves must come to rest.* [38:11]

> *Come, deck yourself out in* **majestic pride** *and dignity.* [40:10]

∿
37:7–9
He has sealed up the hand of every human so that each mortal of his making may know that a beast goes in for shelter and settles down into its lair when the tempest comes out of its chamber, cold from its scattering-place.

Here Elihu likens the way in which man has been sealed up within the sphere of human understanding to a beast settled down in its den for the long winter, when the cold wind blows and nature is inhospitable. The cave is man's only shelter from a world which, no matter what it may be in itself, is only a cold and frightful chaos to man.

   On a topsy-turvy course he steers them to accomplish
37:12–13 *all that he has commanded them upon the face of this fruitful ground, whether by lash or by love, so he founds it upon his land.*

If Job were to face the ways in which God accomplishes his commands and orders this fruitful orb, they would seem to him a wild course totally indifferent to its end.

   Do you know how the clouds are kept in balance, the
37:16–17 *wonders of simple knowledge? Or even how it is that your clothing keeps you warm when the land has respite from the southern wind?*

Elihu means that if even the simplest things, the things we rely on most in our daily lives (and hence the things which are most at hand within the human sphere), in fact evade human understanding—why, then, should any man expect to comprehend what is beyond that sphere?

   Can you beat the nebula into a great expanse, firm
37:18–20 *as a mirror cast like molten metal? Tell us, then: what shall we say to him? We cannot lay out our case because of the darkness. Does anything get through to him when I speak? Can a man speak when he is about to be swallowed up?*

For Elihu there is no court where a man can lay out his case and expect it to be heard and adjudicated. All of Job's daydreams regarding such a court are pointless distraction. Rather, Job should see himself as about to be swallowed up by a totally indifferent nebular world, with no possible way of knowing whether that world is directed by an all-knowing, all-caring God who listens to the prayers and takes note of the needs of man.

Elihu, representing himself as a typical man, says, "Does anything get through to him when I speak?" For Elihu, then, there is no alternative to a steadfast belief in an all-loving God, other than the senseless roar of the stormy nebula which no man can face or consider.

> *Now not a man sees the light, though it shine*
> 37:21–22 *blinding bright in the nebula, not till a passing spirit*
> *shall make them pure. Out of the north there comes*
> *a golden splendor. A frightful majesty rests upon*
> *God.*

Elihu's final belief is that one day a spirit will pass by to purify the nebula. On that day man will see that from the beginning there had always been a blinding light shining bright in the nebula, though not a man could see.

> *The Almighty—none will find him. He is ever*
> 37:23 *multiplying in might and in right, abundant in*
> *judgment, giving neither wrack nor reason.*

This last phrase, *giving neither wrack nor reason,* represents a very complicated play on words which I was not able to reproduce in English by a single word. On the one hand, the verb ענה ('anah) means *to answer*; it is the same word that occurs so often in that stock phrase, "And he answered and said..." (In fact, the very next chapter, which is only one verse away, will begin with the words, "And the Lord answered Job out of the tempest and said...") On the other hand, it can also mean *to afflict* or *to torment or torture,* or even *to corrupt.*

The Book of Ecclesiastes has some wonderful examples of what I consider to be intentional word play on ענה. Ecclesiastes 1:13 might be translated:

> *I applied my heart to seek and to search out by wisdom all that is done under heaven; it is an unhappy business that God has given to the children of man to* **give** **answer** *concerning it.*

But it might equally well be rendered:

> *I applied my heart to seek and to search out by wisdom all that is done under heaven; it is an unhappy business that God has given to the children of man to* **afflict** *themselves with.*

Again, should Ecclesiastes 10:16 read like this:

> *Bread is made for laughter, wine gladdens life, and money* **answers** *everything.*

Or like this?

> *Bread is made for laughter, wine gladdens life, and money* **corrupts** *everything.*

Being unable to find a suitable English pun, I was forced in my translation to render the Hebrew play on words with alliteration; thus "torment" and "answer" became "wrack" and "reason."

The Hebrew pun is a particularly haunting one. A pun usually has a primary meaning, one that is intended to hit the ear first; then there follows a kind of double take when the listener suddenly realizes the second possibility. The first meaning must always precede the second—sometimes by years, but usually by milliseconds. An essential part of punning humor, however, is the unspoken agreement between speaker and hearer as to which is the first meaning and which meaning carries the punch; but in the present case, one cannot tell which meaning is intended to be the first, and there is no double take. The sudden recognition, that a horizon has been shared where one was least expected, is missing; and the humor intentionally falls flat.

The pun, which was not a pun, splendidly captures the relationship between Elihu and Job. For to Elihu there can be no more comforting answer than to know that there is a loving God behind the mute raucousness of chaos; but to Job, there can be no greater torment than to have no answer.

⌒ *Thus mortals hold in awe the one whom even the wise*
37:24 *of heart have never seen.*

These are Elihu's last words, and this is the last time that אֲנָשִׁים (anoshim), the word we have translated *mortals*, will appear in the text; in particular, the Voice of the tempest will never use it. Etymologically, its root אנש (anosh) is in fact rather close to the word *mortal*, since it means *weak* or *sick*— or, when used of a wound or a disease, *incurable*. We have seen it used in that sense already:

The arrow was **mortal**, *though I was without transgression.* [34:6]

In like manner, Elihu's is the last voice in the text to use the word *awe* (ירא).

Discussion of Chapter Thirty-Eight

⁓   *And the* Lord *answered Job out of the tempest and*
38:1–3   *said: Who now is this one that makes counsel dark by*
         words without knowledge? Come, gird up your loins
         like a hero. I will question you, and you must inform
         me.

The chapter begins with a question which is clearly
intended rhetorically; and yet, unlike most rhetorical questions, the answer is by no means obvious. Is the intended
answer *Job*, or is it *Elihu*? Perhaps we are not yet in a position
to ask the question. It is also the first time the name *the* Lord
has been used since Chapter 2.

The phrase "Come, gird up..." is my all-too-poor attempt
to capture the very moving fact that the Lord uses the word
נָא (na). It is roughly equivalent to the English word *please*,
and converts a command into a plea or a request, or (as in
our case) an invitation. Needless to say it is a word the Lord
rarely uses, and each instance requires our close attention.

The Voice of the tempest seems to be reminding Job of his
own first words, urging him on yet to fulfill that high promise which was inherent in his birth. Job had said:

> *May the day of my birth be lost in oblivion and with it that*
> *night in which it was said, "A hero has been conceived."* [3:1]

Now he is being asked to gird his loins and to become that
hero. If Elihu had not been *nearly* right, there would be no
need for Job to gird his loins; and yet, if Elihu were *simply*
right, God's exhortations would have all been in vain.

⁓   *Where were you when I laid the foundations of*
38:4–6   *the earth? Speak up, if you know! Who fixed its*

measurements, if you have any understanding? Who stretched a measuring line round it and into what were its pylons fixed? Who set the cornerstone...?

The Lord begins with a great barrage of questions coming in rapid succession. They are all infinitely beyond Job, and he can only stand in wonderment. But at the same time, the questions are couched in terms such as *foundations, pylons, lines,* and *cornerstones*—words that Job can very well understand. He also learns that measurement, and hence number, was used by God in creation.

〜   *Who closed up the sea behind the double door, when*
38:8–11   *first it burst out of the womb and I clothed it in a cloud and swaddled it in mist, imposing my law upon it, and put up the bars and the double doors, and said: "To this point you may come, but no farther. Here your majestically proud waves must come to rest."*

This word, *burst* (גיח), is often used of the raging seas and of the monsters that inhabit them; also of a child as it bursts forth out of its mother's womb.

> *Daniel said, "I saw in my vision by night, and behold, the four winds of heaven were* **stirring up (bursting)** *the great sea."* [Dan. 7:2]

> *Son of man, raise a lamentation over Pharaoh king of Egypt, and say to him: "You consider yourself a lion among the nations, but you are like a monster in the seas; you* **burst** *forth in your rivers, trouble the waters with your feet, and foul their rivers."* [Ez. 32:2]

> *Though the river rage, he is unalarmed, confident that the Jordan will* **burst** *into his mouth.* [40:23]

> *Yet thou art he who* **burst** *me from the womb; thou didst keep me safe upon my mother's breasts.* [Ps. 22:9]

Writhe and **burst**, *O daughter of Zion, like a woman in tra-*
vail; for now you shall go forth from the city and dwell in
the open country; you shall go to Babylon. There you shall
be rescued, there the Lord *will redeem you from the hand*
of your enemies. [Micah 4:10]

Here, in the Book of Job, the beginning of all things is not
presented as a gentle "Let there be," or as a creation, or as
a making. Instead, by mixing the waters of birth with the
primordial waters of chaos, this passage presents God more
as a midwife, controlling the birth and letting all things
come forth in number and order. As compared to verses 4
through 7, these lines, with words like *burst, womb, clothe,*
and *swaddle,* seem to mark a shift from the arts to those ways
which are older. This movement is away from the masculine workman and his arts, which cause things to come to be
according to the will and design of the maker, through the
application of measurement to a world outside of himself,
and through the forceful fixing of pylons (38:6) into something more solid than themselves.

It is, rather, a movement to another, older, form of coming-to-be, one that brings forth measurelessly from within
itself. Thus far, the movement seems tentative and ambiguous. The Voice of the tempest presents itself as imposing its
law upon the sea, and yet it also shows itself to possess the
more feminine virtues of clothing and swaddling. It does not
speak of itself as trampling on the tier of the sea, but as finding a proper place for its proud majesty.

Another way of looking at the problem is to consider the
distinction between a creating God and a nurturing God.
Fundamental to this question is Aristotle's statement:

Of the things that are, some are by nature, and some are by
other causes. [*Physics*, 192b10]

Foremost among the "other causes" is *art*. Aristotle implies
that the discovery of nature essentially implies that no

conclusion can be drawn, from the things that are made by man and hence rely upon man, concerning things that are not man-made but have within themselves their own source of motion and rest. For Aristotle, the fact that a *painting* of a flower points to an artist outside of itself as its maker does not imply that the *flower itself* carries within any such implication.

The God we meet in the first chapter of the Book of Genesis, the artisan God, has within himself the *to be* of the object. He shapes and molds according to his plan, while the more feminine, nurturing God we meet in the Book of Job allows for the emergence of the *to be* which is in the thing itself.

〜
38:12–13
Have you yet commanded the morning, or taught the dawn to know its place, to grab hold of the corners of the earth and winnow out the wicked?

Winnowing is a strange and interesting process. There is the wheat, which one wants because it is good; and there is the chaff, which one does not want because it is not good. But there they lie, all mixed up together. One's first inclination would be to pick out the unwanted, chaff by chaff. Winnowing, though, is a very different process, and calls for another kind of spirit. In winnowing, the whole is tossed lightly in a blanket. The wind blows and carries off the chaff, or most of it; but the wheat, because it is more stable and weighty, tumbles safely back into the blanket. It falls not because it has been picked out, but merely because it is what it is in itself. The farmer rejoices with his flour though he knows that in spite of all his care, a bit of chaff may have found its way through.

The process of winnowing succeeds in separating the chaff from the wheat precisely because the character of the chaff is different from the character of the wheat. It is this difference in their own characters that causes the separation, in spite of the fact that they are both tossed with the same force and blown by the same wind. The Voice of the tempest seems to be saying that cosmic justice is of that sort.

What Job has seen in the tempest will serve as a reply to Elihu. The world beyond man, the land of the jackal, as it is in itself and apart from the human eye, may not be reducible to the nebula. The beings in it may have their own being, and hence their own striving and ambition apart from any human concern, yet they may be open to human apperception.

⁓   *It is as transformed as clay stamped by a seal, and*
38:14   *fixed as dye in a garment.*

If one looks at the way the author uses the word for *clay*, one can see that it is beginning to be used quite generally as the dead medium out of which, and into which, we come and go. In that sense, it takes on something of what we call matter.

While the imagery of clay often appears in other books of the Bible, especially in Isaiah and Jeremiah, in them man is constantly likened to the clay itself, something to be molded or fashioned; whereas according to the Voice of the tempest, man is more like the object made of clay bearing a seal or signet. The implication is that man, like the pot, but unlike the clay, has his own shape, his own *to-be*:

> *Woe to him who strives with his maker, an earthen vessel with the potter! Does the clay say to him who fashions it, "What are you making?" or "Your work has no handles"? [Isaiah 45:9]*

> *And yet,* LORD, *you are our father; we are the clay, and you our potter; we are all the work of your hand. [Isaiah 64:8]*

> *And the vessel he was making of clay was spoiled in the potter's hand, and he reworked it into another vessel, as it seemed good to the potter to do. [Jer. 18:4]*

O house of Israel, can I not do with you as this potter
has done? says the LORD. *Behold, like the clay in the*
potter's hand, so are you in my hand, O house of Israel.
[Jer. 18:6]

The single word חוֹתָם (chotam), here translated as *stamped*
by a seal, has a most interesting history, of which the reader
should be aware. Originally, it meant *to stop up*:

And this is the law of his uncleanness for a discharge: whether
his body runs with his discharge, or his body is **stopped up**
with discharge, it is uncleanness in him. [Lev. 15:3]

From there the word acquires a feeling of permanence and
safety, either by denoting a thing safe in itself, or as something guarded and therefore safely out of the way:

In the dark he tunnels his way into houses which are **sealed**
up *tight against him by day, since he does not know the*
light. [24:16]

My transgression would be **sealed up** *in a pouch and you*
would plaster over my perversions. [14:17]

Then, in its nominal form, it comes to be used for a signet or
seal placed on a letter:

So he wrote letters in Ahab's name and sealed them with his
seal, *and she sent the letters to the elders and the nobles who*
dwelt with Naboth in his city. [I Kings 21:8]

In that sense, it marks a thing's character and becomes a
kind of guarantee that an object is what it is and will continue
to be what it has become.

And you may write as you please with regard to the Jews,
in the name of the king, and **seal** *it with the king's ring; for*
an edict written in the name of the king and sealed with the
king's ring cannot be revoked. [Esther 8:8]

We have already seen the word moving in that direction in
the Book of Job:

> *He unveils the ears of men and places his* **seal** *upon their conduct, to turn a human away from action and conceal pride from the hero. He will bring his soul back from the Pit, and his life from perishing by the sword.* [33:16–18]

There are, in fact, two Hebrew words for *seal*, or *signet ring*. One of them is our word חוֹתָם. The other is טַבַּעַת (tabba'at). It comes from the biblical root טבע, which means *to dip*: the signet ring is that which is dipped into the wax to give the seal its form. This second word eventually gave rise to the post-biblical word טֶבַע (teva), the word used to translate the Greek φύσις, or *nature*. It is interesting to note that, of the two words, tradition chose the root which emphasizes the fact that the mark is impressed upon the object from the outside. The author of the Book of Job, on the other hand, chooses the one which empasizes the guaranteed character of the object itself. The suggestion is that for our poet, the word חוֹתָם is beginning to acquire the character of the Greek φύσις.

In the phrase, "fixed as dye in a garment," the poet has chosen the very forceful word יְתְיַצְּבוּ (yityatzbu). The root is יצב or וצב, which in Arabic means *to be firm* or *constant*. The grammatical form is reflexive, the only form in which it exists in Hebrew. The word occurs frequently throughout the Bible and has a very strong sense, meaning something like *to take a stand*. Alter and other, earlier, writers argue that it makes no sense for a garment to take a stand. They emend the text (rightly, I believe) to read תִּתְצַבָּע (tit'tzaba), a reflexive form from the root צבע. Within the biblical text this root occurs only once, as a noun meaning *a dyed article*.

The thought seems to be that if a white garment has been dyed red, and the dye stands firm or has been well fixed, then the garment has truly become a red garment. The red color is then as much a part of the object as any of its other essential properties; it would be wrong to think of *white* as the truth lying behind the *red*. In the same way, we are not to consider the clay as the truth lying behind the pot. The seal, or mark, or character, has transformed the clay into a pot, and a pot it now is.

> ∿   *Have you ever come upon the source of the seas, or*
> 38:16   *gone for a stroll down by the cranny in the deep?*

Job had once said:

> *Am I the sea or some monster that you set watch over me?*
> [7:12]

He is now being asked to face the source of that same sea.

With the words "Have you ever ... gone for a stroll down by the cranny in the deep?" we have tried to catch the rather gnarled concatenation here of the relaxed, even inviting character of the verb *stroll* (הִתְהַלֵּךְ, hit'haleych) and the foreboding character of the prepositional phrase which follows it. The verb is in the reflexive form, and so carries with it a sense of aimless freedom and intended joy. When it is used to describe God going for a stroll in the Garden (Gen. 3:8), one immediately senses that he has not come for the sake of checking up on Adam and Eve. It is almost as if the Voice of the tempest were trying to seduce Job into that frightful and forbidden world beyond the world of man.

The verb *stroll* can, of course, be used with great irony:

> "Oh," said the Satan to the LORD, "wandering around Earth. I just went down there to **go for a stroll**." [1:7]

> *His plans will trip him up, for his own feet will lead him into a net, and he will **stroll himself** right into the trap.* [18:8]

> *Clouds have obscured him and he can see nothing as he **strolls round** the circuit of heaven.* [22:14]

> ∿   *Have the gates of death unveiled themselves to you,*
> 38:17–18   *or have you seen the gates of the Shadow of Death?*

Have you pondered the expanse of the earth? If you know all these things, declare them!

Tradition has connected the Shadow of Death with the land of the jackal:

> *Our heart has not turned back, nor have our steps departed from thy way, that thou shouldst have broken us in the land of jackals, and covered us with the shadow of death.* [Ps. 44:18]

The land of the jackal—the world beyond man—has been in the air now for a long time. Job first saw it as a horrid haven of things unwanted, the dark and dangerous place to which Job had consigned the day of his birth with his first words:

> *Then Job opened his mouth and spurned his day. Job answered and said: May the day of my birth be lost in oblivion and with it that night in which it was said: "A hero has been conceived." May that day be a day of darkness. May God from on high not seek it out nor any brightness radiate upon it; but let darkness and the Shadow of Death redeem it...* [3:1–5]

But now Job has been invited just to drop in for a visit. When he does, that day will be there waiting for him; and in it he will learn much about birth and conception. And as we know from the first words that came out of the tempest, his main task will be to become that hero who had been conceived so long ago. Death and the fear of death are central to the theme of the book, and, as we shall see, the remainder of Job's education is nothing more than a stroll down by its gates.

Perhaps nothing that exists can be so transformed or disfigured and contorted as the face of Death, as it steps through the curtain drawn between the world of man and the world of nature. The commonplace becomes the terrifying, and it is not clear that either is the truth behind the other. Which is the face and which the mask?

❧   *Which is the road to the dwelling of light? And which*
38:19–21 *is the place of darkness, that you may take it to its borders and know the way to its home? You know, for even then you were born; and the number of your days is great!*

Job must learn to peer beyond the borders of the light and into the place of darkness. The monsters of the dark cannot be kept out by hiding in a cave as Elihu had suggested. They must be faced and gently escorted home by one who knows the way.

Some take the verse "You know, for even then you were born..." to be intentional sarcasm, but that need not be the case. The Voice of the tempest may be reminding Job of some deep-seated kinship he has with an antique whole.

❧   *By what paths is light dispersed? How is the east*
38:24–25 *wind cast about the earth? Who cleaved canals for the flooding torrent and made a pathway for the voice of thunder...?*

This passage is much more cleverly crafted than I have been able to capture in translation. The three verbs, *dispersed*, *cast about*, and *cleaved*, all mean *to divide into parts*; but the first is a very gentle word, and there is a clear progression to the last, which carries with it much violence. Similarly, there is the motion from *light* to *wind* to *flooding torrent*; and finally, we are at a loss to know what it would take to make a "pathway for the voice of thunder."

God begins Job's education by showing him the forces that were needed to bring the inanimate world into being. They are only a part of the forces which he has laid aside for a time of narrowness and for the days of battle and of war. In this account, more seems to be required than a gentle "Let there be..."

∼   *...that it might rain in no-man land, a wilderness*
38:26–27 *with no human in it, to make a surfeit of the devastation and the devastated, and make a budding field bloom?*

The haunting phrase, "rain in no-man land," is a small foretaste of what Job is to learn. The world beyond man stands as an elegant world whose beauty is there just *to be*, indifferent to whether it be seen by a human eye or no. This passage is the story of that side of the world that Job's friends may be incapable of understanding: a "budding field" which is just there—there for its own sake and not for the sake of man.

∼   *Does the rain have a father? And who begets the*
38:28–29 *drops of dew? From whose belly does ice emerge, and who gave birth to the frost of heaven?*

Again, as we first glimpsed in verse 8, male and female origins are beginning to play an equal role in the foundation of all things. This stance, which comes out of the tempest, is unique to the Book of Job. In rhetoric and imagery, the closest book in the Bible to the Book of Job is the Book of Psalms. Yet even there, if one considers the complete list of its references to bellies and wombs, one sees that, in contradistinction to the Book of Job, the female never quite reaches the level of the divine. The fuller implications of this role are

something we shall not see till we reach the final chapter of
the book.

> *from mortals—by your hand, LORD—from mortals whose*
> *portion in life is in this world. May their bellies be filled with*
> *what you have stored up for them; may their children have*
> *more than enough; may they leave something over to their*
> *little ones.* [Ps. 17:14]

> *Yet it was you who took me from the womb; you kept me*
> *safe on my mother's breast.* [Ps. 22:9]

> *On you I was cast from my birth, and since my mother bore*
> *me you have been my God.* [Ps. 22:10]

> *Be gracious to me, LORD, for I am in distress; my eye wastes*
> *away from grief, my soul and body also.* [Ps. 31:9]

> *The wicked go astray from the womb; they err from their*
> *birth, speaking lies.* [Ps. 58:3]

> *Upon you I have leaned from my birth; it was you who took*
> *me from my mother's womb. My praise is continually of you.*
> [Ps. 71:6]

> *Your people will offer themselves willingly on the day you*
> *lead your forces on the holy mountains. From the womb*
> *of the morning, like dew, your youth will come to you.*
> [Ps. 110:3]

> *Sons are indeed a heritage from the LORD, the fruit of the*
> *womb a reward.* [Ps. 127:3]

> *For it was you who formed my inward parts; you knit me*
> *together in my mother's womb.* [Ps. 139:13]

〰 *Did you bind the Pleiades together with a chain,*
38:31–33 *or untie the reins of Orion? Can you lead out the*
Mazzaroth in its time or guide the Bear with her chil-
dren? Do you know the laws of the heaven, and can
you impose its authority on the earth?

Men were always aware of a world beyond their reach that sparkled over their heads each night while all other things slept. Its vastness and untouchability were awesome. It moved according to its own paths, and no man could stir it or change its course.

Yet God's question to Job would have been banal unless Job were being asked to face those well known, everyday facts in a way in which no man had ever done before. If Job is to step beyond the limits of man, and into the realm of his brotherhood with the jackal—as he shall surely do in the chapters which follow—those banal facts, and others, must be faced again.

In the Book of Genesis, the sun, moon and stars were to be regarded as little more than the servants of man, given to him by an all-loving God to separate the day from the night, and to be for signs and for seasons and for days and years. But the Mazzaroth comes out in its own time, indifferent to good times and to bad times, to times of war, and to times of peace. To some that would have signified an unbearably cold indifference in the stars to human affairs. Not to see them as twinkling for us, but to allow them to twinkle for themselves is Job's first lesson.

〜
38:35
If you send out the lightnings, will they go? Will they say to you, "Here we are!"?

Job must be prepared not only for a world whose inhabitants have ends and ways of their own unrelated to man, there will also be those that strike of a sudden, as if they had intention, but in fact take no aim.

The full force which inheres in the word הִנֵּנוּ (hinenu), "Here we are," can only be felt by reminding ourselves of the conditions under which it has regularly been used. *Readiness* is in the seal of each thing, just as it was in Abraham or Isaac in the land of Moriah, in Moses by the burning bush, and young Samuel in the care of Eli—and in so many others when each of them said, "Here am I."

         Can you hunt up prey for the lioness, and bring to
38:39–41 *fulfillment the life in its cubs as they crouch in their dens or lie in ambush in their lairs? Who prepares a catch for the raven when his young cry out to God for help, while he wanders about without food?*

If Job can gird his loins and stand before all these things, he will see those dreadful forces, all in delicate balance, each a part of that with which it seemed to be at war.

Discussion of Chapter Thirty-Nine

Job has entered far into the Psalmist's "land of jackals" (Ps. 44:18). There he will meet six wild beasts, or species of wild beasts:

Rock-goat and Hind
Wild ass and untamed Jenny
Wild ox
Ostrich
Horse
Hawk and Eagle

None of them is mythical, and each of them is either a close relative of a tame species, or is itself a member of a species capable of being tamed and put to work. It is almost as if we were to learn something about these two worlds by comparing the lives led by each of these brothers—the one of the wild, the other under human control. They remind us of that thin but absolute veil between the world of man and the world beyond the world of man; bear in mind that there were tribes that rode ostriches into battle, like horses, and that the Egyptians used both hawks and eagles in falconry.

⌇   *Do you know when it is time for the mountain goat to*
39:1   *drop? and have you watched the hind writhing in the*
     dance of birth?

The single Hebrew word חוּל (chul), which I have generally translated *to writhe* and have here rendered with the phrase *writhing in the dance of birth*, is a very complex word. Indeed, much of our understanding of the Book of Job will center around our attempt to regain the sense of unity that lies within the complexity of this word.

As far as one can tell, it originally meant *to whirl*:

> *The sword shall* **whirl** *down against their cities, consume the bars of their gates, and devour them in their fortresses.* [Hosea 11:6]

It can also mean *to dance*. Sometimes it is used in a context full of joy and exultation:

> *Let them praise his name with* **dancing,** *making melody to him with timbrel and lyre!* [Ps. 149:3]

But more often than not, things get out of hand; and frequently, when first reading the word, the reader can feel a foreboding thought thickening the air:

> *And as soon as he came near the camp and saw the calf and the* **dancing,** *Moses' anger burned hot, and he threw the tablets out of his hands and broke them at the foot of the mountain.* [Ex. 32:19]

Then too, it comes to mean *to tremble*, or *to quake*:

> *The Voice of the* Lord **shakes** *the wilderness, the* Lord *shakes the wilderness of Kadesh.* [Ps. 29:8]

> *This day I will begin to put the fear and awe of you upon the peoples that are under the whole heaven, who shall hear the report of you and shall* **tremble** *and be in anguish because of you.* [Deut. 2:25]

It often means anguish and pain:

> *When the report comes to Egypt, they will* **be in anguish** *over the report about Tyre.* [Isaiah 23:5]

> *The land* **trembles** *and writhes in pain, for the Lord's purposes against Babylon stand, to make the land of Babylon a desolation, without inhabitant.* [Jer. 51:29]

or even a mortal injury:

> *The battle pressed hard upon Saul, and the archers found him; and he was* **badly wounded** *by the archers.* [I Sam. 31:3]

But, as in our case, it can also mean to be in labor, and hence to give birth:

> You were unmindful of the Rock that begot you, and you forgot the God who **brought you forth**. [Deut. 32:18]

And so the same word that meant *pain and anguish*, can also mean *to prosper*:

> His ways **prosper** at all times; thy judgments are on high, out of his sight; as for all his foes, he puffs at them. [Ps. 10:5]

We can now begin to understand the great admonition, "Gird your loins like a hero." There is wildness and pain present when the signet is put to the clay to create—or bring to birth—a thing of value and worth. Here there is no indication that the pain of birth is the result of a curse or that it is punishment for having taken a bite of an apple. Job, in confronting the nature of birth, is forced to revisit the day of *his own* birth. To venture beyond the realm of man and to see each thing as being what it is, means to come to terms with the unity of all the conflicting associations that the word חוּל contains.

We must look at still one more aspect of these things:

> Behold, the storm of the LORD! Wrath has gone forth, a whirling tempest; it will burst upon the head of the wicked. [Jer. 23:19]

Note the phrase *a whirling tempest*. If the poet intended these words and ideas to come together for his readers as naturally as they do for the English-speaker who knows the word *whirlwind*, we may also recognize in this passage some foundation for the shift we had already begun to feel in the role of the feminine. It is the whirling, dancing, pain-ridden, birthing tempest that speaks to Job. She—for the word *tempest* (סְעָרָה, sa'arah) is a feminine noun—lets Job see that pain

and joy and birth are so interrelated that they cannot be distinguished even in speech.

〰   *Can you number the months they fulfill? and do you*
39:2–4   *know the season for them to deliver, when they couch*
         and split open to give birth to their young and thus
         come to the end of their travail?

If God is a nurturing god rather than a constructing god,
fostering in each being life according to its own signet, then
number and season as well as pleasure and pain are an integral part of the way in which each thing comes to be what it
is, and is what it is. This, then, is the question to Job: Can he
discern number and order in this untrod land?

"...couch and split open...": In using such harsh words, the
Voice is beginning to open Job to a different kind of order.
From the point of view of human justice there is no *a priori*
reason why birth should entail so much pain, and in terms of
human justice it seems to be wrong and even malevolent. Here,
perhaps for the first time, we can begin to see in the world
beyond our world an ordered and numbered whole with its
own necessities, and one which seems to be totally indifferent
to our own sense of order. Yet we can all see that without such
a world, the joys of our world could never come to be.

〰   *Their children thrive and flourish in the wild. They*
39:4   *come out and return unto her no more.*

The Voice here reminds Job that the separation of birth is,
in its own way, as hard and as final as the separation of death.
The child can never return to the comfort of the womb again.
Like Job it suddenly finds itself in a world beyond its world;
and there it thrives.

~   *Who sent the wild ass off to be free? And who has*
39:5–6   *untied the reins of the untamed jenny, whose home I*
          have made the wilderness, and who dwells off in the
          salt lands?

The question is of course rhetorical since, unlike the donkey and the burro, the wild ass has never known either burden or rein. He has, however been mentioned several times in the text. Job has already voiced some care for it in this verse:

Will the wild ass bray when there is grass? [6:5]

while Eliphaz showed no care for it at all:

Hollow man will become thoughtful when the wild ass gives birth to a human. [11:12]

But even Job—notwithstanding that he showed a certain amount of compassion even before he had been invited to enter into the tempest, that land of the jackal—even he did not have quite as much respect as the following lines demand:

They are wild asses in the desert, going off about their labors of snatching up at dawn. [24:5]

~   *He laughs at the bustling of the city, and does not even*
39:7–8   *hear the drivers shout, but roams the hills as his pas-*
          ture, and every green thing is his to search out.

Here the Voice is speaking of the ass; the reader cannot but remember that Job himself had once said nearly the same thing:

There prisoners are wholly at ease, for they do not even hear the driver's voice. Small and great, all are there, and the slave is free of his lord. [3:19]

and there are other passages too that show Job's sensitivity to matters of freedom and bondage:

Like a slave he yearns for the shadows, like a hireling he hopes for his wages. [7:2]

Job acknowledges that slavery is terrible. Nevertheless, like many other men of his position, Job would have had an עֶבֶד (eved), a slave or servant (the Hebrew word does not distinguish between the two):

I called to my servant, but he gave no answer, and now must I curry to him for favor. [19:16]

Whether servants or slaves, however, Job treated them justly and with kindness:

If ever I felt contempt for the cause of one of my slaves, man or maid, when they brought complaint against me—what would I do when God rose up? [31:13]

But now Job is to learn more. Even from within the human sphere, men could always see that slavery was unpleasant, both for those who were enslaved, and for the others. There were always some men who were deeply moved by the pain and suffering it caused, and many of them devoted their lives to alleviating that suffering. But discovery of the notion that slavery is wrong *as such*, whether pain and suffering are involved or not, requires a certain admiration for the wild ass. To put it otherwise, it requires something like the concept of a *signet*, a definite character of its own apart from any human need. It is through seeing the wild ass as being endowed with a life of its own, roaming the hills as his pasture, that its freedom becomes important to us. Later the idea can be apprehended in the form of *natural right*.

Next we meet the wild ox, and again there are questions:

39:9–11   *Would the wild ox agree to serve you? Would he spend the night at your crib? Can you hitch him up with a rope and hold him to the furrow? Will he plow up*

*the valleys behind you? Would you rely upon him?
Remember, his strength is great. Could you leave him
your toils?*

The answer is No! Job can do none of these things; and
yet he did have oxen, five hundred of them, and he did hitch
them up and hold them to the furrow. But:

⌇   *Would you trust him to bring in the grain and gather*
39:12   *it into the barn?*

Of course not. To trust them to bring in the grain would be
out of the question. For the poet, the wild ox always finds a
home; in his prancing he churns and turns the soil, plowing
up the ground and making it ready for the next crop. Human
art is only the vaguest image of what we might call God's
world farm.

This is the only verse in which God speaks of *trust*. It is in
noticeable contrast to what Eliphaz had said:

> *If he puts no trust in his servants and even to his angels lays
> charge of folly, what of those who dwell in a house of clay,
> whose foundation is but dust?* [4:18]

or

> *If he puts no trust in his holy ones and even the heavens are
> not clean in his sight...* [15:15]

Because each thing beyond the sphere of man is what it is,
each thing can be trusted to be what it is. Job sees a world in
which all things are trusted by God rather than watched. The
world farm, chaotic as it may seem, has kept itself in balance
throughout unrecorded time, giving it a legitimate claim to
be much older than Bildad's first generations. The way each
thing is when left to itself, or encouraged to be itself, is prior
to either the arts or tradition.

∾ *The Ostrich whimsically flaps her wing as if she had*
39:13–15, *the pinions and plumage of a stork, but leaves her*
18 *eggs on the ground for the dust to keep them warm.*
She has forgotten that a foot can crush them, or that
a wild beast might trample them down.... She just
flaps her wings as if on high, and laughs at a passing
horse and its rider.

At this point we meet the Ostrich. For Job this must be the
most difficult of the beasts he has encountered thus far; at
least it is the most fearful to write about. Who can help but
be totally charmed by the foolish antics of this silly, silly beast
who knows neither fear nor care? Yet at the same time we are
horrified, and we know that if she were a fellow citizen our
judgment would have been quite otherwise: we would have
to arraign her for child abuse. Our worlds are beginning to
pull apart and to clash, as they have done for Job since we
first met him.

The Ostrich, רְנָנִים (r'nanim) takes her name from a root
meaning *to shout for joy*. Part of the irony at the end of this
passage is that ostriches, in so far as they have been domesticated, have been ridden by some tribesmen as if they were
horses; but our senseless bird is free and can only laugh at the
horse captured by civilization.

A brief note on the stork, חֲסִידָה (chasidah), with whom
Ostrich is contrasted in verse 13. It is not certain what bird is
actually meant, but here is what is known:

> *And these you shall have in abomination among the birds,*
> *they shall not be eaten, they are an abomination: the eagle,*
> *the vulture, the osprey, ... the* **stork,** *the heron according to*
> *its kind, the hoopoe, and the bat.* [Lev. 11:13]

> *The trees of the* LORD *are watered abundantly, the cedars*
> *of Lebanon which he planted. In them the birds build their*
> *nests; the* **stork** *has her home in the fir trees.* [Ps. 104:16]

Even the **stork** *in the heavens knows her times; and the turtledove, swallow, and crane keep the time of their coming; but my people know not the ordinance of the* LORD. [Jer. 8:7]

Then I lifted my eyes and saw, and behold, two women coming forward! The wind was in their wings; they had wings like the wings of a **stork***, and they lifted up the ephah between earth and heaven.* [Zech. 5:9]

〰 *Did you give to the horse its strength, or clothe its*
39:19–24 *neck with a mane? Can you make him leap like a locust when the glory of his snort breeds terror? He digs up the valleys, and exults in his strength as he goes out to meet armed combat. He laughs at fear and is not dismayed, nor is he turned back by the edge of the sword. A quiverful of arrows whizzes by—the flashing spear and the javelin. With clattering and rage, he gouges into the earth.*

With this verse we meet the Horse, but he is far from being the farmer's Old Dobbin. This is the horse as he was before there existed either bridle or saddle.

The Hebrew text of these verses is as moving as any words ever spoken on the field at Agincourt. Why, then, should the human soul find itself so moved by the savage, subhuman might of a beast that can spell only the threat of destruction? And why should the poet wish to arouse in Job admiration for such a beast? Does that not mean raising the very passions in Job that Elihu foresaw, if only in part, when he warned Job not to leave his warm den of hibernation?

It would seem that there are, not one, but two obscure and sometimes interweaving pathways that lure men like Job towards the chinks in the Great Wall of the Human City and reveal its problematic character. Both the highest and the lowest in man have a certain kinship with the lands that lie beyond that wall. If Job is to return safely to the home of man, he must learn to feel and to recognize all sides of the human character, that each may find its proper place.

    〰   *He pays no homage to the trumpet's blast, but when*
39:24–25 *the trumpet call is replete he cries, "Huzzah!" He smells the battle from afar. Oh, the roars of the captains and the shoutings!*

The text at this point is somewhat obscure, and translators differ widely. I take it to mean that, while the horse feels no subservience to the trumpet, once it puts him on to the scent of a battle, he's off.

    〰   *Is it by your wisdom that the hawk soars and spreads*
39:26–27 *its wing out to the south? Does the eagle mount at your command, building its nest on high?*

The hawk, נֵץ (netz), has been domesticated; there is an early bas-relief from Khorsabad showing a falconer bearing a hawk on his wrist. The eagle, too—נֶשֶׁר (nasher)—has been tamed for use in falconry. Throughout this chapter, the animals mentioned are all found in the wild; yet they are also either capable of domestication or have close domesticated relations. Their appearance brings out the strong connection between wildness and civilization—or, one may say, between freedom and slavery.

    〰   *He takes up lodging on the highest pinnacle, making*
39:28–30 *it his stronghold. From there he searches out his prey. His eye spots it from afar, and his fledglings swill down the blood. Whenever death defiles, he is there.*

The last beast, the Eagle, is not so charming as his sister bird the Ostrich; and Job must have felt all but defeated. Elihu's implicit claim, that no man is man enough to face the world of nature, seems to be vindicated. The cold, long-term planning with which the Eagle leads up to his attack makes the resulting carnage all the more grotesque. And then in the final words of the chapter we are even more horrified, but somehow also touched, by the realization that, in all the bloodshed, the Eagle is able to care for his children in a way that the Ostrich, with all her charm, was unable to do for her egg.

Discussion of Chapter Forty

〰️ *And the* LORD *answered Job and said: Should a man*
40:1–2 *of restraint wrangle with the Almighty? One who*
would convict God must give answer.

The LORD treats Job firmly but with dignity, reminding
him of the immensity of the task he has taken onto himself,
and Job has no answer. The Eagle, the violence of the deepest
source of our being, has so horrified him that he has been
numbed as though stung by the *plateia narkē*, the Socratic
torpedofish. Once, Job thought that he knew what justice
was; but he did not. Now he neither knows, nor believes
that he knows. The sight of the six beasts has convinced Job
that Elihu was right, and his warning just. The world beyond
man is no place for a man. Job has been converted from the
"brother to the jackal" (30:29) to one who "would call out
to the muck, 'Thou art my Father,' and call out 'Mother' and
'Sister' to the maggots" (17:14).

〰️ *I have become so weak. How can I answer you? I lay*
40:4–5 *my hand upon my mouth. I have spoken once, but I*
have no answer; twice, but I cannot continue.

If Job's recantation had been what God had wanted, he has
it at this point, and there would have been no need to continue. But the tempest will not let Job go. Again the Voice of
the tempest says: "Gird up your loins like a hero;" and again
its teaching is not a telling but an asking:

~   *Gird up your loins like a hero: I will question you,*
40:7–8 *and you are to let me know. Would you shatter my*
       judgment? Would you condemn me in order that you
       might be right?

God's argument against Job is, I believe, somewhat more specific than one might at first take it to be. It is, as people say, sarcasm; but it is not mere sarcasm.

~   *Have you an arm like God's, and can you thunder in*
40:9 *a voice such as his?*

God seems to base his argument on his power; but Job had always recognized God's greater power. Indeed, that was the problem:

> *If [trial] be by strength, he is the mighty one; and if by court*
> *of law, who will plead my case?* [9:19]

When Job thought that he knew what justice was, he also thought that he had the means to establish that justice. But in the last two chapters it has become clear that Job's understanding of justice was defective: he had not realized that an adequate attempt to address the problem of human justice requires that one journey beyond the sphere of human justice to face the problem of what one might wish to call Cosmic Justice. The next two chapters will deal with the question of the administration of that justice.

~   *Go ahead, deck yourself out in majestic pride and*
40:10–14 *dignity. Put on glory and splendor. Let fly the out-*
        bursts of your anger. Look upon every man of
        majestic pride and abase him. Look upon everyone
        of majestic pride and bring him low and tread down
        the guilty. Bury them all in the dust. Bind their faces

> *in obscurity. Then even I would praise you, for your own right hand would have saved you.*

Appropriately enough, God is joking. He almost seems to be saying "Job, if you think you can do a better job than I have done, give it a try." But the ways of man do not turn out to be the means by which justice is established in the cosmos; and Job still has much to learn of the spirit behind the administration of that justice. Job's search for human justice has led him into a world in which human action no longer seems relevant. Its vast forces are so sweeping that no decking-out would ever be noticed and no outburst of anger ever be felt; and it will take Job some time to see the implications of that kind of justice as it expresses itself within the sphere of human action.

〜 *But look now, here is Behemoth whom I made along*
40:15–19 *with you. He eats fodder just like the cattle, but just look at the strength in his loins. His might is in the muscles of his belly. He can stretch out his tail stiff as a cedar. The sinews of his thighs are all knit together. His bones are ducts of brass, and his limbs are like rods of iron. He is the first of God's ways. Only his Maker can approach him with a sword.*

He was "made along with you," and "eats fodder just like the cattle." He is a normal part of the greater world around us, being neither miraculous nor mythical. He is, however, clearly of mythic proportion. "His bones are ducts of brass, and his limbs are like rods of iron." The visible universe is much larger than any man knows and contains creatures which he did not name and of which he is unaware. Man is not the unquestioned center of all that is visible.

◠   *The mountains yield him produce, and all the beasts*
40:20–23 *of the field come there to play. He lies down under the*
lotuses, hiding in the reeds and the fen. The lotuses
blanket him with their shade, and the willows of the
brook surround him. Though the river rage, he is
unalarmed, confident that the Jordan will burst into
his mouth.

The half-mythic, half-real fabric of the account of the
Behemoth succeeds in leaving the reader feeling that he shares
a world with a living being of monumental stature whom
he has never seen, in a land just beyond his ken. This grand
beast is at ease in the land of the jackal. He finds room for the
pounding, tyrannizing river, making it his drinking fountain.
In this verse we find a creature that is passively ferocious yet
actively gentle. He seems to rule by *play*, שׂחק (sachaq).

God's discourse continues with the famed Leviathan:

◠   *Can you haul Leviathan in with a fishhook? Can*
40:25–27 *you press down his tongue with the line? Can you*
put a ring through his nose, or pierce his jaw with a
barb? Would he make you many pleas, or speak to
you softly?

No, Job cannot haul him in. He came, he saw—but Job, no
Caesar, has not come to be the conqueror of nature.
Eliphaz did once have a dream, not of the conquest of
nature but of peaceful relation with it:

> ... *but at violence and starvation you will laugh. Have no*
> *dread of the beasts of the earth, for you have a covenant*
> *with the rocks in the field, and the beasts of the fields will*
> *bring you peace.* [5:22]

But it was not the right dream, for it could not cognize the
rocks and the beasts apart from their relation to man—as the
Voice implies when it says:

〰️ *Will he make a covenant with you to be your eternal*
40:28 *servant?*

To put it more succinctly, Job has come to learn from nature, not to conquer it. To that extent, he has come to have its ways impressed upon him rather than impressing his ways upon it; and one of the things he learned, as we have seen from the Ostrich, is the importance of freedom. On the question of freedom, consider this passage in the Book of Genesis:

> *And God blessed them, and God said to them, "Be fruitful and multiply, and fill the earth and* **subdue** *it; and* **have dominion** *over the fish of the sea and over the birds of the air and over every living thing that moves upon the earth."* [Gen. 1:28]

It should be noted that both words, *subdue* and *have dominion*, are quite definite and strong:

> *You may bequeath them to your sons after you, to inherit as a possession for ever; you may make slaves of them, but over your brethren the people of Israel you shall not* **take dominion**, *one over another, with harshness.* [Lev. 25:46]

In addition, the Hebrew word for *subdue* also has a sense of completion and finality.

> *Then the whole congregation of the people of Israel assembled at Shiloh, and set up the tent of meeting there; the land lay* **subdued** *before them.* [Josh. 18:1]

> *But afterward they turned around and took back the male and female slaves they had set free, and* **subdued** *them as slaves.* [Jer. 34:11]

〰️ *Can you play with him like a bird or tie him on a*
40:29–32 *string for your young ladies? Or can the dealers get hold of him and trade their shares in the market? Can you fill his hide with harpoons, or his head*

with fishing spears? Merely place your hand upon his
head, and you will remember war no more.

The world beyond man is not a world in which man can
play; it is only a world in which he can learn about play. The
charm of these verses teaches us about innocent jesting, but
the beyond is not ours. We cannot divide it up and use it as
we will. To see it is to see it as *a thing for itself*, not as a thing
for us; but our brush with it will greatly change life in our
little world of man.

Discussion of Chapter Forty-One

Chapter 41 continues the tale of Leviathan:

〜   *Thus, [all] expectation is an illusion.*
41:1

The word translated as *expectation*, תּוֹחַלְתּוֹ (tochalto), is from the root יחל (yachal). Even a reader not versed in Hebrew can probably see that יחל is a near relative of the root חול (chul), which was considered in the discussion of Chapter 39. But חול can suggest a sense of fear, whereas יחל implies expectation or hope.

We have examples of such illusory expectations elsewhere:

Those who despise the sea and those who are determined to lay Leviathan open will curse it. [3:8]

In that day the LORD with his hard and great and strong sword will punish Leviathan the fleeing serpent, Leviathan the twisting serpent, and he will slay the dragon that is in the sea. [Isaiah 27:1]

You crushed the head of Leviathan and gave it to the people of the island as food. [Ps. 74:14]

If abandoning expectation primarily means giving up the specific expectation that Leviathan will one day be crushed, then perhaps we can gain a deeper insight into the interplay between חול and יחל, and begin to address the questions which arose in our discussion of 3:8 concerning those who would "lay Leviathan open." Consider the alternative view of Leviathan that is implied in these passages:

There go the ships, the Leviathan whom you made to play with. They all look to you to give them their food in due time. [Ps. 104:26]

Can you play with him like a bird and tie him on a string for your young ladies? [40:29]

The question is this: Are the frightful things in nature—the lions and tigers and bears—to be destroyed one day by the hand of God so that the world might truly become a world for man? Or do those things have a certain beauty of their own apart from all human need—a frightful beauty, yet one to which man can be open, and under which he first learns to be a human being?

The Voice has introduced us to the second alternative, while denying the first. The second, indeed, has replaced the first. That is to say, it is by giving up the יחל—recognizing that the world beyond man, along with its denizens, has a legitimate being for itself apart from its being for us—that we begin to see our own legitimate being as it is implied in the notion of the חול.

~ *Do men not reel at the sight of him? No one is so brutal*
41:1-2   *as to rouse him up.*

Job has now crossed that veil which separates the human from the nonhuman. His journey had begun some time ago. He first felt it in the form of fear:

...and so I became a brother to the Jackal and friend to the Ostrich. [30:29]

But the forces pulling him back into what the Psalmist calls "the land of jackals" (Ps. 44:18) had, in fact, already begun. Previously in that same chapter, Job had said:

You have turned brutal, and with the might of your hand you persecute me. You hoist me up onto the wind and set me astride to be tossed about in the wreckage. [30:21]

The word אַכְזָר (akhzar), which I have translated as *brutal*, is not a very common word; it occurs only twice outside the Book of Job. One instance reads:

Even the jackals give the breast and suckle their young,
but the daughter of my people has become brutal, like the
ostriches in the wilderness. [Lam. 4:3]

The word *brutal* seems, then, to imply the attempt or
desire to be or become an actor within the realm beyond the
human. But, to see that "[all] expectation is an illusion" is to
see a world which man may admire, but in which he may not
act; one in which he may first learn to recognize a world as
being for itself, apart from the needs of man. But that knowledge can only lead one to say: "No one is so brutal as to rouse
him up." No man can become an actor in that world without
being transformed into a brute.

~ *Now, who is that one who would stand before me?*
41:2–3 *Who confronts me and [demands that] I give exact*
restitution? Is not everything under the heavens
mine?

The root of the word here rendered as *restitution* is שׁלם,
meaning *to be whole or complete*. From it comes the Hebrew
word for *peace*.

So the wall was **finished** *on the twenty-fifth day of the*
month of Elul, within fifty-two days. [Neh. 6:15]

Then the word comes to mean *to pay* (a debt):

She came and told the man of God, and he said, "Go, sell the
oil and **pay** *your debts, and you and your sons can live on*
the rest." [II Kings 4:7]

Here the word for *debt* is related to a word meaning *to lift off*.
To pay a debt, then, is to *make whole*, or to *replace* what one
has lifted off.

This understanding is fundamental to human justice:

Or if it is known that the ox has been accustomed to gore in
the past, and its owner has not kept it in, he shall **pay** *ox for*
ox, and the dead beast shall be his. [Ex. 21:36]

The goal of this kind of justice is to make those who have suffered whole again. To the extent that one must speak of punishment, one charged with a crime is charged to undo what harm he has caused another. This is human justice as it is contained in the notion of שׁלם. If, however, *winnowing* is the prime analogy of cosmic justice, as the Voice had suggested in Chapter 38, then punishment for cosmic crimes can only be punished in terms of the harm the perpetrator has caused to himself through being what he is. In that sense, it does not strictly make sense to demand exact restitution in the case of cosmic justice. As God has said, "Is not everything under the heavens mine?"

Cosmic justice is larger than human justice. It leaves room for Leviathan and insures that there will always be grass even where no man is. But its justice is of the winnowing kind, catching the kind of things that should be caught, letting go the kinds of things that ought to be let go.

〜   *I will no longer be silent about him, or his exploits or*
41:4–9   *the grace of his frame. Who can unveil his outer garment, or come before his double-folded jaw? Who can open the doors of his face—his teeth surrounded by terror! But his pride is the strength of his shields, narrowed up and closed by a seal, each touching the next, and not a breath between them. Each one clings to his brother. They clutch each other and cannot be parted.*

Near the end of Chapter 31 we saw the importance of Job's openness, as exemplified in his open door. But Leviathan is finally closed to man. We can know him from the outside only: "Who can open the doors of his face—his teeth surrounded by terror!" [41:6]

The word מָגִנִּים (maginim), *shields*, is from the root מגן, *to defend*. Here it is taken by all to mean Leviathan's scales. In

any case, it suggests that Leviathan, unlike Job, has the kind
of impenetrable skin that the Satan spoke of in 2:4. He cannot be disturbed by others; he cannot be hurt by others; no
one can touch him. Therefore he cannot learn from others,
and so can never learn to know himself.

The remainder of this chapter is quite dense, and I am not
sure that I can be of much help either to the reader or to
myself. It might be useful, however, to begin by considering
how the word סָגוּר, *closed*, is used elsewhere in the text:

> *May it not see the eyelid of dawn open, for it* **closed** *not the
> doors of my mother's belly but hid my eyes from toil.* [3:10]

> *If he should pass by and separate or* **close up**, *who can turn
> him back?* [11:10]

> *and what he tears down can never be rebuilt. He* **closes in**
> *on a man and nothing is ever reopened.* [12:14]

> *God sets the wicked to* **close in** *on me and casts me into the
> hands of guilty men.* [16:11]

One cannot help noticing that Leviathan finds his strength
in being closed up, while Job's strength lies in his willingness
to stand in the open entranceway. Job leaves himself open
to what is most other; Leviathan does not. Job's openness
first came to light when we saw that he had no skin beneath
his skin [2:4]. This was the vulnerability that let in pain and
anguish. But it also left him open to feeling, and then seeing, a world beyond his own human world. Job has seen
Leviathan, but has Leviathan seen Job? Leviathan's impene-
trability would seem to deny it.

Leviathan's pride, the tightness of his scales [41:7] turns
out to be the same as Job's old foe, *narrowness*, צָר. For Job it
was the oppressive feeling of walls pulling in and sky being
cut off [23:16]. For Leviathan, narrowness is his completion
and perfection. For Job it was the beginning of murk and
confusion.

〜   *Festoons of flesh, fused all together, lie on him cast as*
41:15 *metal, and they do not quiver.*

The way Leviathan's flesh lies makes him appear to be open to otherness; but, like a flower carved in stone, "flesh cast like iron" remains forever locked within itself. Leviathan is immune to suffering. Not so Job, who had asked:

> *Do I have flesh of bronze?* [6:12]

For man, to be made of flesh is to be able to feel pain:

> *Why do you pursue me like God, taking satisfaction out of my flesh?* [19:22]

While to be incapable of feeling pain is to be incapable of understanding pain:

> *Do you have eyes of flesh?* [10:4]

> *For what reason do I take my flesh between my teeth and my life in my hands?* [13:14]

Job understands that it is through the feeling of pain that we come to understand the notion of *importance*, and that without such a notion, nothing in the world can be of any value or consequence. The world becomes meaningful to us insofar as we see ourselves willing to risk pain and death for that which is important:

〜   *When he rises up, the gods are afraid. They shatter*
41:17–21 *and are in confusion. No sword that will reach him can stand, nor spear, nor javelin, nor lance. Iron he counts as straw, and bronze as rotten wood. No son of the bow can put him to flight. Slingstones turn to stubble and clubs are rated as straw. He laughs at the sound of the javelin.*

Nothing can be for Leviathan what it is for itself. Difference, for him, makes no difference. Slingstones turn to stubble. His total unawareness and indifference to the world around him is awesome. Nothing outside himself can be of any use to him: the lights which flash at his sneeze [41:10] he uses neither to see by nor to read by, and yet our soul is arrested and can see only him.

To see things as they are for themselves, not as they are for us—to appreciate the grass which grew where no man was—Job was forced to quit the world of man for a world unstifled by human need and allowed to be itself. But in that world, only man, the stranger, through his weakness and otherness, could learn to let things be. Only then could he return with a fuller understanding of human need.

⁓ *His underparts are jagged shards. He sprawls himself*
41:22–23 *out, implacable, on the mud and makes the deep to seethe like a cauldron.*

Once an old Parmenides asked a young Socrates if he thought mud was anything in itself apart from what it is for us. The question would seem to be a bit absurd. Has mud anything better to do than to be made into a mud pie, or a brick, or a house? And we all stand upon the earth with never a thought of asking its permission. Nonetheless, we can almost feel his jagged shards cutting their gashes into the ground. In this imagery we see the great destruction implied in Leviathan's sheer being.

⁓ *He makes the sea his ointment-pot and leaves a shin-*
41:23–24 *ing wake till the abyss seems all hoary-headed.*

The sea, long in our tale the measureless realm of chaos and confusion which had always threatened to engulf all, has become a mere utensil, instrument of Leviathan's innocent pleasure.

∼ *No one of the dust will have dominion over him, for he*
41:25 *was made to be without fear.*

The word חַת (chat), which we have translated *fear*, is a
very uncommon word, and in fact appears in only one other
passage in the whole of biblical literature. Ironically, the passage reads:

> Panic and **fear** of you shall rest on every animal of the earth,
> and on every bird of the air, on everything that creeps on the
> ground, and on all the fish of the sea; into your hand they
> are delivered. [Gen. 9:2]

But Leviathan was made to be without fear. Thus, Job 41:25
emerges, and perhaps intentionally so, as a correction to
Genesis 9:2.

∼ *He is king over all the sons of pride.*
41:26

The exact meaning of the word שָׁחַץ (shachatz), which we
have translated *pride*, is not very clear. It appears in only one
other verse in the Bible:

> The eye of the falcon has never caught sight of it, nor have
> the sons of **pride** ever trampled it over. The lion can bear it
> no witness, but man has put his hand to the flint and over-
> turned its mountains by the root. [28:7–9]

In Aramaic, the word שַׁחְצָא (shachtza) means *lion*, while
in Ethiopian the root means *to be insolent*. In Arabic, the
root means *to be elevated*, from which root comes the word
sh'chitz, a bulky man or a man of rank.

Thus, there is disagreement among translators as to
whether the Leviathan is king over beasts or over men. The
ambiguity may not be totally unintentional, since it is not so
clear that such a distinction is of any concern whatsoever to

the Leviathan himself. It is not even clear that he knows that he is king, though king indeed he surely is.

This grand beast, above and beneath all malice or ambition, oblivious to all, rules all by the mere weight of his being. In him we recognize our limitations and hence see our definition.

Discussion of Chapter Forty-Two

~   *Then Job answered the* LORD *and said: I know that*
42:1–2 *you can do all and that no design can be withheld*
       from you.

Job has been to the world beyond the world of man, outside
the gates of the city. He knows that while man can do little
to affect that realm, whatever takes place there continually
reverberates within the human sphere. All human thought
must take this one thought as a given.

As a secondary point, let me add a remark on "design"
(mezimah). It is terribly unclear how one should translate
this word. *Mezimah* generally implies evil or wicked intent;
compare Job 21:27. But in the Book of Proverbs, it often
means something more like discretion:

> *I, wisdom, dwell in prudence, and I find knowledge and* **dis-**
> **cretion.** [Prov. 8:12]

Jeremiah, on the other hand, uses the term to describe God's
plans against the wicked:

> *The fierce anger of the* LORD *will not turn back until he*
> *has executed and accomplished the* **intents** *of his mind.*
> [Jer. 30:24]

The verb *withheld* (root בצר)—used in verse 42:2 in
conjunction with *design*—occurs in the passive in only one
other passage in the Bible; there it indicates something that
is to be prevented:

> *And the* LORD *said, Behold, they are one people, and they*
> *have all one language; and this is only the beginning of what*
> *they will do; and nothing that they propose to do can be*
> **withheld** *from them.* [Gen. 11:6]

Here, then, the choice of his verb would seem to preclude taking *mezimah* either in the sense found in Proverbs or in that of Jeremiah, since in neither of those cases is anything being spoken of which one would want to prevent. But the remaining sense—that of evil or wicked intent—is also difficult to attribute to God. Perhaps Job means, however, that we can even accept God's sending something harmful, so long as we know it to be without malice or bad intent.

~ *"Who is this one that conceals counsel without*
42:3 *knowledge?"*

Having set the proper realm of discourse, Job restates the LORD's question of 38:2, a question that Job is bound to answer. His answer is a confession, and for that very reason it is not a confession:

~ *I have spoken though I had not understood. There*
42:3–4 *is a world beyond me, a world full of wonders that I had never known. "Now listen and I will speak; I shall question you, and you will inform me."*

Job is the one who spoke without knowledge. That is, indeed, the reason he spoke: because he was without knowledge. Now he must speak again: In verse 4 Job repeats the LORD's words of 38:3 as a way of signifying that he has accepted and will obey.

~ *I had heard of you as ears can hear; but now my eyes*
42:5–6 *have seen you. Wherefore I have both contempt and compassion for dust and ashes.*

For most of his life, Job had lived by the hearing of his ears. The tradition handed down by the wise, who were well schooled in it, established the foundation and horizons of the world in which he lived and in which he grew and prospered. But now, for Job, those foundations have turned into "bulwarks of clay" (13:12). Job had once said:

> It is I myself who shall see. My own eyes must behold, and not those of a stranger, although the vitals within my bosom are finished. [19:27]

Throughout the text, the two words, *contempt* and *compassion*, have been dancing around each other, each cautiously avoiding the other; but in Job's final words they have at last come together. The two worlds have ceased their clashing. Job, the homeless, is at home now. He is at peace in a very large world in which no man counts for more than the proverbial hill of beans. He is also at peace in a very small world in which each man is of infinite value. He can be at peace in each world only because he is at peace in the other. He also knows that that large and woolly world has in it a kind of love and a kind of laughter which only he and his fellows can re-establish within the realm of the small.

⁓ *The* Lord *said to Eliphaz the Temanite: "My anger*
42:7–8 *fumes against you, and against your two friends: for you have not spoken of me the thing that is right, as has my servant Job. Therefore, get yourselves seven bulls and seven rams, and go to my servant Job, and offer up for yourselves a burnt offering; and my servant Job shall pray for you..."*

Job's eyes have seen, but that seeing took place in a foreign land in which his hands could not act. Job of the wide world is again Job the servant of the Lord, living in a nutshell. He who has seen Leviathan will say a prayer for his friends as they bring their bulls and their rams to be sacrificed. Job's old foe, narrowness, no longer weighs upon him. He has been beyond, and the walls have become transparent. But the

world of seeing turned out to be a world devoid of all meaningful human action; and Job has returned.

〜   *Then all of his brothers and sisters and all of his friends*
42:11   *came to his house and supped with him.*

This atmosphere, to be fully appreciated, must be held in
contrast to that of the book's opening:

> *His sons used to make feasts in the home of each man on his
> day, and send word to their three sisters to come and eat and
> drink with them.* [1:4]

It might be worth mentioning that the only other biblical
character in connection with whom the phrase *brothers and
sisters* is used, with all the sense of equality it implies, was
that wonderful woman of the night, Rahab (Joshua 2:13).

The root אכל (akhal), *to eat* or *to sup*, which had been connected so often with death, destruction and resignation, now
holds together a festive world in which humans can act and
interact. The following examples chronicle a gradual transi-
tion from אכל as destructive to אכל as joyful:

> *All that he has harvested the hungry shall* **devour**, *even
> taking out from under the thorns; and the thirsty shall go
> panting after their wealth.* [5:5]

> *Can what is tasteless be* **eaten** *without salt, or does the slime
> of an egg white have any taste?* [6:6]

> *and it all becomes worn out like a rotten thing—like a piece
> of cloth that the moths have* **eaten**. [13:28]

> *the tents of bribery are a* **consuming** *fire.* [15:34]

> *His skin will be* **eaten away**; *death's firstborn will* **consume**
> *his members.* [18:13]

> *He will be* **consumed** *by an unblown fire, and all shall go ill
> with the remnant left in his tent.* [20:26]

> *Another dies in the bitterness of his soul, never having **eaten***
> *of goodness, yet together they lie in the dust, and the worms*
> *cover them over.* [21:25]

> *Has not our enemy been destroyed, their remains **con-***
> ***sumed** by fire?* [22:20]

> *...then let me sow but another **eat**....* [31:8]

> *It would be a fire **consuming** down to Abaddon, uprooting*
> *all that I have ever accomplished.* [31:12]

> *How could I withhold pleasures from the poor or drain a*
> *widow's eye, or even **eat** a crust of bread alone, not sharing*
> *it with the fatherless, when they had grown up with me for*
> *a father?* [31:16–17]

> *...claims that I have **eaten** its produce without payment and*
> *snuffed out the life of its owners....* [31:39]

Now, at the end of the book, and after Job's return, *eating* can lose its destructive character and become an act of simple joyous unity:

> *But look now, here is Behemoth whom I made along with*
> *you. He **eats** fodder just like the cattle; but look at the strength*
> *in his loins. His might is in the muscles of his belly.* [40:15]

〜 *They consoled him and showed him compassion for*
42:11 *all the evils which the* LORD *had brought upon him.*

We are reminded of what we had read in the beginning:

> *Now when Job's three friends had heard of all the evils that*
> *had come upon him, they came each from his own place,*
> *Eliphaz the Temanite, Bildad the Shuhite, and Zophar the*
> *Na'amathite. They conferred with one another and planned*
> *to come together "to console him and to show him compas-*
> *sion."* [2:11]

What had not been possible before has now become actual. The recognition of compassion that Job gained from beyond the human sphere has had its full effect within the human sphere.

◦   *he also had seven sons and three daughters.*
42:13

We remember:

> *While he was yet talking, another one came in and said, Your sons and your daughters were eating and drinking wine in the house of their oldest brother, when a mighty wind came in from the wilderness and struck the four corners of the house. It fell down on the young people. They are dead, and I alone have escaped to tell thee.* [2:18–19]

This verse echoes alongside the verse just now read:

> *They consoled him and showed him compassion for all the evils which the* LORD *had brought upon him.* [42:11]

No one has forgotten that Job's first children all died.

The Book of Job does not end with a *deus ex machina* or miracle of resurrection. Job recognizes the being of all the things that are, including the being of death itself.

◦   *The first he called by the name of Jemimah; the second*
42:14   *Qeziah; and the third Qeren-Hapukh.*

The first daughter's name, יְמִימָה (y'mimah) is from the word יוֹם (yom), or day. It is a new day for Job, in contrast to the earlier verse:

> *Then, Job opened his mouth and spurned his day.* [3:1]

The second, קְצִיעָה (q'tziyah)—in English, *cassia*—is the name of a fragrant bark of a tree; it can be powdered like cinnamon and used in cooking.

> *Your robes are all fragrant with myrrh and aloes and* **cassia**. *From your ivory palaces, stringed instruments make you glad.* [Ps. 45:8]

קֶרֶן הַפּוּךְ (qeren happukh) is the name of the third daughter. The first two names are clearly intended to be very beautiful. Then too, the very fact that the daughters are mentioned by name gives them a certain being and hence a certain nobility. But what of this name?

The word פּוּךְ (pukh) means *antimony*, which also enjoys a certain association with beauty, as in this verse:

> *So I have provided for the house of my God ... great quantities of onyx and stones for setting, **antimony**, colored stones, all sorts of precious stones, and marble.* [I Chron. 29:2]

In ancient times, antimony was ground into a powder, also called פּוּךְ, and used by women as mascara, eye makeup. In the pens of the prophets, however, "eye paint" became symbolic of feminine corruption:

> *When Jehu came to Jezreel, Jezebel heard of it; and she **painted** her eyes, and adorned her head, and looked out of the window.* [II Kings 9:30]

> *And you, O desolate one, what do you mean that you dress in scarlet, that you deck yourself with ornaments of gold, that you enlarge your eyes with **paint**?* [Jer. 4:30]

Contrastingly, the word קֶרֶן (qeren), *horn*, enjoys abundant associations with beauty, nobility, and strength. A קֶרֶן, for example, contained the oil used to anoint the kings of Israel:

> *Fill your **horn** with oil, and go; I will send you to Jesse the Bethlehemite, for I have provided for myself a king among his sons."* [I Sam. 16:1]

> *Then Samuel took the **horn** of oil, and anointed him in the midst of his brothers; and the Spirit of the LORD came mightily upon David from that day forward.* [I Sam. 16:13]

> *There Zadok the priest took the **horn** of oil from the tent and anointed Solomon.* [I Kings 1:39]

Originally, the word denoted the horn of a living animal; but the root קרן also means *to shine*:

> *And when Aaron and all the people of Israel saw Moses, behold, the skin of his face* **shone***, and they were afraid to come near him.* [Ex. 34:30]

and hence, the word itself can mean *a ray of light*:

> *His brightness was like the light,* **rays** *flashed from his hand; and there he veiled his power.* [Hab. 3:4]

The horns of an animal are his strength and his defense. They give him greater stature and a formidable look; and so the word comes to mean those same attributes for a human being too:

> *The* LORD *will judge the ends of the earth; he will give strength to his king, and exalt the* **horn** *of his anointed.* [I Sam. 2:10]

> *Hannah also prayed and said, "My heart exults in the* LORD; *my* **horn** *exalted in the* LORD. [I Sam. 2:1]

> *For thou art the glory of their strength; by thy favor our* **horn** *is exalted.* [Ps. 89:17]

That is what Job had in mind when he said:

> *I have sewed sackcloth over my skin. I have driven my* **horns** *into the dust.* [16:15]

As was mentioned before, the horn played a central role in the place of worship:

> *And you shall make* **horns** *for it on its four corners; its* **horns** *shall be of one piece with it, and you shall overlay it with bronze.* [Ex. 27:2]

And, of course, it was a prime source of triumphal music:

> *So all Israel brought up the ark of the covenant of the* LORD *with shouting, to the sound of the* **horn***, trumpets,*

and cymbals, and made loud music on harps and lyres.
[I Chron. 15:28]

Thus the third daughter's name, which can be rendered Horn of Mascara, alleviates and even overcomes any negative connotations that may echo from the prophets. The phrase *horn of mascara* also works well linguistically because it easily blends into the language along with such other, affirmative, phrases as *horn of oil* (I Sam 16:13) and *horn of my salvation* (II Sam. 22:3).

To put the argument simply: by conjoining the word קֶרֶן to the word פוּך in such a natural and ordinary way, the poet has silently but forcefully robbed the word פוּך of any sting. Its bare mention is no longer sufficient to conjure up a degrading image of womankind.

The ambivalent connotation of פוּך, which the Book of Job ultimately resolves in the naming of Job's third daughter, mirrors a larger ambivalence with respect to beauty itself:

〜 *In all the land there could not be found any woman*
42:15 *more beautiful than Job's daughters.*

As is the case in the dialogues of Plato, there is here a prima facie assumption that what is beautiful is also good. Plato, of course, was by no means unaware of the problematic character of that assumption—just think of his portrayal of such characters as Meno and Alcibiades—but for him the intimate connection between the Beautiful and the Good ultimately prevails.

In the biblical view, though, the relation of beauty to goodness is highly ambivalent, especially in the so-called historical books, Genesis through II Kings. In those books, when the subject of beauty comes up there is always trouble.

The subject first arises with respect to Sarai, whose beauty twice put Abraham in danger and nearly led to the death of an innocent, though perhaps somewhat naive, ruler:

When the princes of Pharaoh saw her, they praised her to Pharaoh. And the woman was taken into Pharaoh's house.... But the LORD *afflicted Pharaoh and his house with great plagues because of Sarai, Abram's wife.* [Gen. 12:115f]

And Abimelech king of Gerar sent and took Sarah.... Now Abimelech had not approached her; so he said, "Lord, wilt thou slay an innocent people?" [Gen. 20:2–4]

Jacob preferred Rachel's beauty to Leah's soft eyes (Gen. 29:16), but the reader may esteem the sisters differently with regard to goodness. Leah, for example, knows only gratitude each time she has a child:

"Because the LORD *has heard that I am hated, he has given me this son also"; and she called his name Simon.* [Gen. 29:31]

But Rachel only thinks in terms of battle and victory:

Then Rachel said, "With mighty wrestling I have wrestled with my sister, and have prevailed"; so she called his name Naphtali. [Gen. 30:6, 8]

When Rachel finally does have a son of her own, she reacts not with gratitude, but with a demand for another:

and she called his name Joseph, saying, "May the LORD *add to me another son!"* [Gen. 30:24]

Joseph was beautiful; but in his case, too, beauty led to grave problems:

Now Joseph was handsome [beautiful] and good-looking. And after a time his master's wife cast her eyes upon Joseph, and said, "Lie with me." [Gen. 39:6]

The law concerning a beautiful captive woman would seem to depict marriage with her in a positive light:

[If you] see among the captives a beautiful woman, and you have desire for her and would take her for yourself as wife... [Deut. 21:11]

but it must be read in the light of Cozbi, and the possibility that such wives might lead their husbands astray (Num. 25:6–18).

In David's time beauty began to seem less ambiguous:

> *And he sent, and brought him in. Now he was ruddy, and had beautiful eyes, and was handsome. And the* LORD *said, "Arise, anoint him; for this is he."* [I Sam.16:12]

> *And when the Philistine looked, and saw David, he disdained him; for he was but a youth, ruddy and beautiful in appearance.* [I Sam. 17:42]

But that promise did not actualize for David's children; Tamar's beauty caused her disaster:

> *But he would not listen to her; and being stronger than she, he forced her, and lay with her.* [II Sam. 13:1]

Her brother's beauty (specifically associated with his voluminous hair) was his downfall as well.

> *Absalom was riding upon his mule, and the mule went under the thick branches of a great oak, and his head caught fast in the oak, and he was left hanging between heaven and earth, while the mule that was under him went on.* [II Sam. 14:25]

In contradistinction to all these cases, the opening of verse 42:15 appears to present beauty in a very favorable light.

Along with women's beauty, we find that women's status undergoes a significant change in the Book of Job:

〰️
42:15   *...their father gave them an inheritance alongside their brothers.*

Perhaps the best way to understand the significance of this inheritance is to compare it to the case of the daughters of Zelophehad. So far as I know, there is in Scripture no specific statement that only male offspring may inherit; but there are many passages which take it for granted that such was the case.

Zelophehad, who lived in the time of Moses, had five daughters but no sons. When he died, the daughters went up to Moses and said: "Why should the name of our father be taken away from his clan because he had no son? Give to us a possession among our father's brothers."

> *When Moses brought their case before the* LORD, *the* LORD *said to Moses, the daughters of Zelophehad are right; you shall give them possession of an inheritance among their father's brothers and cause the inheritance of their father to pass to them. And you shall say to the people of Israel, "If a man dies, and has no son, then you shall cause his inheritance to pass to his daughter. And if he has no daughter, then you shall give his inheritance to his brothers."* [Num. 27:5-9]

But at the end of the Israelites' long journey, and just as Moses was about to give his last words, the heads of the fathers' houses complained that if their daughters were married to any of the sons of the other tribes of the people of Israel, then

> *"their inheritance will be taken from the inheritance of our fathers, and added to the inheritance of the tribe to which they belong; so it will be taken away from the lot of our inheritance." And Moses commanded the people of Israel according to the word of the* LORD, *saying, "The tribe of the sons of Joseph is right. This is what the* LORD *commands concerning the daughters of Zelophehad, "Let them marry whom they think best; only they shall marry within the family of the tribe of their father."* [Num. 36:4-13]

The daughters of Zelophehad received an inheritance only because their father had no son. Had there been a son, they would have merited only a dowry. Their claim concerns only the preservation of the father's name; whereas Job's daughters inherit in their own right.

The request, "give us a possession alongside our father's brothers," cannot convey the same sense of equality that one feels so strongly in the verse "their father gave them an inheritance alongside their brothers."

Finally, although the words, "Let them marry whom they think best," show genuine concern for the welfare of the women, tribal inheritance proves paramount in the time of Moses, for "they shall marry within the family of the tribe of their father"— thus the inheritance turns out to be little more than a grand dowry. In the case of Job's daughters, however, nothing is said about either husbands or dowries; the inheritance is outright and absolute. Job has established the right of women to own and hold property.

The affirmation of that right reflects a larger change in women's status that develops by the end of the book. Job was born into a world that held women in low esteem; we hardly notice the fact that, while the sisters are invited to parties, they never seem to host them. Job's own harsh outburst, "You talk like a worthless woman" (2:10), expresses an attitude similar to that of Eliphaz's lament, "What is a mortal that he should be clean, or one born of woman that he should consider himself just?" (15:14). Of a like cast is Bildad's "What can cleanse anyone born of woman?" (25:4).

Such thoughts also remind us of Job's early musings:

> *May it not see the eyelid of dawn open, for it closed not the gates of my mother's belly but hid my eyes from toil. Why did I not come out of the womb and die, exit the belly and perish?* [3:9–11]

> *Why did you bring me out of the womb? Had I only perished without ever an eye to see me, I would be as though I had not been, as though I had been led from the belly to the grave.* [10:18–19]

> *Their belly brews deceit* [15:35]

By the end of the book, the womb or belly has become for Job, and perhaps for the reader too, the mighty, turbulent, and often ferocious source from which there has emerged a world full of life and living creatures—a world larger, stranger, and more violent, but at times curiously more tender, than any man had ever seen. But at all times it is breathtakingly beautiful, and we stand in awe of that which does not know us.

> *Who closed up the sea behind the double door, when first it burst out of the womb and I clothed it in a cloud and swaddled it in mist...* [38:8]

> *From whose belly does ice emerge...* [38:29]

In the tempest Job met the nurturing God, the one who clothes in a cloud and swaddles in mist—not just the God who fixed the pylons [38:6], but the one from whose belly ice emerges, and who gave birth to the frost of heaven as well (38:29). When Job returned from the land of the jackal, he remembered the God who, unlike man, *can* trust the wild ox to bring in the grain and gather it into the barn (39:12), and the God who caused it to rain in no-man land (38:26). And so the father who saw the unity in the whirling, dancing, pain-ridden birthing gave his daughters "an inheritance alongside their brothers."

Works Cited

Alter, Robert, *The Wisdom Books: Job, Proverbs, and Ecclesiastes: A Translation with Commentary* (W. W. Norton and Co., 2010).

Gordis, Robert. *The Book of Job: Commentary, New Translation, and Special Study* (Jewish Theological Seminary of America, 1978).

Greenberg, Moshe, tr., *The Book Of Job* (Jewish Publication Society of America, 1980).

Mitchel, Stephen, tr., *The Book of Job* (North Point Press, 1987).

Saadia Ben Joseph (Saadia Gaon), *The Book of Theodicy: Translation and Commentary on the Book of Job*, tr. L. E. Goodman (Yale University Press, 1988).

Sacks, Robert D., *A Commentary on the Book of Genesis* (Edwin Mellen Press, 1990).

The Holy Bible, containing the Old and New Testaments. Authorized King James Version (Oxford University Press, n.d.); abbreviated KJV.

The Holy Bible, Revised Standard Version (T. Nelson & Sons, 1952); abbreviated RSV.

The Holy Bible, English Standard Version (Collins, 2012).

Young's Literal Translation of the Holy Bible, (Baker Book House, 1953).

Index

307

Leviathan, 6, 91–94, 109–110, 172, 278, 281, 284–289, 292
ambivalent Biblical tradition of, 109–110

lightning, 82, 83, 87, 175, 242, 245, 262

loathing, 18n, 22, 74, 133, 139

man, Hebrew names for, *xiii*, 16n, 22n, 79n

Mazzaroth, 86n

mishpat (judgment or case), 131

Mitchell, Stephen, 112n

narrowness, 15, 33, 81, 82, 86, 94, 123, 124, 126, 135, 162, 205, 260, 284, 285, 292

ostrich, 66, 88, 207, 208, 264, 271, 274, 279, 282, 283

perversion, *xii*, 16, 22–24, 29, 31, 32, 39, 43, 45, 49, 67, 69, 73, 139, 140, 142, 143, 151–156, 168, 169, 176, 177, 179, 181, 195, 198, 205, 213, 214, 226, 231, 234, 255
meaning of term, 142–143

Picasso, 147

Pit, 15, 24, 30, 38, 46, 54, 57, 74, 108, 144, 166, 187, 195, 227, 228, 237, 243, 256

Plato, 298
see also Socrates

Ptolemy, 147

Saadia Ben Joseph (Saadia Gaon), 106n

Satan, the, 2, 4, 99–102, 103
as adversary or accuser, 100–101

sexuality, 209

Shadow of Death, 6, 23, 27, 54, 60, 77, 86

sheol, 15n
see also Pit

skin, 4, 15, 22, 35, 39, 42, 66, 101, 103, 104, 170, 171, 172, 173, 186, 285, 293
imagery of, 101, 103
"skin of my teeth," 42, 170–172
"skin beneath skin," 103, 173

sleep, 10, 74, 113, 127, 129, 227

smile, 137, 164

Socrates, 132, 150, 152, 275, 287

stork, 88n, 271–272

surface-view of the world, 107, 113, 115, 116, 118, 121, 127, 132, 135, 137, 138, 142, 145, 147, 149–151, 155, 157, 158, 160, 161, 164, 166, 168, 170, 172–184, 191, 193, 194, 195, 197, 199, 201, 202, 204, 230

tam, 1, 70, 98, 215–219

About Robert D. Sacks

Photo by Berel Levertov
Used by permission

Robert D. Sacks received his undergraduate education at St. John's College, Annapolis, Maryland (B.A. 1954) and his graduate education at The Johns Hopkins University (Ph.D. 1961). He also studied at the Ecole des Langues Orientales Vivantes in Paris, Hebrew University, Jerusalem, and the University of Chicago.

Sacks has taught at St. John's College since 1960, at both the Annapolis and the Santa Fe Campuses; he has been a visiting faculty member at Middlebury College in Vermont and St. Mary's College in California.

Sacks is the author of *A Commentary on the Book of Genesis* (Edwin Mellen Press, 1990) and *Beginning Biblical Hebrew: Intentionality and Grammar* (Kafir Yaroq Books, 2008). An earlier version of the present book appeared as *The Book of Job with Commentary: A Translation for Our Time* (Scholars Press, 1999); the present edition has been extensively revised.